Numerology and the Divine Triangle

ABOUT THE AUTHORS

Dusty Bunker, numerologist and astrologer, is the author of five books, two of which have been translated into foreign languages. A former newspaper columnist on dreams and metaphysics, she consulted on the Time-Life Books series, *Mysteries of the Unknown.* Dusty lectures widely and appears frequently on radio and television talk shows. She and her husband live in New Hampshire with their four children and three grandchildren.

Faith Javane, an internationally recognized authority on metaphysical topics, specializes in numerology, astrology, the Tarot, and symbology, and is particularly noted for her work in synthesizing these sciences. Counsellor, lecturer, researcher, author, and teacher, Javane is also involved in numerous professional societies.

Javane is co-author of *Numerology and the Divine Triangle.* The publication of *Master Numbers: Cycles of Divine Order* marks her fiftieth year in the study of metaphysics. Her current projects include developing advanced features of astrology and preparing further thoughts on the Tarot.

Numerology

and
The Divine Triangle

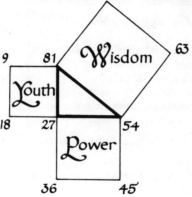

by Faith Javane and Dusty Bunker

A division of Schiffer Publishing, Ltd.
77 Lower Valley Road, Atglen, PA 19310 USA

Published by Whitford Press

A Division of Schiffer Publishing, Ltd.
77 Lower Valley Road
Atglen, PA 19310
Please write for a free catalog.
This book may be purchased from the publisher.
Please include $2.95 postage.

Numerology and the Divine Triangle
by Faith Javane and Dusty Bunker

ISBN: 0-914918-10-9

Rider Waite Tarot Deck Copyright © 1971
U.S. Games Systems, Inc.
Use by permission.

Typeset in 9 pt. Paladium on Compugraphic 7500
Cover Calligraphy by Margaret Shepard
Produced by Josh Brackett & Friends

Manufactured in the United States of America

Omnia in numeris sita sunt.

(Everything lies veiled in numbers.)

CONTENTS

Contents

Acknowledgments

I wish to express my appreciation for the helpful suggestions so generously given by Ellen Hargraves, Linda Stead, Linda Brough, and Carole Winters.

Faith Javane

I wish to thank my husband, a man of love; my children, April, Melanie, Matthew and Sarah, who took over the household duties while I remained in seclusion with my second love, this book; my in-laws, Ginny and Reid, whose inexhaustible faith in me is a continuing source of amazement; and finally the beloved Master Pythagoras, whose gentle nudgings kept me going.

Dusty Bunker

FOREWORD

by Faith Javane

MANY OF MY STUDENTS and a number of people who
have heard my lectures have expressed a desire for a complete textbook on numerology so that they could study their own life patterns in depth. Until now, I have neglected this responsibility, hoping that my classes would be sufficient. Also, I felt such a project to be beyond possibility. However, pressures have convinced me that a full-length text would be both acceptable and fulfilling.

My study of numerology began in the spring of 1938. I found a teacher of astrology who insisted that before she would accept me as a student, I must study numerology. Since I very much wanted to study with her, I agreed to start with the numbers.

Her approach to numerology, however, was like none other. She had received it in a unique way, from what she called the inner planes, which meant that she went outside her body to a mystical

1

school for her instruction. She called this work Kabbalah because it had come to her through the mind and soul rather than from a flesh-and-blood teacher, or from a book. Kabbalah refers to secret information in symbolic form, whether in a numerical, verbal or hieroglyphic pattern.

The biblical books of Ezekiel, Enoch, and IV Ezra contain mystical revelations of hidden knowledge, including speculation about the mystical import of numbers and letters. The Kabbalist knew how to decode the esoteric messages in the Scriptures.

I admit to some skepticism about my teacher's beliefs, but I went along with her teaching. What she revealed we now call the Divine Triangle. It was known in the Pythagorean school, (about sixth century B.C.) as the Life Theorem, and it is now commonly accepted as the proposition that: *The square of the hypotenuse of a right triangle is equal to the sum of the squares of the other two sides.* Pythagoras used the right triangle as a representation of the universe; it was his "Eureka."

According to my teacher, the master K.H., whom she believed to be Pythagoras reincarnated, taught her that the right triangle could also be made to symbolize the world of an individual. This startling revelation is the original basis for the method of numerological delineation of the life pattern of an individual described in this book.

In answer to many requests, I now present to you the secret of the Divine Triangle.

FOREWORD

BY DUSTY BUNKER

I N ANY PROFESSION one is invariably asked the question, "When did you become interested in...?" I have pondered that question long and deeply and now realize that it cannot be answered simply. There is no given moment when one thing ends and another begins. A great thunderbolt from heaven did not strike the ground before my feet, etching words in flame, pronouncing my destiny. Nor did I proclaim at noon on a Sunday, "I am going to begin now." It just happened, naturally and with little fanfare.

Metaphysics is as much a part of me as breath itself. As I studied over the years in one discipline or another, information began to fall into place more and more easily. Just as a child struggles to achieve balance upon those tiny feet, I struggled with many concepts and experiences until I found the proper balance. As the work progressed, the steps became easier and more natural. Now this philosophy I em-

3

brace so respectfully has become my love, my life and my devotion.

I could speculate that it began eons ago in Lemuria or Mu or Atlantis or in the ancient initiation chambers of the Great Pyramid, or even in the sacred halls of the Lyceum with my beloved Pythagoras. Perhaps we do carry deep within our souls memories of past existences that eventually surge into our present incarnations, demanding fulfillment. Certainly, child prodigies are living proof of this possibility. Whatever the impetus driving us into certain professions, we seem to be inextricably bound to continue an evolution that some primal recollection tells us we have begun.

I have been most fortunate along that path, for I was given the greatest of all privileges—a true teacher—that rare and much sought-after creature. In a pupil-teacher relationship, I met Faith Javane, co-author of this book, in 1975. The relationship grew into a bond of respect, admiration and love. We presented our first book, *13 - Birth or Death?* on May 1, 1976, and have now completed this, our second book, inspired by the knowledge that there is a great searching in people's hearts today, a need to comprehend the vast inner spaces as well as the outer spaces. Through this book we believe we can help fill that void with logic, reason, understanding and love. Through the sacred science of numerology, truths can be gleaned and souls can be set at rest. Go with us then, and discover your inner self, your reasons for being and the eternal splendor of the Spirit.

I

INTRODUCTION

THERE IS AN ORDER in the universe, from the atom to the solar system. Awakening interest in the rhythm of this order has called forth new efforts to synthesize the different methods used throughout the ages to understand it. Somewhere between the microcosmic and the macrocosmic, we look for the key that can put our world into logical perspective. We believe that the science of numbers can provide formulae which help clarify the evolving pattern of existence on earth.

Enough ancient wisdom has survived the vicissitudes of time to suggest some basis on which to build new methods of analyzing personality, or at least to cast new light on the systems used in the past.

Our methods, while containing the element of mystery, yet proceed in an orderly and practical way, using the numbers involved in names and birthdates to solve the enigmas of individuality, personality, and the patterns of function and fate carried through life by every human being. We invite you to experiment with this combination of ancient formulae and modern application. While it has not been presented, to our knowledge, in any book, it has been verified by thirty years of actual application and successful experience.

The Divine Triangle, used as a blueprint of one's life, reveals, step by step, from birth to death, what that life should express, indicating the potentials and pitfalls by a series of numbers from 1 to 78.

We are all born at a certain date, hour and minute into the earth's field of energy. The conditions and vibrations of that energy field determine to a great extent the particular actions and reactions that will characterize our entire lives. We are conditioned by the basic set of vibrations that were active when we took our first breath.

The birthdate provides the pattern which we call the *Life Lesson*. The name given at birth, transcribed into numbers by use of the number-letter code used since ancient times and described in this book, provides the three vibrations we call the *Soul Number*, the *Outer Personality Number* and the *Path of Destiny Number* of a given individual. And by placing the name and birthdate formula on the blueprint of the Divine Triangle, we are provided with the key to the incarnation a soul has chosen for the attainment of certain goals. Your numbers tell the state of consciousness which you have reached and record the growth of your soul as well.

One's personal numbers are not isolated clues, but, like all phenomena, are interlocking pieces in the vast puzzle of existence. Therefore, for the benefit of those who wish to broaden their understanding of numerology, this book seeks to synthesize it with the sciences of astrology and the Tarot. To go into the vast and deep correspondences among the three sciences would require volumes; we are simply pointing out certain relationships that we have verified over many years.

This book is divided into two parts. Part I presents the origins and philosophy of numerology. It explains how to determine the numbers that govern your existence and how to make a blueprint of your life by placing these numbers on the form called the Divine Triangle. There is also a chapter entitled More with Numbers, which shows you how to find the right career or determine your compatibility with someone else. A case study of Edgar Cayce, the beloved and well-known psychic who has been called the Sleeping Prophet, follows to illustrate the use of the Divine Triangle. Lastly, Part I presents a look at number symbology in the Bible, both in the Old and the New Testament.

Part II of the book presents delineations of the numbers 1 through 78. Until now, numerology has been limited to the use of the digits 1 through 9 and a few double numbers ranging into the 20's. The number 78 was not chosen at random; rather, it represents a total experience. The number 12 incorporates the basic 1 through 9 cycle, with an additional three steps in which to use the learned experience of the 1 through 9 cycle and bring it out to be shared with others for their benefit. It represents the twelve months of the year and indicates a complete cycle, a whole, a circle, as also exemplified in the twelve signs of the zodiac and the twelve disciples. The next step, 13, takes us into a new level of consciousness. Therefore 78, as an extension of 12 $(1+2+3+4+5+6+7+8+9+10+11+12=78)$, symbolizes a complete round of experience.

In the delineations in Part II, the seventy-eight numbers are fully described as numerical vibrations. They are also synthesized with the seventy-eight Tarot keys and the planets, signs, and decans of the zodiac. As this amazing synthesis unfolds, one can only stand in awe before God's work. Only a cosmic mind could have planned such an intricate pattern in which each science dovetails so exquisitely with the other.

We repeat that to our knowledge this synthesis has never been attempted. The correspondences among numerology, astrology and the Tarot were not chosen at random; they have been tested through years of research and application. We believe they are accurate. We suggest that you try them for yourself, for it is only through personal verification that any belief or process is truly accepted.

1

ESOTERIC NUMEROLOGY

NUMEROLOGY BEGAN when life began, because "in the beginning there was 1." The vibrations then began and the 2 appeared, the first pair, and ushered in the real beginning of universal geometry.

Numbers, by themselves, represent universal principles through which all things evolve and continue to grow in cyclic fashion. The digits 1 through 9 symbolize the stages through which an idea must pass before it becomes a reality. All manifestation is the result of these nine stages.

Esoteric numerology is the art and science of understanding the spiritual significance and orderly progression of all manifestation. Every word or name vibrates to a number and every number has its inner meaning. The letter and number code, when rightly understood and applied, brings us into a direct and close relationship with the underlying intelligence of the universe.

We owe much of our spiritual and scientific understanding of numbers to Pythagoras, the father of mathematics. Pythagoras is most commonly remembered for the Pythagorean theorem, which states that *The square of the hypotenuse of a right triangle is equal to the sum of the squares of the other two sides.* However, Pythagoras was primarily a mystic and a philosopher. He believed that "all things are numbers" and that numbers represent spiritual entities whose presence is felt in all existence.

He discovered the mystical significance of numbers, noting that the numbers 1 through 9 stand, macrocosmically, for universal principles. On the personal level, microcosmically, they stand for characteristics, abilities and events. He saw in number patterns and geometrical ratios the explanations of all natural phenomena, musical harmony and tonal qualities. He knew that the stars and planets as vibrating bodies produced sound which became known as the "music of the spheres."

Pythagoras was born around 582 B.C. on the Greek island of Samos, in the Aegean Sea. As a young man he left home and travelled to Egypt, where he was initiated into certain mathematical doctrines. He is also reported to have studied with Zoroaster, the Persian sage, and to have learned the Kabbalah in Judea. The science of numbers he eventually taught was based on Kabbalistic principles.

Pythagoras finally settled in Crotona in southern Italy and established a school of the mysteries. Before his students could proceed into the Pythagorean mysteries, they had to know the four sciences of arithmetic, music, astronomy and geometry. Plato was a follower of Pythagoras and it is to him that we owe most of our knowledge of the Pythagorean school.

Pythagoras taught that, "Evolution is the law of life; Number is the law of the universe; Unity is the law of God." He believed that everything in the universe was subject to predictable progressive cycles. His means of measuring these cycles were the numbers 1 through 9.

He also taught that numbers have a significance apart from the values denoted by the figures. Numbers are different from figures. *Numbers represent qualities; figures represent quantities.* Numbers operate on the spiritual plane, while figures are for measuring things on the material plane.

A lucid understanding of these digits is essential in the study of numerology because every number over 9 ultimately reduces to one of these digits. With a comprehensive knowledge of the meaning of these numbers, one can understand the orderly progression of all life cycles.

The Numbers 1 through 9

Science claims that in a vacuum where nothing exists, in time hydrogen ions spring into existence. 1, as the first digit in the series, represents the ion, the beginning, the genesis, the first spark of energy emerging from the original source. It stands alone and isolated because it is the first; there is no other. It is independent of outside influences or assistance because it has chosen to seek its own self-expression, and cannot therefore be encumbered or swayed. It is decisive and independent and makes the choices necessary to ultimately determine its destiny.

1 REPRESENTS THE MALE PRINCIPLE, the yang. It is the pioneer, striking out alone, seeking the experiences which will establish its distinct identity. It is in the process of discovering its own abilities. It is raw energy, positive, original and creative, in a state of perpetual motion. Since 1 is alone and is imbued with so much creative energy, it must decide how its energy will be used. It must take command and have the courage to maintain its direction without fear of opposition.

1 is the real I AM of humanity, the unity of all, the unit of vibrational measuring. It is self-consciousness.

Keywords: original, independent, aggressive, individualistic, creative, dominant; the first in a series, the start of any operation or activity, the leader, the pioneer, the boss who likes authority. "He who goes forth."

2 IS THE PAIR, the duo. It is changeable and adaptable and can also be indecisive. It is the agent, the go-between, the diplomat and peacemaker, because unity can only be accomplished through a meeting of the minds, a compromise on each side.

2 represents the feminine principle of receptivity, the yin, which seeks a union of two distinct entities. It is the gestation period in which things begin to form. 2 collects and assimilates. It seeks a balance between opposing forces, and therefore represents co-operation, attachment and partnership. It is the peacemaker, with an avid attention to detail. Because 2 is so keenly aware of opposites, it has a pronounced sense of rhythm and harmony. Music appeals to its sympathetic and emotional nature. The maternal, patient and sensitive characteristics of 2 cause it to place others first, before itself. Union is its goal, not separateness; therefore, it is obedient to and understanding of others. It seeks harmony and assimilation above all.

The hydrogen ions which sprang into existence under 1 are now hurtling through space. They will be drawn toward one another by the law of mutual attraction, or the law of number 2.

Keywords: adaptable, tactful, understanding, gentle, cautious; a follower rather than a leader.

3 COMBINES THE QUALITIES of 1 and 2. It is a fascinating and diversified vibration, carrying the qualities of manifestation and self-expression. The ion, which sprang into existence from 0, sought to assert its individuality under 1 and felt the attraction of others under 2, now awakens to its need for social interaction. 3 is the need to communicate and become involved in the pure joy of living. Through its exuberant response to life, 3 bestows sunny radiance and enthusiasm upon all. 3 is the extrovert whose personal magnetism draws others and inspires them to expand and grow. It is the performer who possesses an innate appreciation of pleasure, romance, art and beauty. Its creative imagination allows all things to be possible; it therefore becomes involved in many emotions and experiences. 3 is friendly and expansive, thriving on sociability and variety. If any of the numbers could be called happy-go-lucky, it would be the effervescent 3.

Keywords: expansive, sociable, dramatic, communicative, diversified, creative.

4 IS STABILITY, a 4-square consciousness, the symbol of law, system and order. It is firmness, security, stability and conservatism. It is the builder who must submit to earthly things where form and substance are the predominant elements. 4 is nature and relates to the earth. The formation of the earth took place on the fourth day in the biblical story of creation.

The attraction the ions felt under 2 led to interaction under 3. Now, under 4, the inevitable concentration of energies occurs. Formation takes place. The ions realize that they can no longer scatter their energies, but must now begin to place them in a productive, orderly system. 4 therefore develops a practical nature, and through self-discipline, binds itself to a conventional routine exercise of its energy.

Keywords: form, work, order, practicality, construction, stability, endurance, discipline.

5 IS FREEDOM, change and adventure. Curiosity and constant activity produce a resourceful, adaptable and versatile entity always ready to take a chance.

Since 5 is the midpoint in the cycle 1 through 9, it allows for decision-making. It might be called the pivotal point in which the ions, now encased in flesh and form, must decide upon their future in the rest of the cycle 6 through 9. It now meets with many opportunities and varieties of experience through which it will be given the information it needs to make that decision.

5 is involved in much superficial interaction with groups and crowds. Because of its past varied experiences, it is the natural promoter and advertiser, fluent in communications, with a little information about a lot of things, and a desire to travel here and there to communicate it. 5 attracts the opposite sex because of an irresistible magnetism, and this attraction sets the stage for the domestic responsibilities which naturally follow under 6.

Keywords: versatility, resourcefulness, adaptability, change, activity, travel, adventure, promotion, speculation.

6 IS CONSCIENTIOUS; it desires to bring harmony, truth, justice and a sense of balance into its environment. Love and compassion are uppermost in its mind, and it can therefore be an effective teacher, counselor or healer. Others are drawn to it because of the understanding which emanates from it.

The ions, under 5, had the opportunity to experience many events and emotional encounters. They are now ready to take on social and family responsibilities, or the 6 vibration. 6 is a domestic and artistic vibration, and, under this number, the ions must adjust to the needs of others.

The 6 desires a close companion, marriage and a home and family where beauty and harmony prevail. A need for group harmony and service to the community follows naturally. 6 settles down, blending into the conservative element of the community, where it can create better standards of living. Gifted in the arts, it can also express its creative potential through its developed sense of balance and become a fine artist in its own unique field.

Keywords: family and social responsibility, service, love, compassion, counseling, healing, creativity.

7 SEEKS ANSWERS. It tries to establish a philosophy by which to live and attempts to penetrate the mystery behind its existence which it has never questioned to this point. Because solitude is necessary for analysis, the 7 feels the need to spend time alone, away from the crowds, in touch with nature. It looks for friendship with those of an elevated consciousness that can match its own.

And on the seventh day God rested. All things rest under the 7 because time is needed in which to think. The ions under 7 feel poised and calm; they realize that they now need to be still and to know. They have established a routine for their energy, and now analysis begins.

7 ushers into the cycle a physical completion without apparent effort. Goals that have been long sought are now magically attained. Spare time is available in which philosophical and metaphysical interests can be pursued. Perfected thinking is the goal of 7, which is why it is called the sacred number. It is also why scientists, philosophers, teachers, mystics and the clergy come under this influence. The physical facet of 7 also relates to the health of the body which is highly sensitized through this vibration.

Keywords: quiet, introspective, intuitive, analytical, inspirational, reclusive, philosophical, mystical.

8 WILL ASSUME POWER, for it now has achieved control and responsibility in its chosen field. Recognition and financial rewards are bestowed, and expansion and growth in the business world take place.

Under 8, karma is king, and the ions will reap what they have sown. Power is the quality associated with 8. Ardor, zeal, steadfastness and the ability to see in broad terms give it the ambition and added qualities needed to achieve material goals. 8 has the drive to overcome all obstacles and eventually to succeed through ability and perseverance. 8 can now go to the very top with the ideas and plans that have been formulated gradually during the last seven cycles. Through fair and ethical standards, good judgment and organizational abilities, it will achieve recognition, power and financial remuneration.

Keywords: power, responsibility, financial rewards, good judgment, recognition.

9 IS SELFLESSNESS and compassion. Encompassing a love for all, it desires to apply its energy to universal service. It bestows an impersonal but just view of life, one that is generous, benevolent and patient. This is the artist and thinker who has developed skills through the preceding cycles and is now ready to share his or her knowledge with the rest of the world.

The ions are in their final state of completion. They have travelled the entire cycle of nine parts, ingesting experiences along the way. Now, in the closing cycle, they reach a total understanding and tolerance of others' views and prejudices.

9 is ready to give back to the universe some measure of what it has learned through the eight previous steps of the cycle. The law of cyclicity allows for no waste, and demands input for output. When this is done willingly, the completion experienced under 9 brings only joy at the gift of life and the freedom with which to enter the next cycle unencumbered.

Keywords: love, compassion, patience, universality, tolerance, selfless service, endings.

2

YOUR PERSONAL NUMBERS

AND PERSONAL YEARS

Y OU ARE ENDOWED at birth with your own four personal
numbers. These numbers tell you the lessons to be learned
during your life and the spiritual growth and development which you
can attain. The four personal numbers are: the *Life Lesson Number*,
the *Soul Number*, the *Outer Personality Number* and the *Path of
Destiny Number*.

Your personal numbers are determined by the numbers in your
birthdate and the letters in the name you are given at birth. To arrive
at the numerical vibration of names, each letter in the alphabet is
given a number value. A is 1; B is 2; C is 3; and so on to Z, which is
26.

To work with the value of the letters beyond I, which is number 9,
we reduce the value to a single digit. For example, L is number 12. We
reduce the 12 by adding the first digit to the second, or $1+2=3$. The

number 12 is then written as 12/3. The letter T is 20. We reduce the 20 by adding the first digit to the second, or 2+0=2. The number 20 is then written as 20/2.

The table below gives the number value of each letter in the alphabet.

A	1	J	10/1	S	19/1
B	2	K	11/2	T	20/2
C	3	L	12/3	U	21/3
D	4	M	13/4	V	22/4
E	5	N	14/5	W	23/5
F	6	O	15/6	X	24/6
G	7	P	16/7	Y	25/7
H	8	Q	17/8	Z	26/8
I	9	R	18/9		

Learn this code thoroughly. Then you won't have to keep referring to the table, which can be a slow and tedious process. The more you work with the code, the easier it will come to you.

Notice that there are patterns you can learn. For example, A, J, and S all reduce to 1; B, K, and T reduce to 2; C, L, and U reduce to 3, and so on. Train yourself by saying over and over, "AJS, AJS, AJS; BKT, BKT, BKT". There are memory tricks you can use. For instance, number 6 is FOX. That's an easy one. GPY sounds something like "gypsy" for number 7, and number 8, HQZ, might remind you of "headquarters". Use your own memory pegs so that the code will be readily accessible when working out the value of words.

We can reduce any word to a number vibration by using our table, so let's experiment with a few words before we begin with names. Place the number value above each letter, add the values, and reduce the total to a single digit, if necessary.

$$3 + 9 + 2 + 9 + 1 + 9 + 7 = 40 / 4$$
$$L \quad I \quad B \quad R \quad A \quad R \quad Y$$

We reduce the 40 by adding 4+0=4, which is written 40/4.

$$6 + 1 + 2 + 8 + 5 + 9 = 31/4$$
$$F \quad A \quad T \quad H \quad E \quad R$$

We reduce the 31 by adding 3+1=4, which is written 31/4.

$$6 + 9 + 9 + 5 + 7 + 3 + 1 + 3 + 5 = 48/3$$
$$F \quad I \quad R \quad E \quad P \quad L \quad A \quad C \quad E$$

We add 4+8=12, but we still have a double digit. We reduce again, 1+2=3. 48 is then written 48/3.

$1 + 1 + 3 + 9 + 1 + 4 + 5 + 5 + 2 + 6 = 37 / 1$
S A C R A M E N T O

Add $3+7=10$; then reduce the 10, $1+0=1$. 37 is then written 37/1.

There are four double digits which are not generally reduced. These are called the *master numbers*. Master numbers offer more opportunity for expression and thus demand more effort from the individual or thing in question. The master numbers are 11, 22, 33, and 44. Whenever you arrive at one of these numbers, retain the master number value. For instance:

$3 + 9 + 7 + 8 + 2 = 29 / 11$
L I G H T

Because "light" vibrates to master number 11, it is written as 29/11 rather than 29/2, which would be the case if we reduced it entirely. However, 2 is still acknowledged as the base number, and the word in question will fluctuate between the vibrations of 2 and 11.

An individual will fluctuate between any master number and its base digit because the vibration of the master number is so intense and so powerful that it cannot be lived under continuously. Therefore, living under the base number for a brief period offers a moment of respite where one gathers one's forces before attempting to work with the master number vibration again. Master numbers demand the greatest output from the individual, and, in return, offer the greatest reward.

A name that vibrates to a master number is:

$4 + 5 + 3 + 1 + 5 + 9 + 5$
M E L A N I E

$4 + 1 + 5 \quad 3 + 3 + 1 + 9 + 2 + 5 = 65 / 11$
M A E C L A R K E

Again, this number would not be reduced further, because it is a master number. However, this individual will fluctuate between her master number 11 and the base number 2.

The word "roses" vibrates to 22:

$9 + 6 + 1 + 5 + 1 = 22$
R O S E S

We do not reduce the 22 because it is a master number.

In this system of numerology, we only use the numbers 1 through 78, for reasons which we explained in the introduction. When totaling a name, if you arrive at a number above 78, simply reduce that number to the next lower double digit or single digit, as the case may be. For example, if a personal number totals 86, add the $8+6$, and work with the 14/5 vibration. Or if the personal number totals 106, add the $1+0+6$, and work with the 7 vibration.

Remember, all double digits that reduce to the same base number have the same basic meaning. The double digit reflects a variation of the single number. You could liken this to living in the same city but on different streets. Therefore, the numbers 12/3, 21/3, 30/3, 39/3, 48/3, 57/3, 66/3 and 75/3 all reflect the basic 3; however, the double digit expresses a variation of the original 3.

Now that you know how to reduce any word, we will demonstrate how to arrive at your four personal numbers and explain what those numbers mean.

The Life Lesson Number

The first of the four personal numbers we will discuss is called the *Life Lesson Number*. It represents the lessons you must learn in this lifetime and is most significant in your choice of a career. (See Chapter Five.) It is derived from your full birthdate. Even a business or idea has a moment of "birth" and can therefore be treated in the same way.

We will use as an example, Ada Wynn Lunt, born November 12, 1940. First, reduce the birthdate to numbers. November is the eleventh month; therefore, Ada's birthdate is written: 11-12-1940. Remember to write the *full year* of birth and not an abbreviated form such as '40. Next, reduce the year to a double digit by adding the year through once: $1+9+4+0=14$. Now we total the birthdate once more:

$11+12+1940$
$11+12+14 \ (1+9+4+0)$
$11+12+14=37/1$

37 is reduced by adding the first digit to the second, or $3+7=10$. Reduce the 10 in the same manner by adding the $1+0=1$. 37 is then written as 37/1. This is Ada's Life Lesson Number.

The Life Lesson Number is a constant and cannot be changed or modified in any way because it is derived from the birthdate. It indicates vocation plus the lesson you came into incarnation to overcome or to learn. It also represents the cosmic gift you are given in order to accomplish your destiny.

Find your Life Lesson Number by following the same procedure. Then read the delineation of the Life Lesson Number single digit below. For a finer delineation of the double digit, turn to Part II of this book.

In our example, Ada has a 37/1 Life Lesson Number. She would read number 1 under the Life Lesson Number section following. She would then turn to Part II, page 120, for the delineation of the 37, a more explicit description of the basic number 1.

1 AS THE LIFE LESSON NUMBER: You must learn to be original, strong-willed, creative and innovative. You should have the courage and drive to go ahead into new fields of expression and be a pioneer. You should always go forward, never turn back. At times you may be dictatorial and stubborn because you do not like to be restricted or directed. You are a good executive, and work best alone. You are usually efficient and well-organized. You are not naturally domestic but can manage well in any situation. You usually like sports and athletics, and enjoy the thrill of winning. You are sophisticated, not emotionally romantic, and always appear at the head of social and commercial groups. By learning the lessons of number 1, you become intimately familiar with the God energy, that probing, seeking, independent spark that moves all creation. You are creative on the physical plane because your pioneer spirit precedes all others, and expresses your unique individuality.

2 AS THE LIFE LESSON NUMBER: You are here to learn to become a good mixer. You are a good salesperson, more persuasive than forceful. You should be a support for those in the leadership role, help them to find their goals in life, and remain behind the scenes if necessary. This quality can be a help to you in business because those who benefit from your talents will in turn help you make use of your abilities. In partnerships and groups, you will encounter the lessons you came to learn in this lifetime. Success is then very possible. You must have consideration for others, and should bring people together for a common cause. Various professions are open to you as you learn to be adaptable to most things that need to be done. You could select a career in finance, music, medicine, religion or statistical analysis and research.

3 AS THE LIFE LESSON NUMBER: You are best in intellectual, artistic or creative endeavors. You need to express, to manifest and to see the results of your work. *Beauty, fruitfulness, luxury* and *pleasure* are your keywords. You should have ambition and pride. You must become conscious of the law, and, by being an excellent disciplinarian, you will achieve a position of authority over others. 3 combines the daring of 1 with the caution of 2. It is a number of self-expression and freedom and is extravagant in using energies to gain freedom. You must guard against becoming a jack-of-all-trades; rather, you should specialize. You could then be successful in artistic, religious or inventive pursuits. You should never do routine work because you dislike restriction. You should work alone for the best results. Business partnerships become too disciplined for your freedom-loving nature. You could write, lecture, teach or find your niche in journalism. Whatever you decide to specialize in, you must use your creative and inspirational talents.

4 AS THE LIFE LESSON NUMBER: You must build a solid foundation on which to base your life. This demands a well-ordered system of conduct and morals. Administration or some sort of management would be the best type of employment for you. You want your home life to conform to the culture in which you live. You will provide well for those within your care, and you expect them to respond with respect and dignity. You should become a diligent worker and honestly earn your success. By being thrifty, you will have an adequate savings account as security against any possible losses. You should learn not to take a chance unless it is a sure bet. You should seek high goals. You might want to achieve concrete results quickly, and therefore should strive for patience and perseverance. Learn to face reality, and base all your efforts on sound practical reasoning.

5 AS THE LIFE LESSON NUMBER: Your keyword is *freedom*. If you have "free rein," you can accomplish wonders, but if you feel bound or limited, you lose your enthusiasm and accomplish little. You would be a good explorer or Peace Corps volunteer, as you learn well by travel and experience. You are a diligent student if interested in the subject, but you may fail in subjects for which you see no useful ends. You should be eager for new experience, and shun monotony. In your quest for knowledge, you will become interested in discovering answers in books and magazines. An avid reader, a fluent talker, and a versatile doer, you are the witty conversationalist, and brighten any group by your mere presence. You are here to learn and to experience the value of freedom, and should not tie yourself down too severely. Your talents, once learned, prepare you for a literary career or a position in sales, and dealing with the public.

6 AS THE LIFE LESSON NUMBER: You are here to learn a sense of responsibility for your family and community. 6 is the love and domestic vibration and requires that you be responsive to the social needs of others. A fine sense of balance must be acquired so that you can equalize injustices. This keen sense bestows artistic abilities as well as judgmental talents which can be utilized in the legal system. You should develop the compassion and understanding necessary to ease the burdens of those who will naturally be drawn to you. You are among those who serve, teach and bring comfort to humanity. A wide choice of professions is yours including nursing,

19

teaching, welfare work, the ministry, medicine, restaurant enterprises, the legal profession and possibly veterinary or animal husbandry. You may also choose to enter a career in the arts, interior decorating or hairdressing.

7 AS THE LIFE LESSON NUMBER: You are here to use and to develop your mind. Your words should be full of wisdom when you decide to talk. Your strong intuition helps in any line you choose and gives insight when needed. You may be an enigma to others, and even to yourself at times. You like to read, think and meditate. Many times you have to rely on your soul-force to solve difficult material problems. You may delve into the occult, the mysterious and the phenomenal side of life. Music and other arts are in harmony with your keynotes. You may be drawn to the church, science or research and analysis. A career in mathematics or investigation could hold your interest. You should learn to spend time by yourself, in the woods or by the seashore, where you can get in touch with your inner self and your deepest thoughts because your destiny is to use your mind.

8 AS THE LIFE LESSON NUMBER: This is the number of power and ambition, the number of the executive, the boss, who lives by brain and brawn. You will learn to work and will want to see everyone else working. You can push people to become successful in their own right. You should lead and show by example how to profit in business. You are here to learn to handle power, authority and money. You can build a business empire and should work to that end. You want success for your family and for the family name as a matter of pride. You want your offspring to carry on your name with honor and dignity. Sports is another field open to you, as this number vibration bestows great strength and endurance. Many famous athletes operate under an 8.

9 AS THE LIFE LESSON NUMBER: You should be the universal lover of humanity, patient, kind and understanding. You are at the peak of life's expression, and must turn and show others the way. You seem to receive wisdom from above; thus you know that the true way of happiness is in service to others. You are the marrying type, strong in passion and compassion. You easily acquire money or wealth, and know how to preserve it. You are never petty but deal in broad concepts and can attain success in the face of difficulties. You are here to show others the way, through your breadth of thinking. You can choose from many professions; education and medicine are the most usual. You may become an orator, writer or lecturer with equal ease. Communication, foreign service, statesmanship and leadership positions are easily within your capacity.

11 AS THE LIFE LESSON NUMBER: the keywords here are *altruism* and *community*. You came into a unique and testing incarnation. You must practice "love thy neighbor as thyself" and use it as your foundation. Your strong intuitions are of value in gaining wisdom and inspiration. 11 is one of the most difficult vibrations because the demand for high standards is constant. You must learn patience and at the same time be able to make quick decisions. Seek for balance between the material, physical life which has to be considered, and the inspirational, spiritual life which underlies your self-understanding. You can succeed in the field of science, because all new inventions and discoveries such as the laser rays, research in the fields of anti-gravity or kirlian photography or any area of electronics would appeal to you. You could choose to be an astronomer or astrologer, or a Bible researcher and interpreter. You may become a teacher or writer in the field of philosophy. You are original and creative, and could become an inspirational speaker. 11 is an esoteric master number of spiritual import. It bestows courage, power and talent with strong feelings of leadership. You must not let this power go to your head, since fame and recognition are likely; instead realize that true mastership is service.

22 AS THE LIFE LESSON NUMBER: You must express a basic building urge, accomplish things in a big way, and work with large groups or business concerns. You would enjoy the import-export business which could demand long-distance travel and meetings with persons of authority. You like to take an inspirational idea and put it to practical use. Self-knowledge is very valuable to you. 22 gives the promise of success. You know how to use your ability to adjust the physical laws of life and living, to demonstrate exoteric wisdom rather than esoteric. You could become an executive in banking or financial affairs in a national capacity, or help to organize businesses for others as an efficiency expert or the like. As an ambassador to foreign countries, you would demonstrate statesmanship. You like to be occupied in some large enterprise to challenge your power to achieve. Your lesson is to learn to take charge of large organizations and corporations and to handle money efficiently and usefully for the benefit of large groups of people.

33 AS THE LIFE LESSON NUMBER: You should be steady and reliable and develop a strong desire to protect others. You would like to live close to nature, and this urge may influence you to choose a life in agriculture. Your goal would be to produce food on a large scale to help provide sustenance for the hungry of the world. You would never be found in any profession that could act destructively to humanity. Your talent may lie along the line of the arts—music to bring harmony, painting to bring beauty, or literature to promote education. Service in the field of medicine and healing could also attract you. Possibly you would choose the law as a way to protect others through justice. Since the 33 consciousness is almost beyond that of humanity, and is Christ-like in expression, a place within the ministry or priesthood could lead you to the realm of your dreams as a world savior. You may be required to sacrifice your own desires for the needs of others in order to fulfill your Life Lesson vibration.

44 AS THE LIFE LESSON NUMBER: This number stands for strength and complete mental control over your life while on earth. It requires discipline in every department of life so that you may be instrumental in promoting the material advancement of the world. Your mind must be trained to let the higher forces work within it, and you must keep your body and your environment in order, so that you are ready for any opportunity to achieve these same results for others. Your high energy potential is meant to further evolution by helping others set their world in order. You should try to promote better ethics and justice in the world of business. You must recognize reality, then use what you learn to alleviate the physical burdens of others. You are the instrument by which this alteration takes place. By displaying bravery, resourcefulness, courage and discipline, you serve as an example for others. See Edgar Cayce (Chapter Six, page 90) as an example of the 44 vibration.

The Soul Number

The *Soul Number* comes from adding the vowels in the name. Always work with the *full name at birth*. Prefixes and suffixes such as Mr., Mrs., Jr., Sr., II, III, Esq. are not considered part of the cosmic name, and are not figured in the total name. Place the number value of the vowels *above* the letter in the name. The vowels are A, E, I, O, and U. The letter Y is a vowel when it sounds like E, as in the name Mary. It is not a vowel in the name May. Y is also a vowel when it is the only vowel in the syllable, as in the name Sybil. W is a vowel when it follows D or G as in the names Dwight or Gwendolyn, because it carries the vowel sound.

We will use our example, Ada Wynn Lunt, born November 12, 1940. To arrive at Ada's Soul Number, we add the vowels in her name:

$$1 \;+\; 1 \quad +7 \qquad\quad +3 \qquad = 12/3$$
$$A\;\;D\;\;A\quad W\;\;Y\;\;N\;\;N\quad L\;\;U\;\;N\;\;T$$

The Y in Wynn is considered a vowel because it is the only vowel in the name. The 12 is reduced by adding the first digit to the second, or 1+2=3. The number 12 is then written 12/3.

Discover your Soul Number by following the same procedure. Then read the explanation of the basic Soul Number (single digit) given below. For a finer delineation of the double digit, turn to Part II.

In our example, Ada has a Soul Number of 12/3. She would read number 3 under the Basic Soul Number section which follows. She would then turn to Part II and read the number 12/3 Personal Number Vibration which gives a deeper look into her real self.

Your Soul Number is your real personality, the you that is known only to you. If one embraces the philosophy of reincarnation, the Soul Number also indicates what you have been in previous lifetimes. This part of your personality is not easily recognized by others unless they know you very well. The Soul Number is what you, in your inner secret self, desire to be. This urge may be so strong that it can overcome other vibrations of your four basic numbers. Since the Soul Number reveals something of accumulated growth in past lives, it becomes an underlying force which influences the actions of your present life. If, however, the soul urge remains repressed by outer circumstances, and the soul fails to accomplish its purpose, it may need to repeat the same vibrational urge in a future life, until it finds true expression.

1 AS THE SOUL NUMBER: The leadership won in past lives now brings a desire to continue striving for higher consciousness. You are independent regarding your beliefs. Your desire for free and independent thinking continues to occupy your innermost yearning. Do not let this strong drive obstruct your attainment of practical goals in the present life. You are always conscious of your inner strength and would have difficulty taking a secondary position among your contemporaries. If marriage or partnership is considered, investigate the inner yearnings of your prospective partner to safeguard the successful outcome of your relationship. If your individuality is too strong, it could express itself as bossiness and be a detriment to personal happiness. So firm is the intensity of your focus and so strong the memory of self-glory from the past that you are apt to stand on your convictions even though it could disrupt important relationships. Your inner strength gives you something to rely on when the going is rough, and you can be a tower of inspiration to others in times of trouble.

2 AS THE SOUL NUMBER: You have a strong desire for peace and harmony. You are considerate and tactful, adaptable and gentle. You are a follower rather than a leader. Tact is a strong point in your makeup; therefore, you are a go-between or agent, helping to bring peace between opposing forces. You avoid hurting the feelings of others to the point of subordinating yourself to their wills. As a

23

result, you appear shy and lacking in confidence. Try to overcome indecision; while you are hesitating, others may forge ahead of you and claim what should be yours. Dare to do what you know is right and do not let emotions deter your purpose. Your sensitivity can be positive when used to tune in to the balancing forces of the universe and bring forth truths which help all people gain understanding.

3 AS THE SOUL NUMBER: You are very conscientious in regard to duty. You are well aware of the law of the Trinity, and know that inspiration and imagination will bring the best results when used to help others. This could easily become your philosophy of life. Follow your urge to create and expand the activities that interest you. You seek happiness and find it in making others happy. If a person feels depressed, a visit with you will bring them hope and courage. Expand your ideals by dedicating yourself to the expression of good cheer and optimism. Work to make your dreams come true, but not to the extreme of becoming impractical. Love is important to you—both in giving and receiving—but try to hold to reason in your loving expansiveness. You become happy and well-adjusted by making others happy.

4 AS THE SOUL NUMBER: You are well organized, a trait which could bring you material success. Your practicality permeates your entire being. Others could set a pattern after your well-ordered program of living. Your loyalty, balance and dependability mean much to those around you. They know where you stand in all things and feel that any dealings with you will be handled squarely. You take matters seriously, whether in business or romance, and can therefore make your dreams come true in a planned, practical way.

5 AS THE SOUL NUMBER: You claim the right to freedom and will not allow any limitations of your ideals or ways of thinking. Variety of self-expression is absolutely essential. You would feel dull and listless without the stimulation of changes and new outlooks. Travel is one of your soul's desires since you believe it to be educational and broadening. Narrowness cannot be tolerated. If you feel yourself falling into a rut, a trip, a new outfit or a vacation could change the vibrations for the better and open new avenues for continued inner growth.

6 AS THE SOUL NUMBER: You respond to beauty, harmony and peace. You are affectionate, sympathetic and loyal to those you love. Your mission could be to teach others to maintain peace and harmony in their lives and to spread the idea of the Golden Rule. You work hard to keep domestic harmony as your ideal way of life. Of all the love vibrations in the various numbers, yours is the most likely to be guilty of a smothering love, so deep is your desire to live for your own immediate family. Learn to allow your family members to express their own desires in life, even if you do not agree with their choices.

7 AS THE SOUL NUMBER: You are quiet and reserved, a good thinker, analyzer and mediator. You need peaceful surroundings and become irritable if your environment is noisy. You are refined, sensitive, secretive and usually psychic. You may live alone and remain unmarried. You could be celibate and join the higher mystical order of humanity. Your true nature is to be calm, to develop depth of character, and thus to benefit humanity through philosophy.

8 AS THE SOUL NUMBER: Ambition is your keyword. You believe in accomplishment and let no obstacle deter you in attaining your goal. Your number is not an easy one to handle, but the rewards are worth your effort. You are one who will tackle a big job in order to rise above the crowd and arrive at the pinnacle. You have the ability to organize large groups and undertakings successfully. Psychology will help you understand the masses with whom you may work. Others expect more of you than of the average person, so you must rely upon your inner self to guide you to stay at the top. This is the number of high-ranking sports figures.

9 AS THE SOUL NUMBER: Intuition is strongly active in your life. You are sensitive and imaginative and can think in abstract terms. Although you may appear vague at times, you are extremely impressionable, compassionate and generous. You need to have and to give love. You are kind and forgiving, with an expansive consciousness dedicated to uplifting humanity. This could be the number of a master or adept from a previous lifetime.

11 AS THE SOUL NUMBER: You have been on the spiritual path for a long time, probably for more than one incarnation. Through spiritual evolution you have learned much of the mysteries of life and death. You have courage, talent and leadership ability. You are understanding, wise, intuitive and often clairvoyant, with extremely sensitive ESP abilities and strong spiritual leanings. You also have the fortitude to contend with many changes and unexpected events.

22 AS THE SOUL NUMBER: With the power of 22, you have the urge to continue the tangible achievements of past lifetimes. You desire material fulfillment. You are the master builder. Your soul's aim is to leave the world a tangibly better place for your having been here, so it follows that you must keep mental balance while expressing your ideals in practical ways. You have higher goals than the average person; you should keep your feet on the ground while your thoughts expand.

33 AS THE SOUL NUMBER: You are ready to sacrifice for humanity. You see clearly a vision of future world conditions and feel ready to help in any way you can to bring peace to all mankind. Sometimes your life lesson vibrations can be in opposition to your soul's urges; nevertheless, you will practice generosity and try to see other people's points of view. This circumstance may force you temporarily to take a background position but the hope remains that you will reach a position to promote your ideals. You stand ever ready to help others.

44 AS THE SOUL NUMBER: Universal concepts are part of your consciousness; they now express themselves as inner urges to accomplish great advances in world culture. You desire to unite the practical with the philosophical. A career within the government or in the United Nations could give you the opportunity to promote these ideals among all peoples. You are willing to shoulder heavy responsibilities. Your inner self realizes that it is adept; now the problem becomes how to manifest it in the outer world. You believe that your soul will guide you into fields where your great expectations can be promoted. You have an innate ability to solve everyday problems and can work with others to help them organize their lives. (For further information on master number 44, see our *13 - Birth or Death?*)

The Outer Personality Number

Now that you have discovered the real you through your Soul Number, let us determine how other people see you. Your *Outer Personality Number* indicates how you appear to others; it is not necessarily what you really are. The Outer Personality Number also shows what people expect from you because of the image you present.

To find the Outer Personality Number, add the values of the consonants in the full name at birth. Consonants are all those letters other than vowels. Place the value of the consonants *below* the name, and add each digit together. In our example:

```
A  D  A  W  Y  N N  L  U  N T
   4     +5  +5+5  +3  +5+2 =29/11
```

29 reduces by adding the first digit to the second, or 2+9=11. 11 is

a master number and is therefore not reduced further. Other people see Ada Wynn Lunt as a 29/11, although this is not what she necessarily is.

As in the preceding section, the basic numbers will be delineated here. Ada would read 11 as an Outer Personality Number, and then turn to Part II of this book for a finer delineation of the basic 11 as a 29/11.

If your Outer Personality Number were 49/4, for instance, you would read 4 as an Outer Personality Number here and then turn to Part II to read 49/4 as a Personal Number Vibration which is a finer delineation of the basic 4.

Personality comes from the word "persona" meaning mask and therefore represents the mask we present to others. It is important because through it other basic vibrational urges are expressed. A pleasing personality is a great asset in all areas of life to help attain spiritual, mental or physical goals. Our body language, mannerisms, and traits—even the way we dress—reveal much more than we realize. They are clues which others use to determine our attitudes and characteristics.

1 AS THE OUTER PERSONALITY NUMBER: You present an independent, capable and executive-type image to the world. Others see you as a unique individual, separate from the ordinary crowd, perhaps a loner in some respects, but definitely different. They expect you to be able to take control of any situation and be able to run an organization or club efficiently. They will look to you to get the job done because you appear to be the leader, the pioneer, the idea person who always knows where to go and what to do. The creation of the correct image is foremost in your mind, and you depend upon the force of your personality as your identification pass into society. You may appear to be overly aggressive and domineering. In this case, your selfish need to assert your individuality is realized at the expense of the free expression of those around you. You, as a number 1 person, dress to be among the first in style. You like exclusive models and never want to look like anyone else. Negatively, you may even dress freakishly or in modes beyond the limits of good taste.

2 AS THE OUTER PERSONALITY NUMBER: You appear quiet and modest and seem to need a peaceful environment in which to live. You are fussy about details; neatness and cleanliness are a must. Rather than make a big entrance, you prefer to remain in the background, working behind the scenes or in cooperation with others. You are attractive and popular with the opposite sex. This is partly due to your desire for companionship and harmony which prompts you to indulge others. You seem incomplete by yourself.

You can appear to be restless and dissatisfied with conditions because of the mental balancing you perform on every situation. You may have difficulty in making decisions because both sides are so clear to you. On occasion, you can display a temper and use cutting words. You dress neatly and inconspicuously, preferring a balanced, pleasing look. You should choose easy-to-wear styles of clothing that reflect your more passive and artistic nature.

3 AS THE OUTER PERSONALITY NUMBER: You are extremely charming, affable and sociable. You have an attractive manner and desire pleasure and fun. Loyalty and honesty enhance your idealistic nature. Communication is a vital part of your personality, and you have a facile manner of expression. An avid conversationalist, you shine in the midst of any group. You are like the sun, lighting up the world of those you encounter, spreading sunshine and optimism wherever you go. Others naturally cluster around your warmth. Your extroverted popularity can become so great that it could cause your downfall through conceit and jealousy. Then your conversational talents may degenerate into gossip, exaggeration and superficiality. If you are a woman, you may be beautiful, with a well-rounded figure. You like personal adornment—jewelry, scarves, makeup—and have an artistic flair in choosing your clothing. On the negative side, you can possess a slovenly beauty and be careless about the styles you choose and the way you care for your clothing.

4 AS THE OUTER PERSONALITY NUMBER: You present a determined, work-oriented attitude to the world. You appear conservative, self-disciplined and practical. You desire an orderly existence through which your ability for physical and mental application will produce conventional and useful results. You are the honest, hard-working type who respects values and industry. You like the earth, nature, your home and country. You can appear so disciplined that there is no time for play, which can isolate you from others. Overly cautious and frugal, you can become defensive and stingy. Crudeness and bad temper could remove you further from social contacts. Or, as an opposite reaction, you could appear completely undisciplined and lazy. Good sports clothes appeal to you, as they are designed for hard use and need little care. You select your clothes for service, insist on good quality materials, and often have them tailor-made. You want to look neat and trim at all times. You are conservative in dress as well as conduct.

5 AS THE OUTER PERSONALITY NUMBER: You are a good conversationalist, bright, sparkling and witty, and will therefore have much interchange with groups of people. You are magnetic to the opposite sex and possess strong sensual appetites.

Because change and freedom are so essential, there may be a quick turnover in your relationships. You like constant activity, variety and change and believe that change is progress. You must be able to do what you want, when and how you want to do it, in order to produce up to your capacity. You have a natural curiosity and are likely to take chances. Others see you as a natural salesperson, advertiser or promoter. Overdoing social interchange and desire for sensual indulgences can lead to excesses in eating, drinking, drugs or sexual contacts. You can become fickle, restless and undependable. You like to be among the best dressed on the fashion list or at least be ahead in style, and you wear bright colors in good taste.

6 AS THE OUTER PERSONALITY NUMBER: You emanate a protective vibration and a sense of responsibility for others. People are drawn to you for counseling, teaching and healing because you have a motherly or fatherly appearance which lends comfort and security. The home seems very important to you. You are optimistic, cheerful and reliable. You appear to love beauty and all things connected with the arts. You have a fine sense of balance and symmetry and can therefore see all the pieces as separate and yet part of the whole. A social consciousness urges you to seek truth and justice. You could become a slave to others, especially in the home, and your social responsibility could degenerate into social irresponsibility or interference in the affairs of others. In choosing clothing, you are careful yet display an artistic flair, preserving a tasteful color harmony in whatever combinations you choose. You prefer comfortable styles which are easy to wear rather than exclusive models, although you are particular in choosing soft and flowing materials. Negatively, you could be a casual housekeeper and be careless about how you dress.

7 AS THE OUTER PERSONALITY NUMBER: You have the appearance of being a loner, enjoying your moments of solitude away from the crowds. Nature and periodic trips into the woods or time spent by the seashore provide the proper climate for your philosophic temperament. There is an air of mystery and secrecy about you. You seem to be the philosopher, mystic, poet, thinker, scientist and researcher whose temporary withdrawals allow time for further probing. A keen power of observation aids you in mentally analyzing any situation. You have an aristocratic air, a personal dignity and a refined manner and seem to possess an unshakable faith in the future. If you become tangled in materialism, you will find only disappointment and lose your poise and become frustrated, gloomy and withdrawn. Confusion, fear and pessimism then take over. You are neat, well-groomed, and inclined towards wearing pastels or dark shades. You avoid loud or brilliant colors and dress in good taste. If you become unhappy, you are then indifferent to the way you dress, and neglect the so-called petty details of color, harmony and matching outfits.

8 AS THE OUTER PERSONALITY NUMBER: You have a dynamic personality and people recognize your authority because you appear affluent and in control. There is an air of the executive about you, one who can manage big business and direct the affairs of commerce. You emanate a personal power and strength which brings recognition wherever you go. You appear authoritative, impartial and ethical. You seem to possess an endless font of physical stamina and endurance. Your personal power could lead you into situations where you might abuse that power. Materialism then overcomes your better judgments and you can become retaliatory and cruel if crossed. A successful appearance is your standard and you insist your clothes be well made and of good materials. You would never wear cheap articles. Carried to extremes, you appear flashy, the gambler or sport, desiring to impress others by wearing loud clothes and by flaunting large rolls of bills. A female might wear too many jewels and exhibit expensive clothes even though they may have come from the thrift shop.

9 AS THE OUTER PERSONALITY NUMBER: You appear to have a breadth of understanding as well as a personal magnetism that is universal in scope. Your warm, friendly and charming manner pleases all you come in contact with, and the selflessness that you emanate makes you loved by many. You seem to have a tolerance and compassion for others that allows you to forgive and forget easily. You are generous towards the needy and exemplify humanitarian traits. Others see you as emotional and romantic, as the idealist who believes that the progress of the world justifies personal sacrifice. Emotionalism can overtake you, and then you become susceptible to every sad story that comes along. At this point, you scatter your energies and emotions wastefully. Bitterness can result. You dress artistically with a dramatic flair, although you desire that your clothes be smooth-fitting and comfortable. You may be beautiful in face and figure, and if you take care of your skin and maintain good posture, you may remain young-looking for years.

11 AS THE OUTER PERSONALITY NUMBER: You are an inspiration to others who see in you a refinement and an artistic genius which moves their very soul. Avant-garde art is your preference and you seem to epitomize unusual and innovative techniques. Recognition and fame may very likely be bestowed upon you because of artistic or humanitarian endeavors. You appear to be the visionary who believes in equal opportunity for all regardless of sex, race, creed or color. Your idealism can degenerate into egocentricity in which case your many talents are dissipated or lie fallow. Your mind then seeks unhealthy outlets for its genius which can bring notoriety. Your eyes emit a spiritual light that can inspire others to achieve their potential, as they witness what you have done. Your dress is original in style and you may design your own clothes because you have the artistic flair and inventiveness to do so, and you prefer to be different.

22 AS THE OUTER PERSONALITY NUMBER: You appear as the masterly, diplomatic type who can handle all situations in a practical, efficient manner. You seem to have control over the material world and have the ability to make profound changes that could alter the course of history. You are a super-power who gives freely of finances to charity and organizations that benefit large groups of people. Your power can extend to the international level; you should perform material service for the world. Unprecedented power placed in your hands can cause you to become power-hungry and, rather than serve others, you may exploit them out of greed. You then become indifferent to the needs of others and are not above committing dishonest acts to achieve your goals. You are usually careful about your dress, choosing high quality materials and conservative styles. Clothes fit you as though they were made especially for you. You wear your clothes; they do not wear you.

33 AS THE OUTER PERSONALITY NUMBER: You strike others as modest, humble and charitable. You always seem to gravitate to places where you are needed and you give more than you receive. Generous at all times, you do not look for rewards; you appear to be a natural giver. You love children and animals, and express kindness and tenderness towards them. People feel they can tell you their problems and you will understand. Sensitivity to the woes of others can lead you into futile self-sacrifice, and you deny yourself for others who often have no intention of bettering themselves. Then your martyrdom is useless, falling on barren ground. You dress in dignified styles, choosing your clothes carefully. Your conduct is proper and refined.

44 AS THE OUTER PERSONALITY NUMBER: You have a disciplined, almost military bearing, walking straight with shoulders held high. This inspires confidence in you from others wherever you go. You seem to know where you are going, what you are going to do, and how you are going to do it. There is a down-to-earth practical quality about you that comforts others. They sense that your common sense can solve their everyday problems and set the material world back in order for them. You may be so earth-oriented that you become mired in drudgery and responsibility. Then you lose sight of the source from which you sprang. At this point, your spiritual progress will suffer. You enjoy wearing a uniform-type outfit and often buy tailored clothing. You may add a military touch, using stripes, bars or distinctive buttons in an effective manner.

The Path of Destiny Number

You have at this point explored your Life Lesson Number (your birth-date), your Soul Number (the vowels in your name) and your Outer Personality Number (the consonants in your name). We will now take the total of your entire name, which is determined by adding the unreduced Soul Number and the unreduced Outer Personality Number together. This is your *Path of Destiny Number*. It shows what you must do in this lifetime, what you came here to manifest.

By adding the unreduced Soul Number to the unreduced Outer Personality Number in Ada Wynn Lunt's name, we arrive at 41/5.

$$1 \ +1 \quad +7 \qquad +3 \qquad = 12/3 \ Soul \ Number$$
$$A \ D \ A \quad W \ Y \ N \ N \quad L \ U \ N \ T$$
$$4 \quad +5 \ \ +5+5 \ \ +3 \ \ +5+2 = 29/11 \ Outer \ Personality$$
$$Number$$
$$41/5 \ Path \ of \ Destiny$$
$$Number$$

Ada Wynn Lunt's Path of Destiny Number is 41/5, and this is what she must do as a lifetime pursuit. Ada would now read 5 as the basic Path of Destiny Number in the following section. She would then turn to Part II and read 41/5 as a Personal Number Vibration, which is a finer delineation of the basic 5 vibration.

This number represents your aim in life; in other words, it shows the path you must walk, what you should accomplish, what you must be. Although you may modify it somewhat by name changes, the birthname destiny is always the power behind any change, and will persist in its desire for expression throughout your life.

1 AS THE PATH OF DESTINY NUMBER: You represent the real "I am," conscious of self as the center of your world, concerned with your individual desires and seeking self-preservation above all else. You use your resources for your own pleasure and have little interest in the needs of others. This is not necessarily bad, since you are here to develop the self but you must not allow this to be carried to the extreme of selfishness. You may be a newcomer to the earth plane where all beginning lessons are to be learned. The words you most often use are "I" and "I am." Leadership is your keyword, and you must accept the destiny of leading while others follow. Your own independent initiative will help you attain success through your determination to stand for your beliefs even under duress. By exhibiting self-reliance and demonstrating your ability to win, you will succeed under all circumstances.

2 AS THE PATH OF DESTINY NUMBER: Your desire for peace puts you in the role of a peacemaker. Your destiny could lead you to act as ambassador of good will to foreign nations and thus bring untold benefits to all mankind. Use your inborn tact and diplomacy to handle difficult situations in life. A mission as peacemaker is a magic gift for creating a better world in which to live.

You also have a keen sense of opposites which allows you to develop your talents along creative lines. By expanding this awareness, you not only maximize your artistic potential, but you also enhance your abilities as a mediator and a useful companion. You become an integral part of any organization or group with which you become affiliated.

3 AS THE PATH OF DESTINY NUMBER: You have talents which give you a choice of occupations or hobbies. Your destiny is that of one who uplifts and inspires others. You should play center-stage and develop your talent for expression and communication through drama, elocution or foreign languages. Explore the arts. Study the religions of the world. This could be a constructive outlet for your energies, since you have a natural inclination toward spiritual philosophies. Your occupation could encompass therapy for others, as well as self-improvement.

If you wish to be a success, use your time wisely. Do not scatter your energies in too many directions at once and thus postpone the accomplishment of a worthwhile destiny. Promote friendship among your peers by being a friend when a friend is needed. You spread joy and sunshine through your ability for self-expression. Keep optimism as your trademark.

4 AS THE PATH OF DESTINY NUMBER: Your destiny is to build tangible and useful products. You need to see what you have built. 4 is the builder of the world, the rock upon which all earthly substance is formed. You are well organized in your thinking and can manage your particular establishment with efficiency. You emanate a quality of stability. As a result, others will rely on you to get the job done efficiently and properly. You handle money well and might therefore find the financial world a fertile spot for your talents.

Your keywords are *impatience, honesty, determination* and *confidence*. You demand obedience in the family and will practice self-denial in order to fulfill duties, either real or imagined. Your keen sense of value makes you dislike the mediocre. You know that what is worth having is worth working and waiting for.

5 AS THE PATH OF DESTINY NUMBER: Many changes occur in your life, and your mission might well be to promote progress through a willingness to accept change. You are definitely not keyed to the old order or to outworn ideas and set principles. You are willing to adopt new concepts and new points of understanding, even to the extent of daring to claim the liberty to suggest new ways of doing things, and you have the ability to present the new in logical and acceptable terms. You make stepping stones of changes and cleverly turn them into growth experiences. You do not, however, forget conventions since you are really not a rebel. Instead, you propose new ideas to promote enlightenment; you have the courage and willingness to let go of the old and experiment with the new. You are very fluent and expressive with words and could find writing, lecturing or selling the perfect outlet for these talents.

6 AS THE PATH OF DESTINY NUMBER: This is a domestic vibration. You love home and family life. You are the marrying type and your family is your main interest. You are morally good and respectable, trustworthy and generous. You like the comforts and luxuries of life. You are a good mixer, a good host or hostess; you greet and mingle with everyone present at any social gathering. You are proud of your possessions and even enjoy showing off your family's talents and accomplishments.

You should train your artistic talents so that you can share your aesthetic sense and appreciation of beauty with others. Many famous individuals in the arts worked under this vibration, expressing fully their deep and abiding love for others through their work.

7 AS THE PATH OF DESTINY NUMBER: Your depth of character and seriousness destine you to be a teacher of ethics. You psychically separate the true from the false and can discover and reveal some of the mysteries of life to a waiting world. You should become the thinker, the philosopher, the scientist, the mystic or the religious zealot whose destiny is the mind. Some may see you as strange and hard to understand, but they will follow your teachings and seek your counsel when they are troubled. Your example and public image could benefit a whole community and eventually the world.

You find strength in solitude, wisdom in moments of silence, and strength in your own knowledge. In ancient days, those born under 7 were placed in the temple to become priests or priestesses because all were aware of their mental powers. Develop your mental powers; the world will benefit.

8 AS THE PATH OF DESTINY NUMBER: You have magnificent courage and stamina, and you will attain your goals through your own efforts. Recognition, success and wealth are your proper destiny. Perseverance in your career and long hours of intensive work backed up by ambition are what carry you to the top executive position in your chosen field. No lesser position would be acceptable to you. You need, however, to couple your material forces with the spiritual, and to attain mastery over yourself before you can attain and hold the position you visualize for your life's work.

Some people with this number vibration use their tremendous strength and endurance in the sports field and become outstanding athletes, thereby expressing their determination to be at the top in sports rather than in the business world. However, many famous athletes end up in business when their sports careers have ended.

9 AS THE PATH OF DESTINY NUMBER: Perfection is your goal, but it is rarely attained on this plane. Your mission is a charitable one. You may meet many tests and setbacks, but the lesson of forgiveness will bring temperance to those situations. The higher you evolve, the more tests you are apt to meet, so guard against losing balance. You strive to live an ideal life and hope to inspire others to do the same. You desire to better the world through philosophy and philanthropy and become impatient when results come slowly. You need to realize that evolution occurs only in long cycles of time.

You will meet many famous people in your lifetime who will be impressed by the breadth of your thinking. You should learn not to cling to old associations. When you have fulfilled your role with an individual, you must move on. You cannot be limited to a small circle of friends. Your broad philosophy must touch and enlighten the lives of many.

11 AS THE PATH OF DESTINY NUMBER: Your gift of prophecy places you in the position where selfless service to humanity can be expressed, a difficult goal to live up to at best. You could work as a leader in public or civic affairs in your community and promote better standards of living for the more unfortunate. Your career drive could express itself through acting on stage or screen, or as a dynamic preacher or teacher. Your own standard of deportment should be above the average.

You should achieve fame or recognition in some way, and since this vibration bestows great creative potential, the arts or inventive professions are your most likely choices. You have the ability to tap the creative source and imbue your work with an inspirational touch that will affect the souls of those who come into contact with whatever you create. You are truly inspired.

22 AS THE PATH OF DESTINY NUMBER: You have confidence in your ability to lead and therefore naturally assume great responsibility. This fulfills your urge for important accomplishments. Once you have assumed your position of great power and wealth, you will want to participate in new mass movements in important civic and community projects. You are the "super-materialist" whose influence can be world-wide. You are a creator on the material plane; you build in a large way. Bridges, hospitals, museums and other such structures are the visible products you leave to the world, products that serve to aid and enlighten mankind. Your influence is so far-reaching that you must guard against unethical motives because you will ultimately affect many lives. Serve well and you will be rewarded in direct proportion.

33 AS THE PATH OF DESTINY NUMBER: Your mission is self-sacrifice and service to others. You often undergo crucifixion in your emotions and suffer for the woes of the world. Your actions are tempered by compassion through your understanding of right and justice. You often find that you must live impersonally with a detached but caring attitude, and realize that the way in which you handle the burdens placed on you will be a supreme example for others. Others sense your understanding nature and are naturally drawn to you for comfort and solace. By answering their needs, you find the fulfillment this number demands of you. If you are not living up to the master number 33, you can live it as a 6. You may then develop a martyr complex and get little appreciation for your sacrifices.

44 AS THE PATH OF DESTINY NUMBER: This master number vibration demands great discipline and perseverance and the ability to make the best of any given situation. You are very resourceful, drawing upon your great wells of common sense and logic to solve any problems that arise. Your destiny is to serve the material needs of the world through productive and sound techniques. Edgar Cayce, a 44, solved the health problems of thousands. He served their material needs. You must gain complete mastery over your mind and body while here on earth. Your desire should be that others may share in universal prosperity and you should set about to construct situations in which this is possible. You seek to better the world in a physical way.

The Significance of the First Vowel in the First Name

The ancients considered vowels the sacred elements in the alphabet. They thought that the first vowel was the vibration upon which the soul entered the body. It has been found that the first vowel does indeed have a profound influence upon the individual, and that, if one has an abundance of that same first vowel throughout the entire name, the quality of that vowel is enhanced.

There are three things to look for when reading the first vowel in your name: 1) the meaning of the vowel itself; 2) how many of that *same* vowel there are in the entire name, and 3) what, if anything, precedes that vowel.

If there are more than three of the first vowel in the whole name, it means that there is too much of that particular characteristic, and the person may be overbalanced in the direction of that attribute.

The following delineation of the vowels is very general and is meant only as a guide to aid in assessing the individuality of the person under consideration within the context of the total numerological analysis.

A AS THE FIRST VOWEL in the first name: You are bold, independent, inquisitive and interested in research. You know what you want and why you want it. If A is the first vowel and there are two A's in the entire name, you are a clear thinker. If A is the first vowel and there are more than three A's, you can be egotistical, cynical and even critical.

E AS THE FIRST VOWEL in the first name: You have an eventful, exciting life. You are versatile and have the ability to learn easily, but may be nervous and temperamental. If E is the first vowel and there are more than three E's in the name, you may have a fickle nature.

I AS THE FIRST VOWEL in the first name: You are intuitive and interested in the arts, drama and/or science. If I is the first vowel and there are more than three I's in the name, you are sensitive, shy and too emotional.

O AS THE FIRST VOWEL in the first name: You are frank, methodical and believe in law, system and order. If O is the first vowel and there are more than three O's in the name, you can be obstinate, slow and monotonous.

U AS THE FIRST VOWEL in the first name: You have a universal mind capable of great ideas and a broad viewpoint. You love to accumulate material things. Symbolically, the U is a cup that holds, therefore you may become a collector. If U is the first vowel and there are more than three U's you may experience loss and selfishness because the cup spills over and the contents are lost. When W is the first vowel in the first name, it vibrates like a double U.

Y AS THE FIRST VOWEL in the first name: It has the same significance as E or I, according to the sound produced. To determine when Y is used as a vowel, consider the pronunciation. In the name May or Wayne, Y is not a vowel but if Y has a separate sound, as in the name Floyd, it is counted as a double vowel dipthong

since the sound of the Y is distinguishable in the pronunciation. In a
name such as Lynn or Wynn, where the Y is the *only* vowel sound, it
is counted as a vowel. In the names Yvonne or Yvette, Y as the first
vowel has the sound of E. Also, in a name such as Mary or Harry, Y is
a vowel because it sounds like E.

One last note on the vowel or consonant Y. Its two-pronged structure could symbolically indicate its double usage in the alphabet. As a
vowel sound, Y could become the twenty-seventh letter in the
alphabet to complete the ninth vibration presently missing. (I=9;
R=18/9; Y=27/9). Pythagoras considered Y such a high mystical letter that at one time he took the name of Yarancharya to experience its
vibration at first hand.

If the name contains two vowels together, as in the name Faith,
then read the qualities of both vowels. For example, Faith indicates a
person who is independent, interested in research (A), and also very
intuitive, a lover of music and the arts (I).

We do not count the vowels in the name beyond the first vowel
combination unless there are identical adjoining vowels later in the
name. In the name Faith May Winter we consider AI as the first
vowel. Because the AI combination appears nowhere else in the
name, the first AI stands as the only one of that vowel. The A in May
and the I in Winter are considered separately. Conversely, should the
name be Faith Daisy Waite, we would have three AI vowels to consider. The following is a list of dipthongs and double vowels in sam-
ple names.

aa Aaron	ea Jean	ia Diane	oa Joan	ua Luanna
ae Mae	ee Lee	ie Pierce	oe Joel	ue Sue
ai Faith	ei Eileen	ii	oi Lois	ui Guido
ao Lao	eo Leo	io Viola	oo Oona	uo Quomodo
au Audrey	eu Eunice	iu Lium	ou Roulo	uu
ay Wayne	ey Heydon	iy	oy Floyd	uy Guy

Triple vowels, such as in the name Louise, would also combine the
qualities of the three vowels.

Other meanings of the vowels will be found in the list of the ABC's
in Chapter Five, which gives the meanings of the individual letters of
the alphabet.

Your Personal Year

We live our lives in nine-year cycles, incorporating the universal principles of the numbers 1 through 9. When we finish the ninth cycle, we
begin again with 1 and proceed again through the nine numbers. This
cycle occurs over and over throughout our lifetime. Look back nine
years from this moment, and you will find that you are experiencing
not the exact events but a similar type vibration. For instance, nine

years ago you might have been saving money to build a home; now you may be saving to send a child to college. The event is different, but the underlying theme is the same: budgeting money. If you know what to expect in any given cycle, you can live in tune with your particular vibration, and make your life easier, happier and more productive.

To find your present *personal year*, simply add the month and day of your birth to the year of your last birthday. For example, November 12, 1940 is the birthdate of Ada Wynn Lunt. To determine Ada's present vibration, we will add the date $11+12+1975$. (1975 is the year of her last birthday as of this writing July 1976.) Remember, we do not use the year of birth, but rather the year of the last birthday. If you were born on February 29, use February 29 regardless of whether the year in question had a February 29th or not.

$$11+12+1975$$
$$11+12+22 \ (1+9+7+5)$$
$$11+12+22=45/9$$

Ada, in 1975, is in a 45/9 personal year. The personal year runs from the birthday of one year to the birthday of the next year, not from January to December as the general calendar runs. Therefore, Ada will be in a 45/9 personal year from November 12, 1975 to November 12, 1976, even though most of her personal year, 1975, runs into the calendar year 1976.

Ada would then turn to Part II, and read number 9 under the section entitled 9 as a Temporary Vibration. She would then read 45/9 as a Temporary Vibration, which is a finer description of the underlying 9 Temporary Vibration. Note that we are not reading the number as a Personal Vibration. The numerical meanings of a Personal Number and a Temporary Vibration are the same; however, you must put them in their proper perspectives. If a number is your Personal Number, it is with you for a lifetime. If it is a Temporary Vibration, you experience it for a short time. So, from her November 12, 1975 birthday to her November 12, 1976 birthday Ada will be temporarily experiencing a 45/9 vibration.

You can follow the same procedure for any given year of your life to find out what happened or what is going to happen. Merely chose the time you are investigating, for instance, the summer of 1946, or the fall of 1987, and from there determine the year of your last birthday at that time. Then add that year to your month and day of birth to find your personal year vibration.

Period Numbers

We can divide the personal year into three equal blocks of time to

Your Personal Numbers determine what is happening in each four-month period of the year. We do this in the following manner.

Place the personal year calculations in the first column. At the head of the second column write the month of the birthday and the fourth month following; in our example, November to March. In the next column, place the following four months, e.g.: March to July, and in the last column place the remaining four months, July to November.

Personal Years	November 12 to March 12	March 12 to July 12	July 12 to November 12
$11+12+1975$	1975	1975	1975
$11+12+22=45/9$	35	37	12
	$2010=3$	$2012=5$	$1987=25/7$
	Add Age	Add Life Lesson Number	Add Soul Number

If the birth month were June, you would place June to October at the head of the second column, October to February in the third column and February to June in the fourth column. This simply divides the year into three four-month blocks beginning with the month of your birth.

To find the experience of Ada's first four-month block in 1975, add her age to the year 1975. She was thirty-five on November 12, 1975, so we will add $1975+35=2010$. We will then reduce 2010 by adding $2+0+1+0=3$. She will be under a 3 vibration from November 1975 to March 1976 of her personal year 45/9.

In the second block, covering March to July, we add the double digit of her Life Lesson Number, 37, to the year 1975. $1975+37=2012$, or $2+0+1+2=5$. From March to July she will be operating under a 5 vibration.

In the fourth column under July to November, we will add the double digit of her Soul Number to the year 1975, or $1975+12=1987$. $1+9+8+7=25/7$ vibration.

Always add the unreduced double digit of the Life Lesson Number to the third column and the unreduced double digit of the Soul Number to the fourth column.

The delineations for these numbers are in Part II of this book under the Temporary Vibrations section of each individual number.

Use the same procedure for any year. For example, using Ada Wynn Lunt, born November 12, we will examine her year for November 12, 1976 to November 12, 1977.

November 12 to March 12	March 12 to July 12	July 12 to November 12	Personal Month
1976	*1976*	*1976*	
=46/1	*36*	*37*	*12*
2012=5	*2013=6*	*1988=26/8*	

...igure your past personal year and period numbers to ... yourself the accuracy of this method?

Personal Month

...sible to find the personal month vibration which reveals ...g trend of each month of the personal year. Simply add the number of the month in question (January is 1, February is 2, through December which is 12) to the double digit personal year number.

Ada, in 1975, is in a 45/9 personal year. If we wish to find her vibration during the month of May, we add 5 for May (the fifth month of the year) to 45 for her personal year and arrive at 50/5 for her personal month. May will be a 50/5 personal month. Then read the delineations of number 5 and 50/5 in Part II under Temporary Vibrations for a more thorough analysis of the energies Ada is working with during the month of May in the year 1975.

Since her birthday is November 12th, we would continue to work with the 45/9 personal year until November. We would then add the value of the month of November, 11, or December, 12, to the 46, rather than to the 45, because Ada entered a new personal year on her birthday.

Ada is in a 6 period from March to July. This indicates a change in the home; Ada might possibly move during that period. We could then narrow it down to the month of May, because the base number 5 indicates change, movement and freedom.

These personal month vibrations are minor and only help to locate the more important events during the year.

Keywords for period numbers and personal months
1 new starts, action, originality, making decisions
2 harmony, cooperation, mediation, passivity
3 scattering, freedom, entertainment, self-expression
4 practicality, work, order, building foundations
5 change, freedom, new intellectual interests, travel
6 family, health, service, listening to others' problems
7 self-analysis, achievement, health problems
8 business, power, responsibility, money

41

Your Personal Numbers

- **9** giving to others, endings, service
- **11** limelight, inspiration, religion
- **22** materialism, large endeavors
- **33** sacrifice, compassion for others
- **44** helping others resolve daily problems, counseling

3

GOD GEOMETRIZES

T HE SYMBOLOGY OF NUMBERS is universal; it contains
eternal principles that cannot be modified by human will.
Every manifestation is the product of the single digits 1 through 9.
Geometry is the visual tool of the spirit world through which we can
uncover any information needed to promote our understanding of
ourselves and the world around us—in short, our evolution. All
answers are there. An occult axiom states, "God geometrizes." In this
chapter, we attempt to explain what is meant by those two simple yet
enigmatic words.

Through the authors' research, logic, work, meditation and intuition, the following concepts have emerged. Many ideas presented
here have been accepted for ages, some are relatively recent, and the
remaining are totally new, surfacing for the first time. They make
sense to us, and, for this reason, we present them to you.

God
Geometrizes

We can best begin by delineating the four basic shapes which form a numerical foundation for all numbers and shapes:

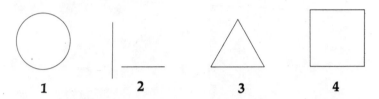

1   2   3   4

The circle represents the Godhead, all that was, is and ever shall be; spirit, the I Am; love because it encompasses, enfolds and contains; balance, because however you turn it, it maintains its shape; and justice, because it is in a state of perfect balance. A circle contains three hundred sixty degrees. $3+6+0=9$. 9 is the highest and final digit in the series of single digits; when multiplied by another number, the result always reduces again to 9 ($2\times9=18/9$, $3\times9=27/9$, $4\times9=36/9$ and so on). A circle has no beginning and no end; it is infinite and endless. The Lord said, "I am the Alpha and the Omega" (Revelations 1:11), the beginning and the end.

The circle symbolizes eternity and the immortality of the soul. This is seen through the laws of nature and cyclicity. Planets revolve around the sun in a circular pattern; nature repeats itself in cycles; and, if we travel far enough out into space, we arrive at the same point from which we started (so scientists claim). The God energy is elliptical or round. It goes on and on, never ending. The ancients said, "God is a spherical intelligence whose center is everywhere and whose circumference is nowhere." Behind the altar in many churches hangs a symbol of the cross surmounted on the God symbol, a circle.

The upright vertical line symbolically represents spirit descending into matter, or energy leaving the Godhead. It has masculine qualities; it is outgoing, dynamic, energetic, fiery, upright and commanding.

Every energy has an opposing polarity, and the horizontal line is such a symbol in relation to the vertical line. It represents the soul energy, the feminine, the receptive and absorptive qualities of mother earth. This line is an ancient symbol for matter and the material world.

The triangle is the first closed form that can be made with single lines. It represents the Trinity, Father-Son-Holy Ghost, father-mother-God, father-mother-child, spirit-soul-mind, super-conscious, subconscious, conscious.

In the two interlaced triangles, the Philosopher's Diamond or the Star of David, geometry captures the axiom, "As above, so below."

We are made in the image of God. The upper triangle of the
Philosopher's Diamond is the father-mother-god which is reflected in
the lower inverted triangle, father-mother-child. The upper triangle is
the world of spirit, and the lower triangle is the world of matter. The
Godhead from above is reflected in the material world below;
therefore, what we see in the material world is merely a reflection of
the truth. It is as if we are gazing into the depths of a cool forest pool,
thinking the images we see are the only truth, although these images
may be distorted by the wind rippling the surface of the water. We in
the material body are merely observers of the shadows cast upon the
walls of Plato's cave. We live in a world of illusion and view things
upside down.

Geometry validates the theory that we see only half the truth. The
following are mathematical truths: the sum of the angles of a triangle
is one hundred eighty degrees; the sum of the angles of a square is
three hundred sixty degrees; and a circle contains three hundred sixty
degrees.

By lowering the downward-pointing triangle of the Philosopher's
Diamond a bit, we have the illustration in the margin. Each of these
triangles has only one hundred eighty degrees, or half the degrees of a
circle or square (three hundred sixty degrees). As we have shown, a
circle contains all truth and wisdom; it is the Godhead. But in the
triangle we have only half the truth. By adding these two triangles
together, or one hundred eighty plus one hundred eighty, we arrive at
three hundred sixty degrees, or all the truth. Symbolically situated in
the lower inverted triangle, we must look to the spirit in the upper
triangle to find all the truth, else we remain in a shadow land where
the ill winds ripple our images and distort our vision of the truth.

If the two triangles are turned to the side, they form a
parallelogram, of four sides, or a modified square.

The square is the second perfect shape that can be drawn with
single lines; it is symbolic of the earth. The 4 appears in a number of
ways: the four points on the compass; the four elements of fire, earth,
air and water; the four points of the cross; the forty days (an elevated
4), spent by Christ in the desert fighting earthly temptations; and salt
crystallizing in cubes, a solidified 4. Finally, as the salt of the earth,
we are all examples of the number 4. These are a few of the many
references relating 4 to earth.

The four sides of the square represent the four parts of the individual—with the physical body added to the triangle of mind, soul
and spirit. Now, spirit has a soul, a mind and a body in which to
work in the material world.

By joining the two triangles of the Philosopher's Diamond shown
above, we arrive at the parallelogram, which like the circle, contains
three hundred sixty degrees or all truths. This shows that complete attainment and fulfillment are possible here on earth in the physical

body because the circle and the square both contain three hundred sixty degrees.

Always remember, however, that spirit is contained within the body, just as the triangle preceded the square and is contained within it. Our body belongs to the earth, but our soul belongs to the spirit. Spirit is immortal because, as we have shown, the triangle existed *before* and *independently* of the square. But the square is *totally dependent* upon the triangle because the square is built upon it, following it in the natural order of things. Spirit cannot operate in the physical world without a material body, but it can operate in other worlds and dimensions. The material body contains and must reflect the Godhead for completion and fulfillment in the material world. "As above, so below."

Futher examination of the Philosopher's Diamond reveals deeper truths. Esoteric tradition teaches that the upper triangle is fire, and the lower triangle is water. We link fire to the spirit with such expressions as the "living flame," the "eternal flame;" and the Bible speaks of the burning bush and the fiery fingers that etched the ten Commandments on Moses' tablets.

Symbolically, water and the emotions are synonymous. We weep tears when we are emotional, happy or sad. Our common expressions equate water with the emotions in such phrases as "rough sailing," "stormy seas," "waves of feeling engulfed him" and so on. The major portion of our planet is water, known to be controlled by the moon, which also affects the stability of the human emotions.

Spirit is linked to the mind, the head area, where the pineal and pituitary glands, the father and mother centers, are located. The watery emotions are centered in the heart. We are told that, "the lion shall lie down with the lamb." What we are being promised is that Leo the lion, ruler of the heart, shall lie with the lamb, or Aries the ram, ruler of the head. We shall have peace when the head and the heart are brought into perfect balance, when we think with our hearts and feel with our heads.

The preceding analysis of geometrical forms has been preparation for the delineation of the Divine Triangle, the basis of which is the Pythagorean Theorem. The explanation of this blueprint can describe the magnitude or destiny of our lives.

The blueprint is formed by the triangle of three parts of mind (mind-soul-spirit) added to the square of the physical body and matter.

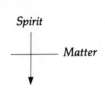

As you can see from the blueprint, the cross is also part of the Divine Triangle. Spirit descends into matter as shown in the illustration in the margin.

We as human beings are stationed at the corner point where the two lines of the cross meet. At this point we are the recipients of the cosmic energy; therefore, these points represent an aspect of consciousness.

The soul enters the body at point A and immediately begins its journey along the path which for the first nine years will cover line AB. It then turns the corner at B and continues from B to C between the ages of nine and eighteen. Upon reaching eighteen, it then turns and travels line CD for nine years, until age twenty-seven. The first square ABDC has been formed.

In this period of time, from age zero to twenty-seven, the mind and character are formed. Psychology and medicine bear this out. Plato said that one gains one's soul at age twenty-eight, and astrologers will note that this closely corresponds to the first complete Saturn return which, at approximately age twenty-nine, has made one circuit on the natal chart, touching every planet, lending structure and form and crystallizing the energies emitted by each planet. As you can see, the soul, at point D, for the first time since entering the physical body, touches the fire of spirit. Therefore, between the ages of twenty-seven and twenty-nine, we are in a precarious position; this is the first time the soul comes into contact with the fire of spirit, whose awareness it lost when it entered the body.

Depending on the past use of our personal energies, it is at this age that we can be burned by the fire of destruction, or transmuted by the fire of spirit. This can be a painful, burning experience for those who are bound to the past and past conditionings, who cannot let go of those habits, opinions and beliefs that can restrict and encase them in the past. But, for those who use the experiences and learning of the past as a firm structure upon which to build the future, it is then that they are touched by the fiery flame of spirit, which reaches into their lives and inspires them to follow their true path of destiny. By observing the experiences in people's lives between the ages of twenty-seven and twenty-nine, we learn a great deal about how the fire can burn and destroy, or rekindle and transmute.

We have established that the youth square of the Divine Triangle encompasses that period of time in which the process of building a sound mental structure is accomplished.

In Pythagoras's original theorem, the sides of the right triangle measured 3, 4 and 5 units of length.

In figure 1, you can see that the youth square is built upon the side with the value of 3, which has an astrological correspondence to the planet Jupiter. With Jupiter as the foundation of the first twenty-seven years of life, the principles of mental and spiritual expansion are at work. The youth square is the cornerstone, the mind, upon which the temple, the body, is built. Solomon, a wise numerologist, spoke of this cornerstone as the block upon which the power square, ages twenty-seven to fifty-four, will be placed.

The power square has as its foundation line the horizontal side of the right trangle, with a value of 4, a number related to the earth. This implies that between the ages of twenty-seven and fifty-four our life is

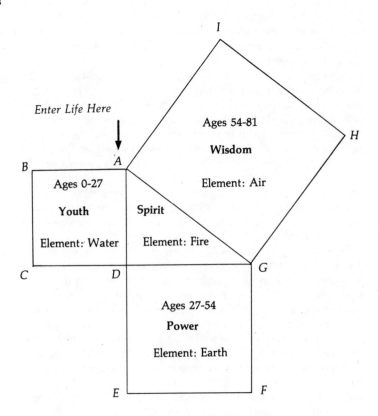

Figure 1 The Blueprint

spent dealing with the material plane and all that it encompasses. Certainly we can agree that most of us spend that portion of our lives using whatever power we have in striving for material gains and comforts in the form of job positions, salaries, housing and personal possessions; each is an aspect of the material plane. It is right and fitting that we should do this. We chose to incarnate in a material body to learn the lessons of the earth plane, and it is here in the power square that we are most intimately in touch with this particular learning process.

You will note, however, that this square is a result of the square of the mind. The earth plane is the base line of this square, but the mind is the overseer, and indeed it is through the mind that we create our environment. It is here in this time span between the ages of twenty-seven and fifty-four that we are free of the psychological restrictions and childhood conditionings of the youth square, free to make decisions about which way we want our lives to go. These decisions rest exclusively with the mind of the individual.

The Bible says, "As a man thinketh, so he is." We cannot deny the profound effect that a positive attitude has upon the direction of our lives. Look around you; what you see is the result of the way you think. It has nothing to do with anyone else; it is yours and yours alone. If you are happy with your situation, then your mind is in order and well balanced. If you are not happy, then you and you alone have the power to change your present environment and relationships by making the decision that yes, you are a worthy person; and yes, you deserve to have all the material comforts you want; and yes, you should be loved and respected. Because it is only when *you* make the decision that you deserve and will have these things, that they will begin to come to you. Romans 12:2 says, "Be ye transformed by the renewing of your mind."

At age fifty-four the second building block has been completed, and the individual has established a body and a mind. We are known by the way we look, and by the way we think. Notice, however, that at age fifty-four we are experiencing the same transitional phenomenon we did at age twenty-seven. This point roughly corresponds to the second complete Saturn return, and brings with it the same choices and results we confronted between the ages of twenty-seven and twenty-nine.

Here again at fifty-four, for the second time in our life, we come into direct contact with the center triangle of spirit, our own true inner self. Will the inner self express approval of our past efforts and reward us with the fruits of our labor? Or will the inner self instead hand us dried dead fruits, scorched by the burning fire of destruction? Whatever we reap, rest assured we have sown. The universal law of balance brings only justice. The law of physics that for every action there is an equal and opposite reaction has precedence here. It is swift and sure and without emotion, pure justice in action, but it is the result of our own past actions. We are always in control. If we have not sown wisely in the past, it is at this point that we can easily make the decision to change our direction. The future is ours to create.

The wisdom square, which is the structure of the soul, is built upon the line assigned the value 5, astrologically a Mercury number. The ages fifty-four to eighty-one, which the wisdom square encompasses, is thus a period in life given to much introspection. We reflect upon the past, its failures and accomplishments; the present, at what station in life we find ourselves; and the future, such issues as death and the immortality of the soul.

In mythology, Mercury was the messenger of the deities, the connecting communication link between the gods of heaven and the mortals on earth. Symbolically, this fleet-footed messenger is the mind, the connection between soul and body, which, in the period of life between fifty-four and eighty-one, must now turn from the material world and build the bridge between the physical world and the world of Spirit. This is accomplished through reflection, reason, order, logic and understanding—all mercurial qualities. This bridge between the physical and spiritual will be achieved through a synthesis of the results of the previous processes.

In the youth square, mind was formed and conditioned and expanded; in the power square, mind had to operate in the world of form on its own, as a single independent entity. Now, in the wisdom square, the mind must analyze the results of the soul's evolution through the various stages up to this point and begin to assimilate these findings into the soul's growth experience up to the time the transition process of death occurs.

For those of us who live through this square and reach the magic age of eighty-one, there is a three-pronged fork at which we must choose a future path.

We may decide to leave the body, at which point we will die and follow the ascending arrow out of the blueprint back to the source from which we came.

Or we may decide to stay in the body, which implies that we will proceed in one of two directions, depending on the type of seeds we have sown in the past. Life past eighty-one is decidedly karmic. If we have wasted our life energies and left naught but destruction and unhappiness in our wake, we may very well take the path we originally trod at birth, that first horizontal line on the youth square, ages zero to nine. Because the line encompasses childhood we too will become childlike (senile) and need to be cared for like an infant.

The third path is for those who have sown wisely, who have used the precious God-given life energies and have honored the body-temple in service to the material world through understanding, compassion and love towards others. On this sacred path, the few are revered and honored because their very presence blesses those near. Their touch is healing, and their words express the music of the spheres, inspiring and lifting the weary heart. Blessed are those who tread this path, for theirs is the destiny of supreme devotion to life.

Chapter Four instructs you in how to place your birthname and birthdate on the Divine Triangle to work with your personal life blueprint.

4

THE DIVINE TRIANGLE

I N THIS CHAPTER, we will explain how to place your birthname and birthdate on the Divine Triangle and discover the events which you will experience in this lifetime. The Life Theorem of Pythagoras is the basis of the Divine Triangle, and as you can see from the blueprint (figure 1), his right triangle is the foundation upon which each of the squares is built.

The information that is about to be revealed to you is unique. To our knowledge it has never been published before. Very likely it was lost in the great fire that destroyed the fabulous library at Alexandria many centuries ago. Priceless parchments containing the wisdom of many masters were lost.

Faith's teacher learned the method for using this blueprint from the master K.H. who, according to some sources, was formerly Pythagoras. Perhaps Pythagoras taught this method to his disciples.

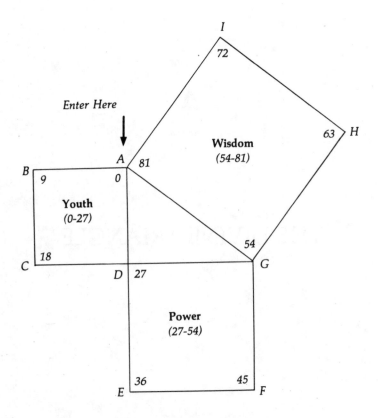

Figure 2: The Blueprint

Regardless of one's belief in such things, the blueprint does work; therefore, in our minds, it is valid. Try it for yourself and see.

Drawing the Blueprint

The blueprint is set up as follows. The right triangle of Pythagoras occupies the center. Squares are built on each side of the triangle. Each of the three lines drawn to complete the square represents nine years of life.

We begin on line AB at the point of entrance indicated by the arrow in figure 2. The lines represent the ages as follows:

Line	Ages
AB	0−9
BC	9−18
CD	18−27
DE	27−36
EF	36−45
FG	45−54
GH	54−63
HI	63−72
IA	72−81

On the blueprint, figure 2, we see that the youth square covers the ages, birth through twenty-seven. The power square covers the ages twenty-seven through fifty-four. The wisdom square covers ages fifty-four through eighty-one. After age eighty-one, we begin again on the youth square, but this time on a higher vibration. See p. 66.

Become thoroughly acquainted with the blueprint before proceeding. If you familiarize yourself with it now, the following process will be much easier to understand.

Labeling the Blueprint

The Birthdate Using our example, Ada Wynn Lunt, we will place her birthdate, November 12, 1940, on the triangle in the center of the blueprint. The birthmonth (11/2) goes on the vertical line AD; the birthdate (12/3), on the horizontal line DG and the birthyear (1940=14/5), on the hypotenuse AG.

We reduce the double digits. Here the number 11 becomes 2, the number 12 becomes 3, and the year 1940 reduces to 14 and then 5. If the birthmonth and birthdate were single digits, such as May 4, you would simply place 5 for May on line AD and 4 for the day on line DG.

The Name The value of the letters in your name is placed on the lines of the squares. Place the letter and its value on each line.

In our example, Ada Wynn Lunt, the letter of the first name, A, and its value, 1, is placed on line AB of the youth square.

Place the second letter, D, and its value, 4, on line BC.

Place the third letter of the name, A, and its value, 1, on line CD.

This completes the youth square, which represents the ages from birth to twenty-seven.

When you come to the end of your first name, place an X on that corner, for it marks an important time in your development. Changes will occur, or a definite event will change your outlook in some way. We place an X at point D because we have completed Ada's first name.

Continue with the power square. Place the next letter of the name, in this case W, and its value, 23/5, on line DE.

Put the following letter, Y, and its value, 25/7, on line EF.

Put the next letter, N, and its value, 14/5, on line FG.

This completes the power square, which represents the ages twenty-seven through fifty-four

On the wisdom square, place the next letter of the name, N, and its value, 14/5, on line GH. At this point we place another X, because this marks the end of the middle name.

The last name is never used on the blueprint, because it is a family vibration and not uniquely your own. Therefore, when you run out

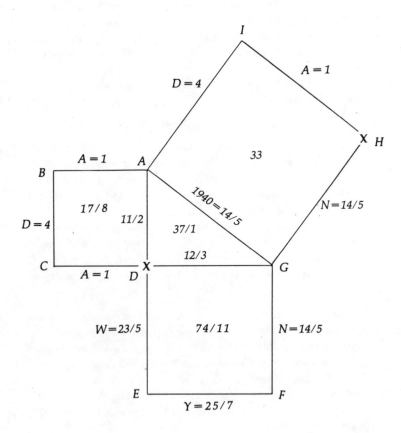

Figure 3: Blueprint for Ada Wynn Lunt, born November 12, 1940

of letters, you begin the first name over again. So, in our example, we begin again with the first name.

Place the first letter of the first name, A, and its value, 1, on line HI.

Place the second letter of the first name, D, and its value, 4, on the remaining line, IA.

This completes the wisdom square which represents ages fifty-four to eighty-one.

If you or the subject is older than eighty-one, begin again on the new square.

The Totals Now that we have placed the name and birthdate on the blueprint, we add the four sides of each square for a total which is placed in the center of the square. Always add the higher unreduced digit in this process.

In the youth square, we add $1+4+1+11$ for a total of 17/8. Place the number 17/8 in the center of the youth square.

In the power square, add $23+25+14+12$ and place the total, 74/11, in the center of the square. 74/11 is a master number and is not reduced further.

In the wisdom square, add $14+1+4+14$ for a total of 33 which is placed in the center of the square. 33 is a master number and is not reduced further.

Now add the three sides of the triangle for a fourth total which is placed in the center of the triangle. Always add the higher digits: $11+12+14=37/1$. Place 37/1 in the center of the triangle. Notice that 37/1 is the Life Lesson Number. The number in the center of the triangle is always the Life Lesson Number.

Figure 3 shows how the blueprint will look when the totals are written in.

The number in the center of the youth square is an umbrella vibration that covers the period of life from birth to age twenty-seven; the number in the center of the power square is the fundamental vibration that covers the ages from twenty-seven to fifty-four; and the number in the center of the wisdom square is the fundamental vibration influencing the years from fifty-four to eighty-one. To find out what each vibration has to offer for that period in your life, turn to Part II of this book and read the Temporary Vibration delineation for that number. Here is one more example:

```
 1  7  5  1  9 5   1   5  =34/7 Soul Number
MARY GERALDINE CHARLES
 4  9  7 9  3 4 5  3 8  9 3 1 =65/11 Outer Personality
                                       Number
                              99/18/9 Path of Destiny
                                       Number
```

65/11 is a master number and is not reduced further. As explained in the introduction, we do not use numbers that exceed 78; so we reduce 99 to 18/9.

May 21, 1927
5+21+(1+9+2+7)
5+21+19=45/9 Life Lesson Number

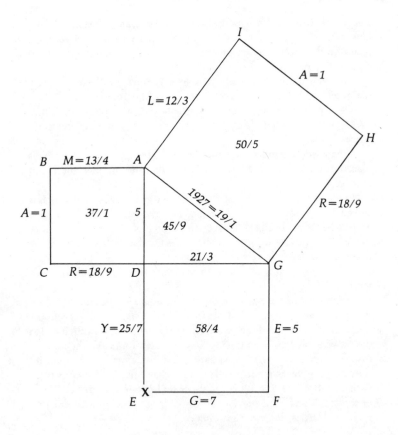

Figure 4 Blueprint for Mary Geraldine Charles

Determining the Line Experiences

We know there are nine single digits, and every double digit reduces to a single one. Consequently, there are only nine phases through which you can pass in life. Each phase lasts nine years; therefore, it takes eighty-one years to complete the nine phases.

Each of the nine lines outside the triangle represents nine years of life; therefore, the number on any given line will influence that nine-year period. For example, Ada Wynn Lunt has a 4 on line BC, which covers the ages nine to eighteen; she will be under the 4 vibration during those years.

Each line of the blueprint reveals eight experiences. Two different methods are used to compute the types of experience to be faced. The first method, which is traditionally called the *major process* yields six types of experience and covers twenty-seven years, giving a wide perspective. The second method, or *minor process*, yields two types of experiences and focuses on a nine-year period to give a more specific delineation. The words "major" and "minor" refer only to the lengths of the time-spans involved. The experiences revealed by the minor process may be just as important as the ones revealed by the major process. However, the minor experiences may have a more current effect, whereas the major experiences have more of a long-range effect.

By the time you reach eighty-one years of age, you will have traveled over nine lines in the blueprint and have had seventy-two experiences. Let us now examine the methods used to arrive at these experiences and the ages at which they will occur. The descriptions for these experiences can be found in Part II under the Temporary Vibration delineations for the numbers.

The Major Process

As we go around the triangle for the experiences revealed by the major process, we will be using three sets of numbers, one set in each step:

Step 1: the numbers in the center of the square
Step 2: the numbers on the side of the triangle
Step 3: the numbers in the center of the triangle

These numbers will be added to or subtracted from the ages on each end of the line we are working on.

We always use a single digit to add or subtract from the ages on the line. If you have a master number, reduce it to its base number. For example, master number 33 would become a 6.

To illustrate, we will use the blueprint of our example, Ada Wynn Lunt, (figure 3) to ascertain what sort of experiences she might have at various times in her life.

Line AB Use 0 and 9, the ages at each end of the line AB.

Step 1: Use the numbers in the center of the square, 17/8. To age 0, *add* the single digit; from age 9 *subtract* the single digit. 0+8=8. 9−8=1. At ages 1 and 8 there was a 17/8 experience.

Step 2: Use the numbers on the side of the triangle, 11/2. To age 0, *add* the single digit; from age 9 *subtract* the single digit. 0+2=2. 9−2=7. At ages 2 and 7 there was an 11/2 experience.

Step 3: Use the numbers in the center of the triangle, 37/1. To age 0, *add* the single digit; from age 9 *subtract* the single digit. 0+1=1. 9−1=8.

At ages 1 and 8 there was a 37/1 experience.

Line BC Use 9 and 18, the ages at each end of the line.

Step 1: Use the numbers in the center of the square, 17/8. To age 9, *add* the single digit; from age 18 *subtract* the single digit. 9+8=17. 18−8=10. At age 10 and 17 there was a 17/8 experience.

Step 2: Use the numbers on the side of the triangle, 11/2. To age 9, *add* the single digit; from age 18 *subtract* the single digit. 9+2=11. 18−2=16. At ages 11 and 16 there was an 11/2 experience.

Step 3: Use the numbers in the center of the triangle, 37/1. To age 9 *add* the single digit; from age 18 *subtract* the single digit. 9+1=10. 18−1=17. At ages 10 and 17 there was a 37/1 experience.

Line CD Use 18 and 27, the ages at each end of the line.

Step 1: Use the numbers in the center of the square, 17/8. To age 18 *add* the single digit; from age 27 *subtract* the single digit. 18+8=26. 27−8=19. At ages 19 and 26, there was a 17/8 experience.

Step 2: Use the numbers on the side of the triangle, 11/2. To age 18 *add* the single digit; from age 27 *subtract* the single digit. 18+2=20. 27−2=25. At ages 20 and 25 there was an 11/2 experience.

Step 3: Use the numbers in the center of the triangle, 37/1. To age 18 *add* the single digit; from age 27 *subtract* the single digit. 18+1=19. 27−1=26. At ages 19 and 26, there was a 37/1 experience.

The table on the next page summarizes the information we derived from Ada Wynn Lunt's youth square.

Now let us see what we can find out about Ada Wynn Lunt's power years, 27-54, by looking at her power square.

Line DE Use 27 and 36, the ages at each end of the line.

Step 1: Use the numbers in the center of the square, 74/11. To age 27 *add* the single digit; from age 36 *subtract* the single digit. (Note: Since we always use a single digit to compute the line experience, we

	Age at Corner	Selected Single Number	Age at Which Experience Occurs	Type of Experience	The Major Process
			Line AB: Ages 0-9		
Step 1:	0	+8	=8	17/8	
	9	−8	=1	17/8	
Step 2:	0	+2	=2	11/2	
	9	−2	=7	11/2	
Step 3:	0	+1	=1	37/1	
	9	−1	=8	37/1	
			Line BC: Ages 9-18		
Step 1:	9	+8	=17	17/8	
	18	−8	=10	17/8	
Step 2:	9	+2	=11	11/2	
	18	−2	=16	11/2	
Step 3:	9	+1	=10	37/1	
	18	−1	=17	37/1	
			Line CD: Ages 18-27		
Step 1:	18	+8	=26	17/8	
	27	−8	=19	17/8	
Step 2:	18	+2	=20	11/2	
	27	−2	=25	11/2	
Step 3:	18	+1	=19	37/1	
	27	−1	=26	37/1	

reduce the master number 11 to its base number 2.) 27+2=29. 36−2=34. At ages 29 and 34 there was a 74/11 experience.

Step 2: Use the numbers on the side of the triangle, 12/3. To age 27 *add* the single digit; from age 36 *subtract* the single digit. 27+3=30. 36−3=33. At ages 30 and 33 there was a 12/3 experience.

Step 3: Use the numbers in the center of the triangle, 37/1. To age 27 *add* the single digit; from age 36 *subtract* the single digit. 27+1=28. 36−1=35. At ages 28 and 35 there was a 37/1 experience.

Line EF Use 36 and 45, the ages at each end of the line.

Step 1: Use the numbers in the center of the square, 74/11. To age 36 *add* the single digit; from age 45 *subtract* the single digit. (Note: Reduce master number 11 to its base number 2.) 36+2=38. 45−2=43. At ages 38 and 43 there will be a 74/11 experience.

Step 2: Use the numbers on the side of the triangle, 12/3. To age 36 *add* the single digit; from age 45 *subtract* the single digit. 36+3=39. 45−3=42. At ages 39 and 42 there will be a 12/3 experience.

Step 3: Use the numbers in the center of the triangle, 37/1. To age

59

36 *add* the single digit; from age 45 *subtract* the single digit. 36+1=37. 45−1=44. At ages 37 and 44 there will be a 37/1 experience.

Line FG Use 45 and 54, the ages at each end of the line.

Step 1: Use the numbers in the center of the square, 74/11. To age 45 *add* the single digit; from age 54 *subtract* the single digit. (Note: Reduce master number 11 to its base number 2.) 45+2=47. 54−2=52. At ages 47 and 52 there will be a 74/11 experience.

Step 2: Use the numbers on the side of the triangle, 12/3. To age 45 *add* the single digit; from age 54 *subtract* the single digit. 45+3=48. 54−3=51. At ages 48 and 51 there will be a 12/3 experience.

Step 3: Use the numbers in the center of the triangle, 37/1. To age 45 *add* the single digit; from age 54 *subtract* the single digit. 45+1=46. 54−1=53. At ages 46 and 53 there will be a 37/1 experience.

	Age at Corner	Selected Single Number	Age at Which Experience Occurs	Type of Experience
		Line DE: Ages 27-36		
Step 1:	27	+2	=29	74/11
	36	−2	=34	74/11
Step 2:	27	+3	=30	12/3
	36	−3	=33	12/3
Step 3:	27	+1	=28	37/1
	36	−1	=35	37/1
		Line EF: Ages 36-45		
Step 1:	36	+2	=38	74/11
	45	−2	=43	74/11
Step 2:	36	+3	=39	12/3
	45	−3	=42	12/3
Step 3:	36	+1	=37	37/1
	45	−1	=44	37/1
		Line FG: Ages 45-54		
Step 1:	45	+2	=47	74/11
	54	−2	=52	74/11
Step 2:	45	+3	=48	12/3
	54	−3	=51	12/3
Step 3:	45	+1	=46	37/1
	54	−1	=53	37/1

The above table summarizes the information we derived from Ada Wynn Lunt's power square. The two righthand columns give the age at which each experience will occur and the number that represents the quality of each experience. To find out what the quality of each of those experiences will be, she would look up each of those numbers as Temporary Vibrations in Part II of this book. For example, at age 29, Ada will have a 74/11 experience. 74/11 as a Temporary Vibration is delineated on page 250.

Now let us look at Ada Wynn Lunt's wisdom square and see what we can find out about her life from ages 54 to 81.

Line GH Use 54 and 63, the ages at each end of the line.

Step 1: Use the numbers in the center of the square, 33. To age 54 *add* the single digit 6 (33 reduced); from age 63 *subtract* the single digit 6. 54+6=60. 63−6=57. At ages 57 and 60 there will be a 33 experience.

Step 2: Use the numbers on the side of the triangle, 14/5. To age 54 *add* the single digit; from age 63 *subtract* the single digit. 54+5=59. 63−5=58. At ages 58 and 59 there will be a 14/5 experience.

Step 3: Use the numbers in the center of the triangle, 37/1. To age 54 *add* the single digit; from age 63 *subtract* the single digit. 54+1=55. 63−1=62. At ages 55 and 62 there will be a 37/1 experience.

Line HI Use 63 and 72, the ages at each end of the line.

Step 1: Use the number in the center of the square, 33. To age 63 *add* the single digit 6 (33 reduced); from age 72 *subtract* the single digit 6. 63+6=69. 72−6=66. At ages 66 and 69 there will be a 33/6 experience.

Step 2: Use the numbers on the side of the triangle, 14/5. To age 63 *add* the single digit; from age 72 *subtract* the single digit. 63+5=68. 72−5=67. At ages 67 and 68 there will be a 14/5 experience.

Step 3: Use the numbers in the center of the triangle, 37/1. To age 63 *add* the single digit; from age 72 *subtract* the single digit. 63+1=64. 72−1=71. At ages 64 and 71 there will be a 37/1 experience.

Line IA Use 72 and 81, the ages at each end of the line.

Step 1: Use the numbers in the center of the square, 33. To age 72 *add* the single digit 6 (33 reduced); from age 81 *subtract* the single digit. 72+6=78. 81−6=75. At ages 75 and 78 there will be a 33 experience.

Step 2: Use the numbers on the side of the triangle, 14/5. To age 72 *add* the single digit; from age 81 *subtract* the single digit. 72+5=77. 81−5=76. At ages 76 and 77 there will be a 14/5 experience.

Step 3: Use the numbers in the center of the triangle, 37/1. To age 72 *add* the single digit; from age 81 *subtract* the single digit. 72+1=73. 81−1=80. At ages 73 and 80 there will be a 37/1 experience.

The following table summarizes the experiences of Ada's wisdom years.

	Age at Corner	Selected Single Number	Age at Which Experience Occurs	Type of Experience
Line GH: Ages 54-63				
Step 1:	54	+6	=60	33
	63	−6	=57	33
Step 2:	54	+5	=59	14/5
	63	−5	=58	14/5
Step 3:	54	+1	=55	37/1
	63	−1	=62	37/1
Line HI: Ages 63-72				
Step 1:	63	+6	=69	33
	72	−6	=66	33
Step 2:	63	+5	=68	14/5
	72	−5	=67	14/5
Step 3:	63	+1	=64	37/1
	72	−1	=71	37/1
Line IA: Ages 72-81				
Step 1:	72	+6	=78	33
	81	−6	=75	33
Step 2:	72	+5	=77	14/5
	81	−5	=76	14/5
Step 3:	72	+1	=73	37/1
	81	−1	=80	37/1

This concludes our discussion of the experiences revealed by the major process. You may have noticed that Ada had more experiences at certain ages than at others, for example at ages one and eight. It is common to find more than one event happening in your life at any given year. Often, many events occur simultaneously, and if they do, the blueprint will reflect this.

Since Ada has many 1's on her blueprint (A=1, and her Life Lesson Number is 1), the 1 will be used more often in addition and subtraction, yielding an abundance of events at the same age. This suggests that some years in our lives will be more active than others, which we know is true.

You will also notice that the numbers in the center of the squares and on the sides of the triangle are often activated, but the Life Lesson Number, in the center of the triangle, is activated on each line of the blueprint. The Life Lesson must be learned; it is therefore repeated more than any number on the blueprint.

The Minor Process

This time we have three steps and two sets of numbers. Again we use the ages at each end of the line, but this time we use the number value of the letters in the name under consideration.

Step 1: Use the single digit on the line to determine the two ages when the experiences will take place.

Step 2: Use the higher number in the center of the square to determine the younger age experience.

Step 3: Use the higher number on the side of the triangle to determine the older age experience.

Since we use our name in the minor process, the experiences are more personal. Whereas two people may have the same birthdate, it is highly unlikely that their birthnames would be identical.

Your birthdate makes up the numbers on your triangle; it also makes up your Life Lesson Number. You always use the triangle numbers to compute your older age experience because the older you are, the more you are dominated by your Life Lesson Number. And, we can assume, the older you are, the more capable you are of coping with your life lesson. Remember, the numbers representing your birthdate are your *most* important numbers.

Now let us apply the minor process to Ada Wynn Lunt's youth square and see what we find.

Line AB Use 0 and 9, the ages at each end of the line.

Step 1: Use the single digit on line AB, which is 1. To age 0 *add* the single digit; from age 9 *subtract* the single digit. $0+1=1$. $9-1=8$.

Step 2: For the *younger* age experience (age 1): *add* the higher number on the line to the higher number in the center of the square. $1+17=18/9$. At the age of 1 there was an 18/9 experience.

Step 3: For the *older* age experience (age 8): *add* the higher number on the line to the higher number on the side of the triangle. $1+11=12/3$. At the age of 8, there was a 12/3 experience.

Line BC Use 9 and 18, the ages at each end of the line.

Step 1: Use the single digit on line BC, which is 4. To age 9 *add* the single digit; from age 18 *subtract* the single digit. $9+4=13$. $18-4=14$.

Step 2: For the *younger* age experience (age 13): *add* the higher number on the line to the higher number in the center of the square. $4+17=21/3$. At the age of 13 there was a 21/3 experience.

Step 3: For the *older* age experience (age 14): *add* the higher number on the line to the higher number on the side of the triangle. $4+11=15/6$. At the age of 14 there was a 15/6 experience.

Line CD Use 18 and 27, the ages at each end of the line.

Step 1: Use the single digit on line CD, which is 1. To age 18 *add* the single digit; from age 27 *subtract* the single digit. 18+1=19. 27−1=26.

Step 2: For the *younger* age experience (age 19): *add* the higher number on the line to the higher number in the center of the square. 1+17=18/9. At the age of 19 there was an 18/9 experience.

Step 3: For the *older* age experience (age 26): *add* the higher number on the line to the higher number on the side of the triangle. 1+11=12/3. At the age of 26 there was a 12/3 experience.

Now let us look at Ada's power square using the minor process.

Line DE Use 27 and 36, the ages at each end of the line.

Step 1: Use the single digit on the line, which is 5. To age 27 *add* the single digit; from age 36 *subtract* the single digit. 27+5=32. 36−5=31.

Step 2: For the younger age experience (age 31): *add* the higher number on the line to the higher number in the center of the square. 23+74=97/16/7. At the age of 31 there was a 16/7 experience.

Step 3: For the *older* age experience (age 32): *add* the higher number on the line to the higher number on the side of the triangle. 23+12=35/8. At the age of 32 there was a 35/8 experience.

Line EF Use 36 and 45, the ages at each end of the line.

Step 1: Use the single digit on line EF which is 7. To age 36 *add* the single digit; from age 45 *subtract* the single digit. 36+7=43. 45−7=38.

Step 2: For the *younger* age experience (age 38): *add* the higher number on the line to the higher number in the center of the square. 25+74=99/18/9. At the age of 38 there will be an 18/9 experience.

Step 3: For the *older* age experience (age 43): *add* the higher number on the line to the higher number on the side of the triangle. 25+12=37/1. At the age of 43 there will be a 37/1 experience.

Line FG Use 45 and 54, the ages at each end of the line.

Step 1: Use the single digit on the line, which is 5. To age 45 *add* the single digit; from age 54 *subtract* the single digit. 45+5=50. 54−5=49.

Step 2: For the *younger* age experience (age 49): *add* the higher number on the line to the higher number in the center of the square. 14+74=88/16/7. At the age of 49 there will be a 16/7 experience.

Step 3: For the *older* age experience (age 50): *add* the higher number on the line to the higher number on the side of the triangle 14+12=26/8. At age 50 there will be a 26/8 experience.

And finally, we will use the minor process to examine Ada Wynn
Lunt's wisdom square and foresee the kinds of experiences she will
have from ages 54 to 81.

Line GH Use 54 and 63, the ages at each end of the line.

Step 1: Use the single digit on the line, which is 5. To age 54 *add* the
single digit; from age 63 *subtract* the single digit. $54+5=59$.
$63-5=58$.

Step 2: For the *younger* age experience (age 58): *add* the higher
number on the line to the higher number in the center of the square.
$14+33=47/11$. At age 58 there will be a 47/11 experience.

Step 3: For the *older* age experience (age 59): *add* the higher number
on the line to the higher number on the side of the triangle.
$14+14=28/1$. At the age of 59 there will be a 28/1 experience.

Line HI Use 63 and 72, the ages at each end of the line.

Step 1: Use the single digit on the line, which is 1. To age 63 *add* the
single digit; from age 72 *subtract* the single digit. $63+1=64$.
$72-1=71$.

Step 2: For the *younger* age experience (age 64): *add* the higher
number on the line to the higher number in the center of the square.
$1+33=34/7$. At age 64 there will be a 34/7 experience.

Step 3: For the *older* age experience (age 71): *add* the higher number
on the line to the higher number on the side of the triangle.
$1+14=15/6$. At the age of 71 there will be a 15/6 experience.

Line IA Use 72 and 81, the ages at each end of the line.

Step 1: Use the single digit on the line, which is 4. To age 72 *add* the
single digit; from age 81 *subtract* the single digit. $72+4=76$.
$81-4=77$.

Step 2: For the *younger* age experience (age 76): *add* the higher
number on the line to the higher number in the center of the square.
$4+33=37/1$. At age 76 there will be a 37/1 experience.

Step 3: For the *older* age experience (age 77): *add* the higher number
on the line to the higher number on the side of the triangle.
$4+14=18/9$. At age 77 there will be an 18/9 experience.

This completes our discussion of the line experiences of an individual from birth to age 81.

We suggest at this point that you select the names and birthdates of
your family and friends, place them on the blueprint, and work out
their line experiences. This will accomplish two goals: 1) you will
become familiar with the procedure, and 2) you will be able to cor-
relate what you find with the individual's past experiences and
discover for yourself how effective the blueprint really is.

After Eighty-one

Those not in possesion of their mental faculties at age eighty-one must begin their youth squares over again with the first letter of the first name, as in childhood.

Assuming that Ada keeps her wits about her after eighty-one, we do the calculations in the same way but with new letters on the lines. Since Ada left line IA with a D on it (see figure 3) we begin her new youth square with the second A of ADA WYNN on line AB. A=1. W=23/5 goes on line BC. Y=25/7 goes on line CD. The number on the side of the triangle (her birthmonth) is still 11. The total for her new youth square is 1+23+25+11=60/6.

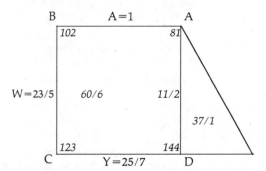

Figure 5: New Youth Square for Ada Wynn Lunt after Age 81.

After age eighty-one, if you are still mentally alert, each line of your new square equals twenty-one years, rather than nine as in the first youth square. Up to age eighty-one, you have completed nine cycles of nine years. After eighty-one, you live under a trinity or three seven-year spiritual cycles. You have reached a higher level of consciousness; therefore each new line covers twenty-one years.

Applying the major process to the first line of the new youth square, here is what we find.

Step 1: We use the 60/6 from the center of the square and the ages at either end of line AB. 81+6=87. 102−6=96. She will have 60/6 experiences at ages eighty-seven and ninety-six.

Step 2: We use the numbers on the side of the triangle, 11/2, and the ages at either end of line AB 81+2=83. 102−2=100. At ages eighty-three and one hundred she will have 11/2 experiences.

Step 3: We use the numbers in the center of the triangle, 37/1, and the ages at either end of line AB. 81+1=82. 102−1=101. She will have 37/1 experiences at ages eighty-two and one hundred one.

Now we will apply the minor process to Ada's new youth square.

Step 1: We use the single digit on line AB, 1, and the ages at either end of the line. 81+1=82. 102−1=101.

Step 2: To determine the younger age experience, we add the unreduced number on the line to the unreduced number in the center of the square. $1+60=61/7$. Ada will have a 61/7 experience at age eighty-two.

Step 3: To determine the older age experience, we add the unreduced number on the line to the unreduced number on the side of the triangle. $1+11=12/3$. Ada will have a 12/3 experience at age one hundred one.

5

MORE WITH NUMBERS

T HIS CHAPTER DISCUSSES four additional techniques based on your personal numbers. It would be impossible to contain within one book all the possible methods one could employ to work with numbers and number combinations. Here are just a few. We hope you enjoy them.

The ABC's

You have seen how to make a life analysis by using the number found in your name and your birthdate on the Divine Triangle. Along with this method, in which the numbers represented by each letter in your name are added to each other to get the Path of Destiny Number, it is also possible to delineate further by evaluating each letter separately and in sequence. The numbers represented by each separate letter have an underlying influence on your life and affect the total energies at work at any given time. You should read the delineations of each number in your name in conjunction with the information on your blueprint.

When a number represented by one of the letters in your name is found on a line of your blueprint, that letter is emphasized and that age span is called a *peak cycle*. A letter is also emphasized if it appears three or more times in your name or if it is the first vowel or the first letter of your name. A letter acts as a health factor whenever the letter is at peak cycle

The 1's

A IS THE HEAD LETTER, powerful and complete. You are good intellectually and require several outlets for your energies. You are not a builder but a planner, and you want others to carry out your plans. You have lots of ideas and begin many projects but do not always finish them. A is a letter of initiative, self-reliance and will power.

A at a peak cycle brings activity and the opportunity for new starts. You can achieve leadership in business or in the community. This is a time to learn the lessons of self-reliance and double your resolution to get ahead through your own efforts.

A as a health indicator means to watch out for the lungs or diseases of the respiratory system.

J IS A STEPPED UP NINE DEGREES; therefore, it is a more intense vibration. Materially and spiritually, it is full of high aspirations, which are necessary to develop more profound powers. You are honest, benevolent, brilliant and often inventive.

J at a peak cycle nearly always means gain and advantage in some form. You should extend a helping hand to those less fortunate and keep your spirits high if you want to enjoy good fortune in the rhythm of J. Willing or not, you will be put in a position of leadership, and if this extends to business, promotions will result. You may also be a leader in family affairs. Through the letter J you will almost always experience gain and advantage in some form.

J as a health factor gives a feeling of well-being.

S IS A LETTER OF ENDURANCE. The ancients called it "the letter of surrender." You are spiritually intense and can sting or charm. S brings love and new starts into life and attracts money, but it is not always a happy letter.

S at a peak cycle will triumph over obstacles to attain ambitions. There will be many turnings in your life's path. If you are responding negatively to this letter, there will be emotional upheavals, failure and uncontrolled impulses. Be positive.

S as a health factor may sharpen an illness but it also tends to bring recovery and reduce trouble, thus creating better conditions.

The 2's

B IN A WOMAN'S NAME indicates mother love. B in a man's name means love of nature and domesticity. It is not a strong material letter. You can go to great heights and equally great depths. You are emotional and fixed in your opinions. Your instinct is to follow others. You are hospitable, but if B is negatively expressed, you become selfish.

B at a peak cycle is influenced by psychological currents. This letter brings strong desire for partnerships or marriage. The lesson is patience, calmness and serenity of mind. Decisions should be left to others. This is a cycle of hidden development which may not be recognized by others.

B as a health factor can cause nervousness, headaches and emotional upsets.

K MEANS EXTREMES in fortune, health and spirituality. You are very versatile, idealistic and intuitive. You either enjoy great success or suffer abject misery. The solution is service to others. Use your leadership abilities for humanity and not for self-glorification.

K at a peak cycle displays creative inspiration and idealism. It should be directed toward a positive goal, or this cycle may result in conflict. There is great emotional force here for either intense romantic experience or spiritual exaltation. It brings travel and change and can bring success if caution is used.

K as a health factor indicates nervousness, which may come from overactivity. But it is a good force, giving strength and endurance.

T WILL EITHER BUILD or break down, save or slay the human race. You like to control everyone within your influence, to shape things to your own liking. You have to learn self-control, as you are very emotional and can be swayed. If positive, you develop high spirituality, as the quality of the 2 is reinforced by the 0 of God's protection.

T at a peak cycle represents reconstruction. This influence creates a sense of restlessness unless ideas are expressed through practical activity that can benefit humanity. Time should not be wasted nor idleness tolerated. This is a time to work for better world conditions. It is also a time of spiritual growth.

T as a health factor indicates stress through change or travel. If it is with an A, there can be accidents and operations.

C IS SCATTERED ENERGY. 3 is a scattering vibration because it wants to go in many directions at once. If C is the first letter, you have a jovial nature but are apt to have an emotional life. You find it difficult to save money. You like to have several lines of effort going at once. You are a good talker and promoter and seldom worry over anything. At times, you can be impatient, irritable and impulsive, and if negative, careless and immoral.

C at a peak cycle favors artistic, political or business success. It is good for self-expression, productivity and growth. There should be rich emotional experiences, prosperity and happiness. This is a strong marriage vibration.

C as a health factor may cause concern with the throat, thyroid and vocal cords.

L GATHERS where C scatters. You always bring to completion anything you start. You are generous but want returns from your giving. L as a whip symbol indicates action, and since you have executive ability, you are a leader. You are moral, balanced, honest and intellectual, and you may attain spirituality. L indicates travel.

L at a peak cycle brings service and self-sacrifice, but also rich rewards in human relationships. Creative ideas bring profit. This letter can bring marriage and increasing concern with financial matters.

L as a health factor suggests paying attention to the throat, which is true under all 3's. Two L's together tend toward accidents or falls.

U HAS THE UNIVERSAL spirit of both the C and the L. U is shaped like a cup that holds the gifts of talent, charm and luck, but if you become greedy and try to fill your cup too full, you may lose through selfishness. You are an enthusiastic collector and you will be tenacious in holding onto the things you accumulate. U is called the rocker letter, and you can be a victim of indecision. While you are deciding, someone else may take things away from you. You have a good memory and should make an effort to have a positive attitude.

U at a peak cycle indicates a time for subconscious development. There may be delays and restrictions now, and family responsibilities can increase, but there is a growing sense of security and protection. Marriage is activated. Be cautious under a U, because things tend to slip away, often through a personal fault, such as overlooking and neglecting to grasp an opportunity. Matters should be examined carefully, and a lawyer consulted in business deals.

U as a health factor tends to bring loss and anxiety. Worries cause other ills, such as high blood pressure. Strive to remain calm and at peace within.

D IS BALANCE; it acts as a good anchor. You are strong in material matters, determined and stubborn. You have good business ability. You are a good worker, steady and practical, a builder who takes responsibility well. These qualities may bring you a position of authority and power.

D at a peak cycle represents a striving to lay a firm foundation for the future. Temporary delays are possible, but valuable lessons in patience can be learned. Speculation should be avoided and conservatism practiced. Travel is possible.

D as a health factor is not notable unless there are two D's together. That can indicate unhappy travel situations and unfortunate probings into your business or personal affairs, which could adversely affect your health.

M SPIRITUALIZES the attributes of the D and is more idealistic. You are not a leader but will carry on for others. You have psychic powers. You may have to carry burdens in this life, but there is no one who bears the cross more bravely and with so little complaint. You have a receptive nature and may bear burdens for others because of the sacrificial aspects of this vibration. You like home and security above all.

M at a peak cycle looks for regeneration and renewal. It is a reconstruction period when old ideas are swept away to make room for better ones. Unexpected changes can occur now, and they should be recognized as a door to progress where a new phase of happiness will open.

M as a health factor can indicate temper, causing rash behavior and headaches. Because of the potential for drastic changes, more than one M can be dangerous unless dealt with carefully. Two of any letter doubles its effects.

V IS THE MASTER BUILDER. You are fixed in your opinions, firm in your friendships and square in your dealings with others. You are an excellent worker. Since you are both possessive and emotional, you can be either very practical or very impractical and unpredictable. Your dual nature needs to become steadfast. You are the marrying kind.

V at a peak cycle has the potential of wanderlust coupled with too much generosity or extravagance with money. If V appears together with U there could be losses in speculation or gambling. At the worst, there could be dissipation and excess—at best, courage in the face of difficulties.

V as a health factor can cause nervous and emotional breakdowns through overactivity. Cultivate peace within.

The 5's

E IS A STRONG VOWEL ruled by Mercury, the cosmic messenger. You are fine when in harmony but changeable when in discord, because many of your best qualities are then reversed. You are more attracted to the worldly than to the spiritual. You are entertaining but may be impulsive. Freedom is a necessity, and you find it difficult to settle down to specialize. Your versatility results in many changes, and often brings travel. Your fine intellect is capable of high honors if applied seriously. If you are drawn to the spiritual, you become idealistic, hopeful and intuitive.

E at a peak cycle will have to choose among many chances for change. There will be constant activity, new people and new situations. If you are single, there is the opportunity now for marriage, but you should be sure it is true love rather than emotional impulse.

E as a health factor indicates good health. The heart feels free, but impulsiveness should be controlled.

N IS THE ANCIENT SYMBOL for a scribe; therefore, this letter implies a person with a vivid imagination who can bring inspired messages to the world. You must remain positive, or instability will result. You like to enjoy the pleasures of life, and when self is overcome, you can rise to the heights. Envy, jealousy and divorce are common to someone whose name contains an N.

N at a peak cycle brings variety, change and experiences. It is favorable for commercial or political enterprises and may involve much competition.

N as a health factor can cause irritability because of emotional upsets brought on by thoughts of marriage. If N occurs with a G, marriage has a very good outcome. If N and T are together, marriage prospects and harmony after marriage are certain.

W TO EXPRESS ITSELF, must follow the divine law of love. You have great persistence and hate to give up. You are a good mixer, charming, magnetic and intuitive. If negative, you can be selfish, greedy and too daring.

W at a peak cycle signifies an alternation between the heights and the depths. This is a time for self-evaluation and for finding your potential. This cycle can bring marriage.

W as a health factor can bring headaches due to the nervous and impulsive vibration of the letter.

The 6's

F HAS THE STRONG characteristics of Venus. You are kind, home-loving, hospitable and friendly. Since you take responsibility well, you are a good organizer of social affairs. Compassion for others is an outstanding trait. If F is expressed negatively, you are sad.

F at a peak cycle centers your attention on family matters and duties connected with loved ones, whether married or not. It is time to learn the meaning of willing service, because the alternatives may be disappointing. Wise choices are necessary.

F as a health factor indicates trouble, including nervous conditions of the heart. If F is with an N, illness is possible. If F is with U or O, watch your financial matters, or losses may occur.

O IS PATIENT, persevering and strong willed. You are a good student, absorbing knowledge easily and retaining it well. Jealousy can cause upsets in marriage relationships and home conditions; therefore you must learn emotional control. O stands for virtue or vice—there is no middle path. You are either a saint or a sinner.

O at peak cycle presents an opportunity for progress by allowing a release from present limitations. A radical change in viewpoint may occur, and fears can be erased. If O is with a G, there is gain. If O is with a U, losses are possible, and if O is with a D, there will be expenses incurred through necessary travel, plus the possibility of changes in the home.

O as a health factor can cause worry and depression if you are responding to its negative side. Slowing down can prevent heart irregularities and despondencies. O is compatible with religious matters; therefore, prayer can help and inspire.

X IS A DUAL LETTER—the upper half is open to receive the better things in life, the lower half is open to overindulgence, especially of the sexual nature. If positive, you can advance mentally and spiritually. If negative, you are angry, unfaithful and sensuous.

X at a peak cycle flashes a danger signal at the crossroads, a warning of deceit. If the positive side is expressed, financial matters will be beneficial, and good relations with people of influence will be established.

X as a health factor indicates a danger of falls and/or injury to the back. It is better not to ride a horse during this period, or to travel to high places. Mountain climbing should be postponed.

The 7's

G IS RELIGIOUS and mystically inclined with a deep understanding. You are inventive, intuitive and extremely methodical. Since your will is so strong, you are hard to convince. You also dislike advice.

G at a peak cycle is a time of expansion, productivity and material success. It is favorable for the arts, music, drama or literature.

G as a health factor is always good. If illness occurs, there is help toward recovery. G occurring with a D or an F indicates financial gain.

P CONFERS POWER of expression, either in speaking or writing. You are clever, clear-sighted and intellectual. You can be dominating and rather impatient if restricted. If negative, you will be selfish and unsympathetic.

P at a peak cycle presents bright prospects for the future. Because of your creative talents, good fortune is in store. Plan wisely and aim toward the future during this cycle.

P as a health factor indicates that you should not overwork while under this letter. If P is with a G, health is good; if with a T or B, nervous conditions may arise.

Y NEEDS FREEDOM—physical, mental and spiritual. You hate bondage in any form. You have a love of beauty and philosophy, and you desire achievement. Pythagoras referred to the letter Y as the two roads which require that choices be made.

Y at a peak cycle brings sudden change, since it is a branching cycle quick decisions are necessary. Decide firmly and refuse to look back or regret the past. Make the best of things after the choice is made.

Y as a health factor gives a feeling of well being and protection while on water.

The 8's

H MUST CREATE and fulfill. You attract success and money, but will either be very wealthy or very poor because your good judgment fails at times. You are a lover of nature and do not need others for your happiness. H is a power letter, sufficient unto itself. If negative, you are selfish.

H at a peak cycle acts as a gate to the path of life, a gate which can be either a barrier or an opening. This is a time when the cosmic laws are working toward completion of karma. There is concern with financial or legal affairs and with the physical and material side of life.

H as a health factor can bring personal strain. If H is with an N, nervous strain and even illness are possible.

Q HAS MORE ORIGINALITY than H and more intensity of feeling. You are a leader. You have a fine mind, and you like to talk. A relationship with unknown forces gives you secret strength and an air of mystery. You are deep.

Q at a peak cycle grants great mental vitality, intuitive power and

75

creative attainment. There is opportunity for outstanding leadership
and distinction in your career. This is a good time for public activity
and travel. Encourage others unselfishly.

Q as a health factor indicates a period of strong health.

Z HOLDS ALL THE QUALITIES of H and Q but it is more
spiritual. You have aspiration and inspiration, hope and
guidance. Since you are intuitive and perceptive, you understand
human nature. You have the power to achieve. Diplomacy and
discretion make you a good mediator.

Z at a peak cycle runs a zig-zag course in a cycle of hidden progress.
Though there are setbacks, you are advancing to a higher level. In
this period, learn patience and its rewards.

Z as a health factor gives control over illness. There may be a need
to control others or to carry out secret missions in healing.

The 9's

I IS A LAW unto itself. Your tendency is to finish whatever you
start. You can be very obstinate if limited, and you chafe under
dictatorship. Since I is an artistic vowel, you like to use the pen or the
needle (writing, fashion design etc.). You make a good lecturer but
can also do clerical work. You can become loving, compassionate, intuitive and humanitarian. Runs of luck, either good or bad, follow
you. If negative, you have a nervous, quick temper.

I at a peak cycle creates an interlude of ups and downs. By standing
firm on your convictions, great inspiration results. Wavering will
bring fluctuations in fortune, resulting in new beginnings. This is a
period when personal feelings are paramount; sensitivity, sympathy
and intuition are high.

I as a health factor brings nervousness, probably caused by overexertion. Intense emotions can cause exhaustion.

R HOLDS ALL THE POSSIBILITIES of the I, except that it
represents the brighter side of the 9's. You are tolerant and like
to help humanity. You are very active. If negative, you may have to
guard against losses. If R is followed by an I, you may be touchy and
irritable.

R at a peak cycle provides an opening for new plans and ideas, calling for a new occupation in life. Resolve to attain status through this
period. Since the pace is fast, there is a need to slow down somewhat.

R as a health factor is called the growler letter, indicating undercur-
rent rumblings, but not very harmful unless two R's are stimulated into action at the same time. If negatively expressed, accidents may occur through rashness or carelessness, which can bring on sickness.

Your Career

Choosing a career is an important step in your life. If you have more than one talent, you may have difficulty deciding what career course to follow. This is when a study of your numbers and their particular vibrations can help. Your numbers indicate your abilities; use them to plan your future.

Your career number is your Life Lesson Number. To find it, add the numbers in your birthdate. Always add the whole number of the month and day, without breaking them down to a single digit. Add the year number through once and use the total in your computation. For example, $1945 = 1+9+4+5 = 19$. Use 19 for the year 1945.

November 12, 1940 is a career number 1: $11+12+14$ $(1+9+4+0=14) = 37/1$

If your birthdate totals a master number, do not reduce it.

Many times the same vocation is found under different numbers. In those cases, look at the other careers in that career number to help you determine how you would use that particular vocation. For example, lawyer appears under numbers 2, 3, 6, 7, 8 and 9. In number 3 it would be expressed as a court lawyer, in number 7 as a divorce lawyer, in number 8 as a corporate lawyer, patent attorney or financial advisor, and so on.

Now read the descriptions below to find out your compatible careers.

1 AS A CAREER NUMBER: Inventor, designer, aviator, leader of a group, department or business organization. Ambassador, director, program planner, store owner, officer in the military. Producer of motion pictures, television or theater productions. Lecturer, promoter, sales manager, engineer, executive, explorer. Creative work of all kinds.

2 AS A CAREER NUMBER: Diplomat, agent, caterer, clerk, lawyer, insurance adjuster or any position that demands arbitration. Architect, bookkeeper, bill collector, custodian, legislator, librarian, minister, foreign minister, politician, teacher.

3 AS A CAREER NUMBER: Artist, musician, nurse, dietician, physician. Writer, entertainer, cosmetician, salesperson of cosmetics or art supplies. An artisan in any line. Lawyer, judge, engineer, pastor, priest, playground director, athletic coach, scout director, vocational school teacher, philosopher. A 3 should avoid positions of close confinement or long hours, as self-expression is necessary for happiness and best work.

4 AS A CAREER NUMBER: All building trades, numerologist, farmer, miner, industrialist, mason, draftperson, mechanic, ac-

countant, undertaker, efficiency expert, executive, professional box-
er, engineer, mechanic, chemist, laboratory technician.

5 AS A CAREER NUMBER: Salesperson, advertising executive,
investigator or detective, writer, teacher, lecturer, copy reader,
news columnist, editor, any career in communications. Graphologist,
proofreader, publisher, playwright, TV or radio operator, actor,
secretary, consultant, psychology or language teacher, interpreter,
import-export dealer.

6 AS A CAREER NUMBER: Actor, host or hostess, homemaker,
teacher, writer, nurse, doctor. Interior decorator, artist, florist,
singer, voice teacher, tutor. Beautician, dressmaker or designer,
fashion expert, musician, perfumer, incense chemist, herbalist. Any
branch of theater work. Marriage counselor, divorce attorney. The 6
needs to be in service to others in some way.

7 AS A CAREER NUMBER: Archeologist, astrologer, engineer,
healer, preacher, author, dentist, farmer, lawyer, photo-
grapher, psychic investigator, any sort of research work. Could do
library work as cataloger or indexer. A 7 dislikes manual labor and
does best in an atmosphere of refinement and culture.

8 AS A CAREER NUMBER: Banker, financier, engineer, undertaker, chemist, carpenter, crime investigator, druggist, exter-
minator, firearms or dynamite expert. Lawyer, organizer, supervisor,
philanthropist, manufacturer, architect, broker.

9 AS A CAREER NUMBER: Researcher, electrician, explorer, magician, narcotics agent, scientist, doctor, teacher,
preacher, lecturer, surgeon, diplomat. Iron worker, artist, musician,
lawyer, spiritual healer, horticulturist, landscape gardner.

11 AS A CAREER NUMBER: Inspirational writer, teacher,
lecturer, promoter, sales manager, leader in public affairs.
Professional in metaphysical work, astrologer, astronomer,
numerologist. Electrician, space age electronics expert, astronaut.

22 AS A CAREER NUMBER: Executive, diplomat, ambassador, government agent, adjuster, mediator,
humanitarian, librarian, school superintendent. A 22 belongs in
public service or in an advisory capacity in some way.

33 AS A CAREER NUMBER: Professor of Bible interpretation, public servant. A 33 birthdate is usually destined for
sacrificial service in some capacity. It could be a life of nurturing or of

giving up one's own career in order to serve a parent, a community or
the world.

44 AS A CAREER NUMBER: Farmer, builder, doctor, nurse,
dietician, soldier, politician, banker, businessman, social
worker. A 44 must contribute to the world in a substantial,
materialistic way.

Number Compatibility

Many people like to determine their compatibility with someone else.
We can do this by comparing Life Lesson Numbers. This is the
number that has the heaviest influence on our lifes.

Here we will use only the single digit of the Life Lesson Number. If
you have a master number, reduce it to a single digit and work with
that single number. For those who do not wish to reveal their birthdate, simply have them figure their own Life Lesson Number and give
only the number to you.

The following list offers all possible Life Lesson Number combinations. Can a 3 be compatible with a 5? Let's find out.

1 WITH A 1: Since leadership is the keyword for both of you, you
would be a dynamic combination. You would both want the
same thing at the same time and would join ranks in competition with
other forces. You might have to work at harmonizing your personalities since you both tend to be aggressive. This is a combination
that requires cooperation, and the necessary endurance to see a project through to its conclusion.

1 WITH A 2: The 1 person has the plans, initiative and leadership
qualities, whereas the 2 person has the tact and the co-operative and
supportive talents to carry out the plans and ideas initiated by the 1.
The 1 person is innovative and the 2 person is supportive, and a
perfect agent or promoter for those innovations. As partners, mates
or co-workers, you will be winners because each has what the other
lacks.

1 WITH A 3: By combining the originality and leadership abilities of the
1 person with the 3 person's charm, magnetism and know-how in expanding an idea and making it into a real success, this combination
can bring honor and fame as well as happiness. The only real danger
is that the 1 person can be impulsive, and the 3 person can scatter his
or her energies, but by concentrating their combined talents, almost
anything can be accomplished.

1 WITH A 4: This combination gives a firm foundation for business
success. The 1 person acts as the decision maker, plus supplying

creative, inventive and original talents. However, the 1 person needs the practicality, thoroughness and steadying support of the 4 person as a restraint on impulsiveness. The 1 person can irritate the 4 with impulsivenesss, whereas the 4 person can irritate the 1 with extreme caution. But, all in all, this is a good combination.

1 WITH A 5: Both of you are active, changeable and original, with a dash of versatility. The two of you can have the world by the tail, and can learn and earn a lot together. The 5 person can sell the ideas of the 1 person. Educational projects would be ideal for you as a team, but let the 5 person take care of the publicity.

1 WITH A 6: The number 6 person loves art, socializing, beauty and luxury, and these worlds can be opened by the 1 person who provides the sparkle, drive and leadership for fruitful outcomes. There can be friction if the 1 person insists on his or her own way, so a co-operative effort in a cultural field such as interior decorating, landscape gardening, gourmet cooking or the like could be rewarding for this team.

1 WITH A 7: A spiritual or metaphysical relationship could work well here. The 1 person must not be too demanding or hasty, because the 7 person needs time for privacy, analysis and thought. Where the 1 person is the extrovert, the 7 person is the introvert, and each should be aware of the other's need for independence. The 7 person should communicate ideas and follow the leadership of the 1 person, acting as a brake for the impulsiveness of the 1 person. This can be a powerful combination.

1 WITH AN 8: You are both aggressive, used to making your own decisions, so it's either cooperate willingly or become rivals and antagonists. If you calm down as a unit and use your combined powers wisely and with careful analysis, there is great power and courage in the face of difficulties. Pool your energies and talents and be winners together, otherwise you may destroy each other. This is a strong business combination.

1 WITH A 9: The 9 person's depth of vision and breadth of understanding combined with the originality and dash of the 1 person can create a combination of inventive genius. The 1 person is the pusher in this partnership, supplying the diverse ideas which fall upon seasoned and wise ears. Together the courage and wisdom of this combination make it one that will go far towards success.

2 WITH A 2: Perfect equilibrium and equal sharing are the watchwords here. You both like to build experiences, and are able to give and receive understanding. Learn to work with, rather than for, the other, and you will both share in the material benefits of your partnership. You are both extremely aware of the other person's point of view, and must not become so bogged down that you cannot effectively make decisions and take action.

2 WITH A 3: This is a popularity combination. While the 2 person knows how to win friends and contracts and keep things running harmoniously, the 3 person can expand upon friendships and inject life and spontaneity into them. The 3 person's creative talents can be effectively managed and balanced by the 2 person's ability to stay in the background and take care of the practical aspects of keeping things on the right track.

2 WITH A 4: There is no competition or friction in this combination of numbers. In fact, you each bring out the best side of the other. There is great harmony and understanding in whatever endeavors you undertake. The 2 person acts as a harmonizer and co-ordinator, and the 4 person plans the practical basis for solid foundations. You would both do well in home building, real estate, farming and other related professions.

2 WITH A 5: This partnership will produce an "all or nothing" experience. The 2 person would be better off to take second place, waiting until his or her strength is needed. The 5 person can talk and plan for both, and friction could occur if the 2 person pours cold water on the 5's wit and brilliance. If he or she can hold the 5's attention and interest, the 2 person can sustain the 5's ideas and help bring them into fruition.

2 WITH A 6: This can be an extremely successful combination of numbers. The tact and magnetism of the 2 person combined with the love of beauty and the appreciation of home and family of the 6 person can attract the confidence of others who see these two people as sensitive, caring, artistic and co-operative. The public will respond to your combined charms. You would do well in charity work, financial drives or any organizational work to do with homes, children or domestic affairs.

2 WITH A 7: This is an extremely harmonious combination and creates no friction; rather the need is to guard against too much serenity. There is agreement in occult, philosophical and mystical studies, and much potential for growth on the spiritual plane together. The 2 person understands and knows how to co-operate, and the 7 person needs periods alone to meditate and perfect ideas that eventually can be shared beneficially by both.

2 WITH AN 8: Your combined energies can take you far towards material success as this is an excellent money and financial combination. As a team you can build prestige, and enjoy a fine reputation for honesty and fair dealings. You are both efficient, and if the 8 person is careful not to overshadow and overwhelm the 2 person through his or her dynamic vibration, a good friendship can develop. The 8 person can rely upon the diplomacy and tact of the 2 person in all business dealings.

2 WITH A 9: The mediating and balancing capabilities of the 2 person coupled with the insight and vision of the 9 person can produce a winning combination. Each contributes harmoniously to the other, and when both are working for a cause, the momentum is increased through having a common goal. The 2 person's ability to see both sides of a situation lends a firm foundation to the imagination and humanitarian instincts of the 9 person, and together they can do much to advance the needs of the world.

3 WITH A 3: This is a combination to watch out for. Since you both are apt to take too many chances, and believe in luck, which you have to a certain extent, you may extend yourselves too far. Your urge towards big ideas and expansive methods of operating your affairs can lead to waste and frivolousness. There is a bit of the gambler in both of you. If these qualities can be toned down and controlled, you can tackle just about anything.

3 WITH A 4: For these two persons to co-exist, a compromise is necessary. Each one must listen to the other, for the 3 person is expansive and free thinking, and the 4 person is saving and conservative, and these qualities can clash. A lasting association is possible if the 3 person is aware of the partner's need for stability and caution, and if the 4 person eases up and listens to the broadening ideas of the 3. Together they can implement sparkling ideas with a firm foundation.

3 WITH A 5: These vibrations are harmonious, and almost anything you try together is bound to succeed. You are both set for full speed ahead. "Do it now" is your motto; the only danger is in being too hasty with your ideas. You are both full of ideas which the 3 person can display effectively, and the 5 person can sell easily. You may find yourselves carrying on more than one business at a time to supply outlets for your numerous ideas.

3 WITH A 6: This should be a very good relationship because you are both congenial, and fond of pleasure and socializing. Understanding and harmony exist between you because you have similar personality traits which should develop into a lasting friendship where you feel safe in making long range plans and investments together. Businesses

which promote friendship and love, such as planning engagement or wedding parties, would appeal to you both.

3 WITH A 7: The 3 person supplies the energy and inspiration in this relationship whereas the 7 person gives understanding and deep insight. This is a winning combination in which the mystical 7 benefits from the lively traits of the 3, and the 3 learns to examine his or her own scattering tendencies and deal more productively with his or her talents. The 3 needs to socialize, and the 7 needs time alone. With each other's needs in mind, this partnership can be ideal.

3 WITH AN 8: If handled constructively, there is nothing that can stop this combination. The 3 person has the talent for ideas, communication and effective advertising; the 8 has the power and drive in big business and philanthropic projects. Each supplements the other's needs. If your aims are compatible, this is an unbeatable combination, and your highest hopes can be attained through 8's practical business sense and 3's social talents.

3 WITH A 9: There is much idealism in these two numbers and work in the material world can be neglected for the social pleasures of the 3, and the philanthropic leanings of the 9. Co-operation and mutual understanding abound here, and perhaps the combination is too compatible. As a team, you must bring your idealism into focus, and realize that practicality is essential, and that the material world is as important as the spiritual.

4 WITH A 4: This can be an extremely lucky and compatible combination, bringing financial success and material comfort. You are both builders in the material sense, and like to have visible products at the end of your endeavors. Your work must have practical value. Be careful that you don't become too immersed in the physical side of life, neglecting the spiritual side of your development. This is a danger as you are both so much alike.

4 WITH A 5: This can be a good combination chiefly because you are so different. The 4 has the practicality and solidity to stabilize your combined efforts. The 4 is the balance wheel in this partnership. The 5 person supplies the wit and a variety of ideas. The 5 also has many contacts because he or she communicates so well with others. The 5 person can more easily adjust a mood to blend harmoniously with the 4, and the results will be worth the effort.

4 WITH A 6: You are both serious and practical, yet you love pleasure enough to keep a balance between your work and your play. Thus you create an atmosphere of happiness and joy. The 4 person is will-

ing to work for gains, and the 6 person loves the home and the arts. Your combined talents might take you into professions that involve beautifying your surroundings. Your work would be appreciated and enjoyed by others.

4 WITH A 7: The 4's talent for strong practical planning and thoroughness coupled with the deep insight and imaginative talents of the 7 person can create a combination of powers that can add up to great achievement. This is a good balance, because the 4 person lives in a material world whereas the 7 lives in a mental world. By combining these two aspects wisely, perfect balance can be achieved.

4 WITH AN 8: Where the 8 person thinks in terms of great power and large business deals, the 4 person can be a perfect balance with the ability to see the small details and add the practical stability that must shore up any large enterprise. You both tend toward physical and material achievement; the 4 moves in a more cautious and conservative manner, while 8 progresses in a larger and more sweeping way. But as a team you balance each other well.

4 WITH A 9: The 4 person has a valuable chance in this partnership to learn the lessons of life because the 9 person has much wisdom and insight to offer which can lift the 4 from the material world and show the value of work in a higher sense. The 9 person learns the lessons of practicality and work on the material plane from the 4. There is an exchange of ideas and philosophies in this combination, and a melding of brilliance with reason and judgment.

5 WITH A 5: You are both temperamental and excitable and when you work in conjunction these qualities come to the surface. If you wish to work well together, you will have to suppress outbursts that arise from nervous energy. Channel your combined energies into work that is adventurous and exciting, which might involve travel, or at least something that offers you both change and intellectual stimulation. Neither of you likes to be tied down for long, and if you are to be successful as a duo, you must find outlets for your energies.

5 WITH A 6: The 5 person intellectually stimulates and brings out the domestic and artistic qualities of the 6 person. The 6 lends form, beauty and order to the variety of ideas and the impulsive nature of the 5 person. The home would be well cared for and tastefully decorated, and much activity would take place there. This is a stimulating yet comfortable combination that puts others at ease.

5 WITH A 7: Too much talk and excitment on the part of the 5 person

can turn the 7 person off. The 7 needs periods of quiet introspection and meditation and can be a calming influence on the 5. The 5 can add the "zip" and "zest" that the 7 person might lack. Together, through mutual respect and understanding of the other's innate qualities, this combination can be extremely successful in the world of ideas.

5 WITH AN 8: This combination might be called "greased lightning" if you combine your vibrations wisely. You are both highly charged, the 5 in the realm of ideas and communication, and the 8 in the worlds of business, finance and sports. There is a great desire for adventure, and the 8 provides the underlying strength to shore up any projects. You both may need to listen to inner promptings and restrain your dynamism at appropriate moments.

5 WITH A 9: This can be a winning combination in that the 5 provides the versatility and promotional abilities to present the 9's insight into the realm of science and research to the world at large. The 5 has the energy and the contacts and the know-how to advertise the expertise and wisdom of the 9 person, whereas the 9 person has the balancing qualities to turn the 5's adventures into reliable and sustaining results.

6 WITH A 6: Beauty, art and comfort are paramount in the nature of the 6, and too much sweetness and roses can be tiresome if there is no real constructive stimulation to go with it. The danger here is that the sameness of your natures is apt to let things go along peacefully, while avoiding work. By combining your talents wisely, you can create an atmosphere of incredible beauty in the home or the community. There is great gentleness and love of the home in this combination.

6 WITH A 7: This can be a difficult combination in that the 6 person is involved in the domestic and artistic world much to the exclusion of all else, and the 7 person is also immersed in separate worlds of mind and thought. The danger here lies in failure to communicate with each other at all. Cooperation and the determination to communicate with one another must be decided upon from the outset.

6 WITH AN 8: This combination has strong possibilities. The 6 person offers the loving support and the spark of imagination that will benefit the 8 person in whatever profession is chosen as a goal. The 8 person with the stronger financial and commercial tendencies, will most likely take the lead in this partnership, and the 6 can offer creative methods for handling and presenting those ideas, plus the domestic background support that makes the end of the day a joy.

6 WITH A 9: Here is a chance for lasting friendship or partnership. You

enjoy mutual feelings about most subjects, and both believe that marriage demands the spirit of give and take. The 6 supplies the beauty, the 9 the truth; and together you can learn much from each other in the realm of the "domestic 6," the microcosmic unit, and in the realm of the "universal 9," the macrocosmic unit. Each teaches the other the importance of the smaller and the greater.

7 WITH A 7: Peace is the key word here. You are both mature in your emotions and no disruption or argument between you could endure for long. You both tend to live in a world of ideas, and realize the transitory nature of the material world. The danger here lies in your rejecting the physical world as illusory, and consequently spending all of your time in your minds, with no one to pay the bills and keep the wolf from the door.

7 WITH AN 8: This could be an excellent partnership. The fire and strength, heat and force of the 8 can overpower the quiet 7, but 8's organizational and executive abilities can greatly enhance the insight and vision of the 7 person. Thus the 8 provides the strength while the 7 predicts the outcome and adds the calm intellect that enhances the daring qualities of the 8. Together this can be a most effective partnership.

7 WITH A 9: Great depth and sympathies exist in this pair. Inner growth is a goal you both seek, and the universality of ideas brings harmony, understanding and peace to you both. This is an almost perfect combination as you have a meeting of mind, heart and soul in harmony. A mystical relationship could develop and your combined talents could produce benefits for all humanity, in which your wisdom could enhance the lives of all those you contact.

8 WITH AN 8: This is a perfect pair for a revolution. As power meets power head on, the sparks may fly. On the other hand, you could have the opposite effect and extinguish each other. As with all energies, this combination can be used wisely. Handled with great care, your combined strength and executive capabilities could present a united front to the world that could not be beaten by any ordinary opposition. This is a partnership that could accomplish almost anything in the world.

8 WITH A 9: This is a good partnership for scientific or philanthropic research and activity. The creative qualities of the 9 combined with the power and practicality of the 8 make this a tremendously successful combination in research and financial or economic circles. At the same time you could contribute much to each other in a spiritual sense since the 8 supplies the stability and values of the material world while the 9 exemplifies the universal philosopher.

9 WITH A 9: This may be said to be a combination of destiny, as you are both intuitive, clear-sighted and imaginatively creative. You both know the value of enhancing your own lives through the teaching and caring of others, and some great benefit to humanity should result from this partnership. A deep bond will grow between you, and you will gain much enlightenment from one another.

Missing Numbers in Your Name

The missing numbers in your name, sometimes called the *karmic* numbers, indicate the qualities you must develop in this lifetime. They represent the qualities and attitudes we must adopt in order to expiate the shortcomings of our past lives.

In our example, Ada Wynn Lunt has the following number vibration:

```
1 +1    +7      +3    =12/3 Soul Number
A D A  W Y N N  L U N T
  4   +5 +5+5+3+5+2=29/11 Outer Personality
                              Number
                    41/5 Path of Destiny Number
  11+12+14 (1+9+4+0)=37/1 Life Lesson Number
```

To these we will add a new number vibration. Add the double digit Path of Destiny Number to the double digit Life Lesson Number. The result is the *Power Number*.

```
41/5     Path of Destiny Number
37/1     Life Lesson Number
78/15/6  Power Number
```

The Power Number represents a vibration that comes into play through your 30's and 40's. It is a combination of all your talents.

If we examine the number vibrations in Ada's name, we see that she is missing the numbers 6, 8 and 9. If any of these numbers is present in her four personal numbers, her Power Number, or a nickname she may use, then that vibration is already present in her life. Her four personal numbers are 12/3, 29/11/2, 41/5, 37/1, and her Power Number is 78/15/6. From the missing group of 6, 8 and 9, we can eliminate the 6, which she has as a Power Number. So Ada is only missing numbers 8 and 9. The qualities represented by these numbers must be incorporated into her life.

Remember that in addition to the personal numbers and the Power Number, a nickname or some other name change may fulfill a missing number vibration. Therefore, check all possible name and number combinations before deciding that you lack a certain number or numbers. In this case, master numbers can be reduced to fulfill vibrations. An 11 fulfills a 2 vibration, a 22 fulfills a 4, a 33 fulfills a 6, and a 44 fulfills an 8.

Find your missing numbers, if any, and read the following delineations to determine what qualities must be built into your character. For further delineation, look up the number in Part II.

1 AS A MISSING NUMBER: You need to build in the qualities of leadership, courage and daring. It is important that you learn to make decisions and take control of any given situation which requires your effort. You need to assert your individuality so that you will be heard and listened to. You must learn to be first and best at something, and to step out into new and untried situations. Exert your pioneering instincts, and dare to be yourself.

2 AS A MISSING NUMBER: You must learn the fine art of co-operation, tact and diplomacy. Working in partnership with another requires giving on your part; learn to stay in the background when necessary. When you understand how another person thinks and feels, you can get in touch with your own emotions and feelings, because you can view the reaction you have upon others. By developing an awareness of opposites, you will enhance your own creative potentials.

3 AS A MISSING NUMBER: You need to learn to express yourself. Develop your communicative talents by training yourself in the art of speaking through acting, elocution, foreign languages, and so forth, so that you can be an influence in the lives of others. You should develop a happy optimistic outlook and spread enthusiasm and sunshine wherever you go. More socializing and entertaining are necessary in your life. Travel, broaden your mind and examine new opportunities. Be aware of your appearance because this has a distinct influence upon those you meet.

4 AS A MISSING NUMBER: You must develop an orderly, systematic life style which produces a structured existence. You must translate your energies into tangible forms through hard work and discipline. Budget finances and keep accounts in order. Become thrifty and practical, steady and reliable. Use reason to arrive at conclusions. Learn what it means to be "the salt of the earth," because your life needs a strong foundation set upon the cornerstone of order, logic and hard work.

5 AS A MISSING NUMBER: You need to learn to adjust to changes and to become more versatile. You must develop your freedom, physically, mentally and spiritually so that the more adventurous side of your nature can express itself. You need to travel and socialize with many types of individuals so that your own perspective on life can be enhanced and broadened. Develop your mind and learn to communicate effectively with others. Your mind is your greatest resource, and should be utilized to its fullest potential.

6 AS A MISSING NUMBER: You must express more love for others. 6 is the domestic vibration, and the lack of it indicates a need to deepen ties of affection with those in your immediate family and environment. You should develop a personal sense of responsibility for those who depend upon you, and a social sense of responsibility for the welfare of those in your community. By becoming aware of the needs of others, you increase your ability to see both sides of an issue and therefore sharpen your talent for making keen judgments. This acute sense of balance heightens your artistic sense and may help you realize hidden creative abilities. The artist in you may then emerge.

7 AS A MISSING NUMBER: You need to develop your mind, and your intuitive and philosophical side. You must abandon the material world on occasion and learn to go within yourself, to meditate and ponder upon the substance of your being. Trips alone into the countryside or to the seashore should be part of your yearly schedule. During these isolated periods, your creative imagination can roam freely to explore the world of thought. Develop your perceptions so that you will not be fooled by outward appearances. Study philosophy, religion and metaphysics to expand your mind.

8 AS A MISSING NUMBER: You should channel your energies into the material world to attain a position of leadership. Develop your business sense. Your role should be that of the "big boss," the executive who organizes and manages big business. Your ambition should carve a niche for you in the financial world where wealth can be easily accrued. This number bestows strength and will, and by using these qualities you could easily become an outstanding athlete. The proper use of this vibration will bring you recognition in either the financial or sports world because, by embracing its gifts, you have the strength and determination to overcome all obstacles and attain your goals.

9 AS A MISSING NUMBER: You must become the universalist, the humanitarian whose primary concern is for the welfare of others. You should develop breadth of thinking, and universal love for others. Close personal ties may have to take second place to your first priority, which is sharing your spiritual knowledge with the world and inspiring those whose lives seem dark and hopeless. You must become an example for others through your compassionate and sympathetic nature. Allow no limits upon your thinking. Dare to dream the highest dream, and perform the impossible task. Become charitable, loving and understanding.

6

THE LIFE OF EDGAR CAYCE

W E WILL DEMONSTRATE, through the life of the famous
psychic Edgar Cayce, (pronounced *Cay*-cee), how the processes described in the previous chapters of this book can be implemented to delineate an individual's life. Rather than begin at birth
and work through his entire life, we have chosen some of the major
events in Cayce's biography. Through them we will establish the
validity of the Divine Triangle as a blueprint of his life. We will present only basic biographical information because Edgar Cayce is well-
known, and written material on his life is plentiful. (See
Bibliography.)

Edgar Cayce was born near Hopkinsville, Kentucky, on March 18,
1877. Although poor and uneducated, he was to become a beloved
figure known as the "sleeping prophet." A deeply religious man, he
lived a devout Christian life and used his remarkable psychic talents

to benefit others. Putting himself into a trance, Cayce would diagnose the illnesses of those who consulted him, and then recommend treatments and cures. He also possessed the ability to read the *akashic records*. It is said that every sound, thought and vibration since the beginning of time is registered on these records, including the first sound vibration which called forth manifestation. Based on the akashic records of those individuals who applied for such a reading, he brought out information on their past lives that was useful in their present incarnation. In this way he helped thousands of people regain their health and conduct their lives in more constructive patterns.

Edgar Cayce expressed his belief that the name indicates the soul's place in evolution. He said in reading #281-31*:

Each entity, each soul, is known in all the experience through its activities—as a name to designate it from another. It is not only then a material convenience, but it implies. . .a definite period in evolution of the experience of the entity in the material plane.

In reading #261-15 he says:

As related to individuals these each vibrate to certain numbers according to their name, their birthdate. . . . Then when these appear, they become either as strengths or as losses or as helps or as change. . .but. . .they are rather as the signs, or the omens; and may be given as warnings. . .in any manner that they may be constructive in the experience of the individual.

In reading #311-3 he says:

In any influence, will. . .a self, the ego, the I AM. . .is the greater force to be dealt with, but as numbers do influence. . .a knowledge of same certainly gives an individual a foresight into relationships. . .

We chose Edgar Cayce to demonstrate the application of double digit numerology and the Divine Triangle because his life clearly demonstrates the truth of the above quotes. By delineating Edgar Cayce's name and birthdate we arrive at his four personal numbers: Soul Number 12/3; Outer Personality Number 33; Path of Destiny Number 45/9 and his Life Lesson Number 44.

---

*All quotes are from the actual readings Cayce gave. They are stored in the custody of the Edgar Cayce Foundation, a subdivision of the Association for Research and Enlightenment (A.R.E.) Virginia Beach, Virginia. and are protected by copyright: © 1971 by Edgar Cayce Foundation. All rights reserved.

Edgar Cayce

$$5 \;+1 \;+1 \;+5 = \quad 12/3 \; Soul \; Number$$
EDGAR CAYCE
$$4+7+9+3+7+3 = \quad 33 \; Outer \; Personality \; Number$$
$$45/9 \; Path \; of \; Destiny \; Number$$

March 18, 1877
$$3+18+23 = \quad 44 \; Life \; Lesson \; Number$$

Soul Number 12/3: This is a very high spiritual vibration. It represents a conscientious individual who is innately aware of our spiritual relationship to God and who has a great desire to help others. Through his ideals, Cayce was inspired to dedicate his life to the betterment of humanity. He had a heartfelt interest in all who sought his advice, and his greatest desire was to help them find health and happiness. He taught the value of prayer and meditation and practiced this in his own life. For many he was a living example of a truly spiritual human being.

Outer Personality Number 33: 33 is a master number which carries an almost Christ-like vibration. In his outer physical life, Cayce worked constantly, giving both diagnostic and life readings through which he brought out the theory of reincarnation, and revealed knowledge of astrology and numbers as related to the lives of human beings. He interpreted the Bible as well. Because he was seen by many as a savior, he felt the need and obligation to work for the good of others, even though his own fortunes would suffer.

Path of Destiny Number 45/9: This number indicates that his mission in life was highly spiritual and mystical. He was not satisfied with worldly success alone. This Path of Destiny Number signifies one who loves to teach and serve others. It endowed Cayce with the courage and fortitude to face the changes and emergencies in his life, giving him faith that everything would work out with God's help and guidance. This number also indicates one who is willing to work hard, even at the expense of his own health. Cayce's theme seemed to be, "Let me ever be a channel of blessings, today, now, to those I contact in every way," (#262-3).

The Life Lesson Number 44: This number, derived from the birthdate, indicates what a person should learn in this life. This master number 44 is called Atlas. In mythology Atlas "supports the heavens on his shoulders." (See our book *13—Birth or Death?*) In other words, Cayce would take responsibility for others, attend faithfully to duty and make the best of any situation which had to be met. He possessed common sense and foresight in order to make fair judgments. He was very understanding in his dealings with others, anxious to please and help in any possible way. He believed that service was the way toward mastership, and his life and works are ample proof of this.

To choose which numbers are important in the delineation of events in a lifetime, select those that coincide with the four personal numbers (in our example, 12/3, 33, 45/9 and 44). The personal numbers are activated whenever they are energized by corresponding numbers. Thus a 12/3 event would energize Cayce's 12/3 Soul Number, as would any type of 3—a single 3, a 21/3, a 30/3, a 39/3, etc. Therefore any variation of 3, 6, 8 or 9 would activate the corresponding personal number; however, it would activate it according to the double digit variation. In addition, it seems that often one's

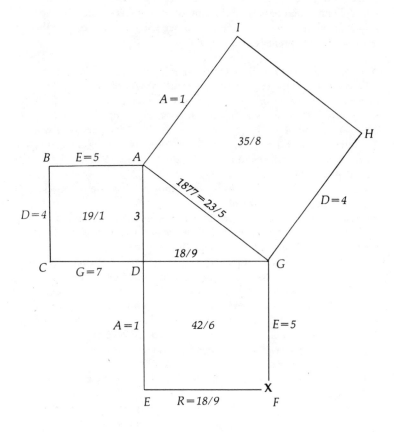

Figure 6: Edgar Cayce

master numbers, e.g. Cayce's 33 and 44, are triggered by any of the four master numbers: 11, 22, 33, 44 or by their base digits 2, 4, 6 and 8.

To see how Cayce's life is reflected in his numerological blueprint, we examine each nine-year cycle in two ways. First, we will look at the correlations between events in his life and the experiences under the major process and the minor process which are operating during each nine-year cycle. Secondly, we can see whether any of the events correspond with the personal year and the three four-month period numbers also operating during that time.

We will discuss here only the most significant events of Cayce's life. - We will, however, list all the experiences under the major and minor process for each nine-year cycle; in addition we will list each personal year and that year's division into the three four-month periods. You will then have before you all the temporary numbers which affected Cayce throughout his life, even though we will discuss here only the most significant events of his life.

Age: Birth to Nine: To calculate the experiences of Edgar Cayce's first nine years by the major process, (see figure 6) we will work with the number in the center of the square, 19/1, the number on the side of the triangle, 3, the number in the center of the triangle, 44, and the ages at each end of line AB, 0 and 9. $0+1=1$. $9-1=8$. At ages 1 and 8, Cayce had a 19/1 experience. $0+3=3$. $9-3=6$. At ages 3 and 6, Cayce had a 3 experience. $0+8=8$. $9-8=1$. At ages 8 and 1, Cayce had a 44 experience.

To calculate the experiences by the minor process, we work with the numbers in the center of the square, 19/1, on the side of the triangle, 3, and on the first line, 5, and the ages at either end of line AB. $0+5=5$. $5+3=8$. At age 5, Cayce had an 8 experience. $9-5=4$. $5+19=24/6$. At age 4, Cayce had a 24/6 experience.

We do not have much information about Cayce's first nine years. We do know that, according to his mother, even as a small child he saw and talked with invisible playmates. At age four the death of a much loved grandfather proved to be a very emotional experience. A few months later he claimed that his grandfather appeared and talked with him. This occurred under a minor process 24/6 experience, a love and family vibration. On the period table, at age four all basic numbers are energized.

Here are the calculations for the yearly periods from birth to nine.

Personal Year	March to July	July to November	November to March
$3+18+1877=44$	1877	1877	1877
	0	44	12
	$1877=23/5$	$1921=13/4$	$1889=26/8$

$3+18+1878=45/9$

1878	1878	1878
1	44	12
1879=25/7	1922=14/5	1890=18/9

$3+18+1879=46/1$

1879	1879	1879
2	44	12
1881=18/9	1923=15/6	1891=19/1

$3+18+1880=38/11$

1880	1880	1880
3	44	12
1883=20/2	1924=16/7	1892=20/2

$3+18+1881=39/3$

1881	1881	1881
4	44	12
1885=22	1925=17/8	1893=21/3

$3+18+1882=40/4$

1882	1882	1882
5	44	12
1887=24/6	1926=18/9	1894=22

$3+18+1883=41/5$

1883	1883	1883
6	44	12
1889=26/8	1927=19/1	1895=23/5

$3+18+1884=42/6$

1884	1884	1884
7	44	12
1891=19/1	1928=20/2	1896=24/6

$3+18+1885=43/7$

1885	1885	1885
8	44	12
1893=21/3	1929=21/3	1897=25/7

Ages Nine to Eighteen: To calculate the experiences of these years by the major process, we work with the number in the center of the square, 19/1, the number on the side of the triangle, 3, and the number in the center of the triangle, 44, and the age at each end of line BC, 9 and 18. 9+1=10. 18−1=17. At ages 10 and 17, Cayce had a 19/1 experience. 9+3=12. 18−3=15. At ages 12 and 15, Cayce had a 3 experience. 9+8=17. 18−8=10. At ages 10 and 17, Cayce had a 44 experience.

To calculate the experiences by the minor process, we work with the number in the center of the square, 19/1, the number on the side of the triangle, 3, the number on the line, 4, and the ages on each end of line BC, 9 and 18. 9+4=13. 4+19=23/5. At age 13, Cayce had a 23/5 experience. 18−4=14. 4+3=7. At age 14, Cayce had a 7 experience.

At age ten, in a 45/9 personal year, Cayce began work as a church sexton. This year corresponds to his Path of Destiny Number, 45/9, and the experiences of this particular time were indicative of his future path.

At the age of twelve or thirteen, Cayce was playing in one of his favorite spots by a brook. He sat down to read the Bible which he always kept with him. He turned to the Book of Judges (13:2-22) to read about the vision of Manoah and, while perusing the passage, he heard a strange sound, saw a bright light, and then heard a voice saying, "Your prayers have been heard—what would you ask that I may grant your wish?"

Cayce answered, "Just that I may be helpful to others, especially children who are ill, and that I may love my fellow man."

The next day, he could not keep his mind on his school work. Because his spelling was unsatisfactory, his teacher made him stay after school and write a misspelled word on the blackboard five-hundred times. That night his father decided to drill him on the spelling homework, but Cayce did not do well. It was late and he was getting sleepy. Just then Edgar seemed to hear a voice within him saying: "Sleep a little and we may help you."

He laid his head on the spelling book and slept for a few minutes. When he awoke he knew how to spell every word in the entire book. This is his story of how universal consciousness came to him.

A few days later he was hit by a baseball. He returned home, dazed, and asked his mother to make a certain poultice for the back of his head. She did, and in the morning he was well. This was his first insight into successful health prescriptions.

During these two years, his basic Soul Number, 12/3, was being activated. At age twelve, he had a major-process 3 experience on the blueprint, and at age thirteen, he was in a 39/3 personal year. During that 39/3 personal year, he experienced a 12/3 period number between November and March, which energized again his Soul Number, and illustrated graphically how his inner talents and abilities from past lifetimes were being filtered into his consciousness.

At age fifteen Cayce quit school and went to work on a farm. At this time, he was also under a major-process 3 experience on the blueprint, which showed that his latent talents were being awakened. Perhaps a formal education would have disturbed his growing psychic talents. Also on the period table this occurred under a 17/8 four-month period. This relates to his Life Lesson Number, 44. Basically the 8 (a master number, 44, reduced) means that the serious business of the Life Lesson is being energized. 8 is a disciplinary number, and it means that work and responsibility are now necessary for accomplishment.

Here are the calculations for the yearly periods nine to eighteen, which reflect the portion of Cayce's life described above.

Personal Year	March to July	July to November	November to March	Nine to Eighteen
3+18+1886=44	1886 _9_ 1895=23/5	1886 _44_ 1930=13/4	1886 _12_ 1898=26/8	
3+18+1887=45/9	1887 _10_ 1897=25/7	1887 _44_ 1931=14/5	1887 _12_ 1899=27/9	
3+18+1888=46/1	1888 _11_ 1899=27/9	1888 _44_ 1932=15/6	1888 _12_ 1900=10/1	
3+18+1889=47/11	1889 _12_ 1901=11	1889 _44_ 1933=16/7	1889 _12_ 1901=11	
3+18+1890=39/3	1890 _13_ 1903=13/4	1890 _44_ 1934=17/8	1890 _12_ 1902=12/3	
3+18+1891=40/4	1891 _14_ 1905=15/6	1891 _44_ 1935=18/9	1891 _12_ 1903=13/4	
3+18+1892=41/5	1892 _15_ 1907=17/8	1892 _44_ 1936=19/1	1892 _12_ 1904=14/5	
3+18+1893=42/6	1893 _16_ 1909=19/1	1893 _44_ 1937=20/2	1893 _12_ 1905=15/6	
3+18+1894=43/7	1894 _17_ 1911=12/3	1894 _44_ 1938=21/3	1894 _12_ 1906=16/7	

Ages Eighteen to Twenty-seven To calculate the experiences by the major process, we work with the number in the center of the square, 19/1; the number on the side of the triangle, 3; and the number in the center of the triangle, 44; and the ages at each end of line CD, 18 and 27. 18+1=19. 27−1=26. At ages 19 and 26, Cayce had a 19/1 experience. 18+3=21. 27−3=24. At ages 21 and 24, Cayce had a 3 experience. 18+8=26. 27−8=19. At ages 19 and 26, Cayce had a 44 experience.

To calculate the experiences by the minor process, we work with the number in the center of the square, 19/1; the number on the side of the triangle, 3; and the ages at each end of line CD, 18 and 27; and the number on the third line, 7. $18 + 7 = 25$. $7 + 3 = 10/1$. At age 25 Cayce had a 10/1 experience. $27 - 7 = 20$. $7 + 19 = 26/8$. At age 20 Cayce had a 26/8 experience.

At age eighteen, Cayce met Dwight L. Moody, an itinerant evangelist, whose advice changed the course of his life. The event occurred in a 44 personal year. By the minor process we find Cayce had a 26/8 experience at age 20, the year he fell in love and proposed marriage to Gertrude Evans. Not only does the 8 correspond with the Life Lesson Number (44 reduced), but also 26/8 is the number of karma. Their marriage was definitely karmic, as revealed in later readings which depicted their past incarnations together. It was destined for both of them to work out their former lives in their present relationship.

Here are the calculations for the yearly periods, ages eighteen to twenty-seven which reflect that portion of Cayce's life:

Personal Year	March to July	July to November	November to March
$3 + 18 + 1895 = 44$	1895 18 $1913 = 14/5$	1895 44 $1939 = 22$	1895 12 $1907 = 17/8$
$3 + 18 + 1896 = 45/9$	1896 19 $1915 = 16/7$	1896 44 $1940 = 14/5$	1896 12 $1908 = 18/9$
$3 + 18 + 1897 = 46/1$	1897 20 $1917 = 18/9$	1897 44 $1941 = 15/6$	1897 12 $1909 = 19/1$
$3 + 18 + 1898 = 47/11$	1898 21 $1919 = 20/2$	1898 44 $1942 = 16/7$	1898 12 $1910 = 11$
$3 + 18 + 1899 = 48/3$	1899 22 $1921 = 13/4$	1899 44 $1943 = 17/8$	1899 12 $1911 = 12/3$
$3 + 18 + 1900 = 31/4$	1900 23 $1923 = 15/6$	1900 44 $1944 = 18/9$	1900 12 $1912 = 13/4$

$3 + 18 + 1901 = 32/5$

1901	1901	1901
24	44	12
1925 = 17/8	1945 = 19/1	1913 = 14/5

$3 + 18 + 1902 = 33$

1902	1902	1902
25	44	12
1927 = 19/1	1946 = 20/2	1914 = 15/6

$3 + 18 + 1903 = 34/7$

1903	1903	1903
26	44	12
1929 = 21/3	1947 = 21/3	1915 = 16/7

When Cayce was twenty-two, he obtained a job as a traveling salesman. This was during a 12/3 period. After some months he became ill and decided to return to Hopkinsville. He was unable to speak above a whisper, the story goes, and a traveling hypnotist, hearing of the case, suggested using hypnotism to determine the cause of the ailment. Cayce underwent hypnosis easily, and talked naturally while under its influence. He described his own condition as a partial paralysis of the vocal cords and also prescribed the cure. He said, "The body should increase circulation to the affected part for a short time."

To everyone's surprise, his throat turned red, then redder, until Cayce said in a clear voice, "Suggest that the circulation return to normal and the body awaken."

This was a turning point in a technique that he was to develop and use countless times to help others. He was now twenty-four years old. He was operating under a major-process 3 experience, activating his Soul Number, 12/3. There was also in operation a 17/8 period number which corresponded to his Life Lesson Number, 44.

He moved to Bowling Green, Kentucky, at age twenty-five, and took a position in a book store. Stories of his strange gift were spreading. At this time in his life he was asked to give a reading for a school superintendent's five-year-old daughter. Her mind had stopped developing and she suffered various other ailments. Many doctors had been consulted but none could find a way to help the child. Cayce agreed to give a reading, and, while in trance, he related the cause and prescribed the treatment for the ailment. He found that the child had struck her spine when she stepped down from a carriage. This had caused an impingement of some nerves. After a few treatments she could talk again, and eventually she returned to normal.

This was another turning point in Cayce's life, as news of this remarkable case spread swiftly. Notice the minor-process 10/1 experience in indicating a turn for the better, at the same time as he was experiencing a 33 personal year which corresponded to his Outer Personality Number. Increased public attention would require increased responsibilities.

Cayce married Gertrude Evans on June 17, 1903. He was twenty-six. The wedding occurred during a 21/3 period number, relating to his Soul Number 12/3. He was also under a 44 experience on the blueprint, a number which ties in with his Life Lesson Number. In addition, his wedding date matches his Path of Destiny Number, 45/9. June 17, 1903 reduces to $6+17+13=36/9$. All 9's relate to emotional experiences, and the 36/9 particularly brings added responsibility.

Ages Twenty-seven to Thirty-six To calculate the experiences by the major process, we work with the number in the center of the square, 42/6; the number on the lower side of the triangle, 18/9; and the number in the center of the triangle, 44; and the ages at each end of line DE, 27 and 36. $27+6=33$. $36-6=30$. At age 30 and 33, Cayce had a 42/6 experience. $27+9=36$. $36-9=27$. At ages 27 and 36, Cayce had an 18/9 experience. $27+8=35$. $36-8=28$. At ages 28 and 35, Cayce had a 44 experience.

To calculate the experiences by the minor process, we work with the number in the center of the square, 42/6; the number on the lower side of the triangle, 18/9; the number on line DE, 1; and the ages at each end of line DE, 27 and 36. $27+1=28$. $1+42=43/7$. At age 28 Cayce had a 43/7 experience. $36-1=35$. $1+18=19/1$. At age 35, Cayce had a 19/1 experience.

On March 16, 1907, two days before Cayce's thirtieth birthday, a son, Hugh Lynn, was born. This date falls under a 19/1 period number, a number which is known as a love number. Because it is a basic 1 it shows a new beginning coming into his life. As his thirtieth birthday arrived, he came into a 38/11 personal year with a 20/2 period. These two base digit numbers activate his two master numbers, his 33 Outer Personality Number and his 44 Life Lesson Number. This was a time of far-reaching importance, as the numbers energized most areas of his blueprint and number table. Also, at age thirty, under the major process, we find Cayce under the influence of the 42/6 experience; the 6 corresponded to the base digit of his master number 33. Any 6 means some kind of domestic or home condition change. Not only did the 42/6 vibration operate in this relationship, but Hugh Lynn helped to maintain his father's image in the world, thereby fulfilling the outer personality tie between the time of his birth and the period under which his father was operating at the time. (Note that there is no exact cut-off date between one period and another, as events can occur shortly before the new period begins.)

Also, Hugh Lynn's Life Lesson Number, 36/9, tied in with his father's Path of Destiny Number 45/9. This has been confirmed over the years. From 1940 to the present, this son has been the prime factor in promoting the work of the Edgar Cayce Foundation, and in building the organization into the successful entity it now is.

At age thirty-three, an article about Cayce's ability, published in the *New York Times*, gave him nationwide publicity. Not only did his age, thirty-three, correspond to his Outer Personality Number at the time of this event, but he was also operating under a 17/8 period number, which tied in with his Life Lesson Number, 44. He was also working in a major process 42/6 experience, thus activating his Outer Personality Number again. He was working in the limelight now, and his public image became an issue in his life. He was learning the lessons that accompanied this unexpected fanfare.

The following year a second child was born and died. His wife, Gertrude, became ill with tuberculosis. His readings saved her life and convinced Cayce of their value. This same year, at age thirty-four, he was investigated by Dr. Munsterberg of Harvard University. These events all occurred during a 33 personal year, which is also his Outer Personality Number. He was required to fulfill a role others expected of him.

Here are the calculations for the yearly periods, ages twenty-seven to thirty-six, which relate to the experiences of Cayce's life described above.

Personal Year	March to July	July to November	November to March
$3+18+1904=35/8$	1904 27 $1931=14/5$	1904 44 $1948=22$	1904 12 $1916=17/8$
$3+18+1905=36/9$	1905 28 $1933=16/7$	1905 44 $1949=23/5$	1905 12 $1917=18/9$
$3+18+1906=37/1$	1906 29 $1935=18/9$	1906 44 $1950=15/6$	1906 12 $1918=19/1$
$3+18+1907=38/11$	1907 30 $1937=20/2$	1907 44 $1951=16/7$	1907 12 $1919=20/2$
$3+18+1908=39/3$	1908 31 $1939=22$	1908 44 $1952=17/8$	1908 12 $1920=12/3$
$3+18+1909=40/4$	1909 32 $1941=15/6$	1909 44 $1953=18/9$	1909 12 $1921=13/4$

$3+18+1910=32/5$	1910	1910	1910
	__33__	__44__	__12__
	$1943=17/8$	$1954=19/1$	$1922=14/5$
$3+18+1911=33$	1911	1911	1911
	__34__	__44__	__12__
	$1945=19/1$	$1955=20/2$	$1923=15/6$
$3+18+1912=34/7$	1912	1912	1912
	__35__	__44__	__12__
	$1947=21/3$	$1956=21/3$	$1924=16/7$

Ages Thirty-six to Forty-five To calculate the experiences by the major process, we work with the number in the center of the square, 42/6; the number on the lower side of the triangle, 18/9; the number in the center of the triangle; 44; and the ages at each end of line EF, 36 and 45. $36+6=42$. $45-6=39$. At ages 39 and 42, Cayce had a 42/6 experience. $36+9=45$. $45-9=36$. At ages 36 and 45, Cayce had an 18/9 experience. $36+8=44$. $45-8=37$. At ages 37 and 44, Cayce had a 44 experience.

To calculate the experiences by the minor process, we work with the number in the center of the square, 42/6; the number on the lower side of the triangle, 18/9; the ages at each end of line EF, 36 and 45; and the number on line EF, 18/9. $36+9=45$. $18+18=36/9$. At age 45, Cayce had a 36/9 experience. $45-9=36$. $18+42=60/6$. At age 36, Cayce had a 60/6 experience.

The year Cayce was thirty-seven, his son Hugh Lynn, then six years old, injured his eyes while playing. Doctors recommended the removal of one eye and were apprehensive about saving the other. The little boy asked his father for a reading, which was given. A method was prescribed for saving his eyes and restoring sight. Following his father's advice, Hugh Lynn recovered entirely; he still has very good eyesight today. This same year Cayce himself underwent an appendectomy. These events occurred under a major-process 44 experience, which is his Life Lesson Number.

In the last days before Cayce's birthday in 1918, another son, Edgar Evans, was born. The date was February 9, 1918, which yielded a 30/3 Life Lesson Number for the new child. Cayce was then ending a 39/3 personal year and a 21/3 period number and entering a 24/6 period number, which tied in his Soul and Outer Personality Numbers during that period of time. With a 30/3 Life Lesson, the new son's destiny was woven in with his father's Soul Number. We have found that quite often families express the same number patterns.

Here are the calculations for the yearly periods, ages thirty-six to forty-five, which relate to the experiences of Cayce's life described above.

Personal Year	March to July	July to November	November to March	Thirty-six to Forty-five
$3+18+1913=35/8$	1913 36 $1949=23/5$	1913 44 $1957=22$	1913 12 $1925=17/8$	
$3+18+1914=36/9$	1914 37 $1951=16/7$	1914 44 $1958=23/5$	1914 12 $1926=18/9$	
$3+18+1915=37/1$	1915 38 $1953=18/9$	1915 44 $1959=24/6$	1915 12 $1927=19/1$	
$3+18+1916=38/11$	1916 39 $1955=20/2$	1916 44 $1960=16/7$	1916 12 $1928=20/2$	
$3+18+1917=39/3$	1917 40 $1957=22$	1917 44 $1961=17/8$	1917 12 $1929=21/3$	
$3+18+1918=40/4$	1918 41 $1959=24/6$	1918 44 $1962=18/9$	1918 12 $1930=13/4$	
$3+18+1919=41/5$	1919 42 $1961=17/8$	1919 44 $1963=19/1$	1919 12 $1931=14/5$	
$3+18+1920=33$	1920 43 $1963=19/1$	1920 44 $1964=20/2$	1920 12 $1932=15/6$	
$3+18+1921=34/7$	1921 44 $1965=21/3$	1921 44 $1965=21/3$	1921 12 $1933=16/7$	

Ages Forty-five to Fifty-four To calculate the experiences by the major process, we work with the number in the center of the square, 42/6; the number on the lower side of the triangle, 18/9; the number in the center of the triangle, 44; and the ages at each end of line FG, 45 and 54. $45+6=51$. $54-6=48$. At ages 45 and 51, Cayce had a 42/6 experience. $45+9=54$. $54-9=45$. At ages 45 and 54, Cayce had an

18/9 experience. $45+8=53$. $54-8=46$. At ages 46 and 53, Cayce had a 44 experience.

To calculate the experiences by the minor process, we work with the number in the center of the square, 42/6; the number on the lower side of the triangle, 18/9; the ages at each end of line FG, 45 and 54; and the number on line FG, 5. $45+5=50$. $5+18=23/5$. At age 50, Cayce had a 23/5 experience. $54-5=49$. $5+42=47/11$. At age 49, Cayce had a 47/11 experience.

At age forty-six, after much traveling, Cayce returned to Selma, Alabama, to give readings as his life work. At this time he obtained the secretarial services of Gladys Davis. That same year he moved to Dayton, Ohio, to work with Arthur Lammers, to give readings on mind and soul, as well as illness. Thus began his life readings with information on reincarnation, numerology, astrology and similar subjects. The year was 1923. Cayce was working under his Life Lesson Number, 44, activated by a 44 experience under the major process on the blueprint.

Cayce's readings advised that a move to Virginia Beach, Virginia, would be helpful in many ways. There he could build a hospital to give the treatments prescribed. More and more people became interested in Cayce's work. Morton Blumenthal, a man with much influence, made arrangements for the family to move to Virginia Beach. Cayce was forty-eight years old. During this period a major process experience on the blueprint was in action, activating his Outer Personality Number, 33. Because of the outer evidence of his abilities, he was aided by a prestigious individual.

The hospital opened on November 11, 1928, a day with a 42/6 vibration. Cayce was also under a major-process 42/6 experience at that time, which activated his Outer Personality Number, 33. The 42/6 is a strongly religious number oriented toward helping others.

In 1931 Cayce realized that the hospital was failing and subsequently had to be discontinued. This was one of the saddest times of Cayce's life, for his hopes had been so high. Cayce was in a 35/8 personal year which activated his 44 Life Lesson Number. Although he experienced some disappointments that year, it was also a year which gave birth to an event perhaps more significant than he had imagined—the incorporation of the Association for Research and Enlightenment (A.R.E.) in July. This event occurred under the number 22 in Cayce's chart (period number for July to November 1931). This is the master number of the material plane, showing a down-to-earth and business-like vibration. Although only a few hundred members were enrolled in the Association in 1931, it now has over 10,000 active participants.

Here are the calculations for the yearly periods, ages forty-five to fifty-four, which relate to the experiences of Cayce's life discussed above.

Personal Year	March to July	July to November	November to March	Forty-five to Fifty-four
3+18+1922=35/8	*1922* *45* *1967=23/5*	*1922* *44* *1966=22*	*1922* *12* *1934=17/8*	
3+18+1923=36/9	*1923* *46* *1969=25/7*	*1923* *44* *1967=23/5*	*1923* *12* *1935=18/9*	
3+18+1924=37/1	*1924* *47* *1971=18/9*	*1924* *44* *1968=24/6*	*1924* *12* *1936=19/1*	
3+18+1925=38/11	*1925* *48* *1973=20/2*	*1925* *44* *1969=25/7*	*1925* *12* *1937=20/2*	
3+18+1926=39/3	*1926* *49* *1975=22*	*1926* *44* *1970=17/8*	*1926* *12* *1938=21/3*	
3+18+1927=40/4	*1927* *50* *1977=24/6*	*1927* *44* *1971=18/9*	*1927* *12* *1939=22*	
3+18+1928=41/5	*1928* *51* *1979=26/8*	*1928* *44* *1972=19/1*	*1928* *12* *1940=14/5*	
3+18+1929=42/6	*1929* *52* *1981=19/1*	*1929* *44* *1973=20/2*	*1929* *12* *1941=15/6*	
3+18+1930=34/7	*1930* *53* *1983=21/3*	*1930* *44* *1974=21/3*	*1930* *12* *1942=16/7*	

Ages Fifty-four to Sixty-three To calculate the experiences by the major process, we work with the number in the center of the square, 35/8; the number on the side of the triangle, 23/5; the number in the center of the triangle, 44; and his age at each end of line GH, 54 and 63. 54+8=62. 63−8=55. At ages 55 and 62, Cayce had a 35/8 experience. 54+5=59. 63−5=58. At ages 58 and 59, Cayce had a 23/5 experience. 54+8=62. 63−8=55. At ages 55 and 62, Cayce had a 44 experience.

105

To calculate the experiences by the minor process, we work with the number in the center of the square, 35/8; the number on the side of the triangle, 23/5; the number on the line GH, 4; and the ages at each end of line GH, 54 and 63. 54+4=58. 4+35=39/3. At age 58, Cayce had a 39/3 experience. 63−4=59. 4+23=27/9. At age 59, Cayce had a 27/9 experience.

When Cayce was fifty-five, the family moved again, this time to a house on Arctic Circle. This was to be his permanent home for the rest of his life. It was there, in June of 1932, that the first Congress of the A.R.E. was held, an annual event that has continued to this day. We can see that it was a karmic experience that the first congress occurred during a 36/9 year which activated Cayce's Path of Destiny number, 9, and his Life Lesson Number, 44.

Mrs. Cayce's mother died the same year that Edgar Evans Cayce entered college. When Cayce was sixty, his father died. When he was sixty-two, a man named Thomas Sugrue came to live with the Cayces. Although Mr. Sugrue was ill, he wrote a biography of Edgar Cayce after living with him for two years. The book is called *There Is a River* and was published in 1942.

When Cayce was sixty-three years old, an office was added to the Cayce residence, providing him with the privacy he needed for his readings. It is significant that the yearly table showed his Life Lesson Number, 44, overshadowing the whole year, while the period numbers, 5, 22 and 8, indicated change (5), then great progress materially (22) and finally the carrying out of the basic 8, (his Life Lesson number 44 reduced) which vibrationally pervaded many dominant periods throughout his life.

By that time, Hugh Lynn had taken over management of the A.R.E., and Cayce was quite content to be free of that responsibility.

Here are the calculations for the yearly periods, ages fifty-four to sixty-three, which relate to the experiences of Cayce's life mentioned above.

Personal Year	March to July	July to November	November to March
3+18+1931=35/8	1931	1931	1931
	54	44	12
	1985=23/5	1975=22	1943=17/8
3+18+1932=36/9	1932	1932	1932
	55	44	12
	1987=25/7	1976=23/5	1944=18/9
3+18+1933=37/1	1933	1933	1933
	56	44	12
	1989=27/9	1977=24/6	1945=19/1

$3+18+1934=38/11$	1934	1934	1934	**Fifty-four**
	$\underline{57}$	$\underline{44}$	$\underline{12}$	**to**
	$1991=20/2$	$1978=25/7$	$1946=20/2$	**Sixty-three**
$3+18+1935=39/3$	1935	1935	1935	
	$\underline{58}$	$\underline{44}$	$\underline{12}$	
	$1993=22$	$1979=26/8$	$1947=21/3$	
$3+18+1936=40/4$	1936	1936	1936	
	$\underline{59}$	$\underline{44}$	$\underline{12}$	
	$1995=24/6$	$1980=18/9$	$1948=22$	
$3+18+1937=41/5$	1937	1937	1937	
	$\underline{60}$	$\underline{44}$	$\underline{12}$	
	$1997=26/8$	$1981=19/1$	$1949=23/5$	
$3+18+1938=42/6$	1938	1938	1938	
	$\underline{61}$	$\underline{44}$	$\underline{12}$	
	$1999=28/1$	$1982=20/2$	$1950=15/6$	
$3+18+1939=43/7$	1939	1939	1939	
	$\underline{62}$	$\underline{44}$	$\underline{12}$	
	$2001=3$	$1983=21/3$	$1951=16/7$	

Ages Sixty-three to Seventy-two To calculate the experiences by the major process, we work with the number in the center of the square, 35/8; the number on the side of the triangle, 23/5; the number in the center of the triangle, 44; and the age at each end of line HI, 63 and 72. $63+8=71$. $72-8=64$. At age 64 (and 71, had he not died) he had a 35/8 experience. $63+5=68$. $72-5=67$. At age 67 (and 68, had he not died) he had a 23/5 experience. $63+8=71$. $72-8=64$. At age 64 (and 71 had he not died) he had a 44 experience.

To calculate the experiences by the minor process, we work with the number in the center of the square, 35/8; the number on the side of the triangle, 23/5; the number on line HI, 7; and the ages on each end of line HI, 63 and 72. $63+7=70$. $7+23=30/3$. At age 70 Cayce would have had a 30/3 experience. $72-7=65$. $7+35=42/6$. At age 65, Cayce had a 42/6 experience.

According to the major process calculations, Cayce's basic number 8 (44 reduced) is activated twice, indicating that this was a time for him to experience his Life Lesson. At age 65 the *Search for God* books became available. These books are still used by all A.R.E. study groups both in the United States and abroad.

Here are the calculations for the yearly periods, ages sixty-three to sixty-seven, which relate to the experiences of Cayce's life mentioned above.

Edgar Cayce	Personal Year	March to July	July to November	November to March
	$3+18+1940=35/8$	1940 63 2003 = 5	1940 44 1984 = 22	1940 12 1952 = 17/8
	$3+18+1941=36/9$	1941 64 2005 = 7	1941 44 1985 = 23/5	1941 12 1953 = 18/9
	$3+18+1942=37/1$	1942 65 2007 = 9	1942 44 1986 = 24/6	1942 12 1954 = 19/1
	$3+18+1943=38/11$	1943 66 2009 = 11	1943 44 1987 = 25/7	1943 12 1955 = 20/2
	$3+18+1944=39/3$	1944 67 2011 = 4	1944 44 1988 = 26/8	1944 12 1956 = 21/3

A personal year runs from birthdate to birthdate; thus Cayce was still in his 1944 year when he died. The actual deathdate was January 3, 1945, a 23/5 experience.

Cayce's last reading was given September 17, 1944, during a 26/8 period. On January 3, 1945, Cayce's work in the physical body was completed. He died at 67 years and 10 months of age, in a 39/3 personal year and a 21/3 period number, which shows that the transition occurred under his Soul Number, 12/3.

Even after his death, Cayce's influence is still felt by many. Some of his predictions have been fulfilled; some have not yet occurred. The A.R.E. continues to thrive and in 1956 was able to buy back the old hospital building in Virginia Beach. This is now the location of the headquarters and it is open to the public. In 1975 a beautiful new library was opened, dedicated to the work of the A.R.E. Within its doors can be found all the information from Cayce's readings, sorted and filed in encylopedic form, thus making available the vast information which came through the instrumentality of one man, Edgar Cayce.

7

BIBLE SYMBOLOGY

THE BIBLE is a veritable mine of number symbology. Both the Old and New Testaments reveal, by use of numbers, depth of meaning and hidden concepts which commonly escape the casual reader.

The Zohar, a collection of mystical kabbalistic writings, states that, "The Universe was created by three forms of expression—Numbers, Letters and Words." The letters in all alphabets represent definite powers. To study the vibratory value of numbers and letters is to study the divine creative energies in various degrees of manifestation. Every name in the Bible describes a deeper meaning regarding the person or place to which it applies. Similarly certain words are made to have hidden significance.

Old Testament

To read through the Old Testament, the Torah, Kabbalah, and other sacred Hebraic writings is to become well aware of how the Hebrews used the science of names and numbers in their number-letter code. By this code they wished to obscure their meanings from the uninitiate, and at the same time to reveal their inner teachings to the initiate.

Each letter of the Hebrew alphabet has several meanings—for example the letter *Aleph* (A) means "life-breath, power, source;"while the letter *Beth* (B) means "house, shelter"—and so on with every letter. The symbology allowed hidden teachings to be evident to those who knew how to read the deeper message contained in the names of all persons and places described. Scholars could also penetrate the mask of allegory and receive or give divine guidance through numbers and letters.

For example, the story of Cain slaying Abel is about fraternal rivalry. But symbolically, the name Cain means body and materialistic human desires, while Abel stands for the soul and idealistic human nature. These characters were so named to warn that materialism would kill spiritual ideas; hence Cain was said to have killed Abel (Genesis 4:8).

Many biblical characters who reached periods of spiritual growth and development in their lives were given new names by divine direction. Thus Abram became Abraham (Genesis 17:5) and Sara became Sarah (Genesis 17:15). In both cases, the Hebrew *Heh* (H), a letter meaning "light" and having a vibration of 9, was added to the name to denote the attainment of spiritual light.

New Testament writers also made name changes to point out an individual's spiritual progress. For example, Saul became Paul after his conversion to Christianity (Acts 9:1-22 and 13:9). This symbolized the removal of the Hebrew *Shin* (S) and its replacement with the Hebrew *Peh* (P). Shin means "tooth or fang of a serpent."Peh means "mouth." After this change, Saul became Paul, the spokesman for Christ (Acts 13:9). As Proverbs 22:1 states, "a good name is rather to be chosen than great riches."

A further use of numbers in biblical language involves recounting the number of years a person lived, begat and died. These numbers did not refer to the person's age in years, but rather to progress in spiritual attainment. The meaning of the name of the begotten indicated the development of a characteristic. Cycles also were indicated by the generations of descent. For example, from Adam to Noah there were nine generations, and from Noah to Abraham there were also nine generations. That made Noah the ninth from Adam,and Abraham the ninth from Noah.

Adam had three sons—Cain (body), Abel (soul) and Seth (replacement for Abel to carry the spiritual light). In a parallel situation, Noah also had three sons—Shem (spirit), Ham (physical nature) and Japhet (mental nature). These names represented the growth of humanity in consciousness after eighteen cycles of change.

Abram meant "father," while Abraham implied the added faith in God which he had come to realize. At ninety-nine years of age, Abraham begat Isaac, whose name meant "joy in divine sonship." Isaac begat Jacob, whose name meant "illumination through unfolding soul." Jacob's twelve sons (Genesis 35:22-27) refer to the twelve types of consciousness represented by the twelve character types in the signs of the zodiac.

To study the whole Bible in this light is to have a lifetime of fascinating discovery. It can be said that Hebrew, more than any other language, offers us a great opportunity to study the profound power and significance of names.

Here is a short list of keywords for the numbers in biblical times:

0. Source before manifestation.
1. God, the one immutable divine unity.
2. Duality—human, not divine.
3. Attributes of $1+2=3$—union of divine and human qualities.
4. The idea of solidity—steadfastness.
5. Humanity with its five developed senses.
6. Equilibrium, fitness, peace.
7. Humanity's septenary nature, cyclic fullness.
8. Accumulation, strength, power, augmentation.
9. Consolidation, conservation, humaneness. (The true mission of the 9 is to serve as a minister of God on earth.)
10. God and humanity, father-mother-deity, completion.

Modern numerology has grown partly from these concepts. The numbers and letters reflect meanings from the past coupled with many added spiritual interpretations. Meanings of our names today have deep significance and can be delineated letter by letter and number by number as we attain cycles of expression year by year in our own lives. These are fully explained in earlier chapters of this book.

0 GENESIS, which means "first cause," relates to the primordial source. The first few verses of Genesis pertain only to the one God, as divine creator, who brings the world into existence out of the void, or from the unmanifest.

1 "LET THERE BE LIGHT" (Genesis 1:3). The first spiritual emanation was light. If our soul continues to follow the light, we will get back to our source. 1 stands for a beginning, a new start and unity.

2 "...AND GOD DIVIDED the light from the darkness" (Genesis 1:4). In 2 there is duality, day and night, heaven and earth, man and woman and all pairs of opposites. Thus the development of *choice* began between good and evil, true and false and positive and negative.

Pythagoras says, "2 is the imperfect condition into which 'being' falls, when it becomes detached from the monad, God." Manly Hall in *The Mystical Christ*, states, "When the eyes of the both are opened, the sight of the soul is obscured."

3 THE FIRST TRINITY—Adam and Eve and child. Thus 3 means manifestation and expansion. Other trinities survive in our world—body, soul, and spirit, and the three divisions of mind—conscious, subconscious and super-conscious.

4 MANY BIBLICAL REFERENCES are taken from the cycles of the natural world. The symbology of the four seasons and four winds is embodied in Ezekiel's vision of the four living creatures—the face of a man, the face of a lion, the face of an ox and the face of an eagle (Ezekiel 1:5-14). These four relate to the four fixed signs of the zodiac.

The four elements appear symbolically as the birds of the air, the fish of the sea, the fire of the Lord and the products of the earth. Genesis 2:10-14 tells of the "river out of Eden which parted into four heads." The rivers were named Pison, Gihon, Hiddekel and Euphrates. Metaphysically these names mean spirit (fire), breath (air), body (earth) and blood (water). These symbolize spirit, mind, body and soul which are the four principles that vitalize the material body during the earth life.

5 METAPHYSICALLY a "river" represents vital force. Human beings are the container of this force, as a "garden" symbolizes the body. The river of Genesis 2:10-14, described under number 4, represents the flow of humanity itself throughout the earth, which divides and divides until it covers all the earth. The 5 is the number of humanity with our five developed senses. The five senses are introduced in the early chapters of Genesis to indicate that the senses are essential in human creation; and therefore 5 is the number of humanity.

Five plays an important part in the story of David and Goliath. "...and David chose five smooth stones out of the brook" and "David took a stone and smote the Philistine (Goliath) in the forehead. The stone sunk into the forehead and he fell to the ground, (I Samuel 17:40). The five stones represent the spiritualization of David's senses. David believed in the indwelling God of love and had learned to depend upon the spiritual power within himself. According to a mystical legend, when David touched the five stones they became as one stone, thus combining the total powers of his senses. The name Goliath means material power; thus the story is meant to demonstrate the power of the spiritual over the material.

6 THE PREPARATIONS for the emergence of humanity had all been made during the five days of creation, so on the sixth day, God made human beings. "In the image of God created He him, male and female created He them," (Genesis 1:27). So 6 is associated with generation, motherhood, fatherhood, domesticity and service. Home, family and children are the concerns of 6; human relationships and love abound.

Moses, the first lawgiver, patterned the Ten Commandments after the Lord's example of creating the universe in six days. "Six days shalt thou labor and do all thy work" (Exodus 20:9). Therefore 6 is related to labor and service, as shown by the sixth sign of the zodiac, Virgo.

Through love, the sixth sense is to be developed as people demonstrate their godliness. The Book of Ruth is keyed to the number 6 and to love. In Ruth 3:15, Boaz gives Ruth six measures of barley, symbolic of love and protection.

7 IS THE PRINCIPLE NUMBER in the Bible; it is used innumerable times (some say over three hundred sixty) throughout both the Old and New Testaments. "But the seventh day is the Sabbath of the Lord thy God....For in six days the Lord made heaven and earth...and rested the seventh day; wherefore the Lord blessed the seventh day and hallowed it" (Exodus 20:10-11).

One of the most profound examples of the use of the symbolic number 7 is related to the fall of Jericho in the Book of Joshua, 6:1-20:

> And the Lord said unto Joshua, "And ye shall compass the city...and go round about the city once. Thus shalt thou do six days....And the priests shall bear before the ark seven trumpets of rams' horns: and the seventh day ye shall compass the city seven times, and the priests shall blow with the trumpets....When they make a long blast with the ram's horn and when ye hear the sound of the trumpet, all the people shall shout with a great shout, and the wall of the city shall fall down flat.

It becomes evident that the fall of Jericho was not by warfare but rather was by the principle of the 7. Victory was achieved by means of the positive vibration of sound which had been built up to a tremendous power.

8 THE MYSTERY of the 8 is that of eternal and continuous spiral motion, which is constant throughout the universe. The life-force currents sweep through the body in the form of a figure 8, following the cerebro-spinal and the sympathetic nervous systems, like radiations of light. This is why in deep meditation one sees a real light within. The symbol ∞, the horizontal 8, means "as above, so below." It is a symbol of power. In Genesis 17:10 the rite and covenant of circumcision was to be performed on the eighth day of a man-child's life. This was considered one of the most important covenants between God and humanity.

9 IS THE ULTIMATE, containing the forces of all the other numbers. It stands for a complete cycle of growth. The nine generations from Adam to Noah and from Noah to Abraham indicate stages of growth and development. Noah was the ninth from Adam, and Abraham was the ninth from Noah.

When Abram received his covenant from God and his new name, Abraham, he was "ninety and nine years old" (Genesis 17:1-5). Symbolically, his age reduces to a 9, to indicate that this was a period of time in which a spiritual cycle had been completed. The addition of the Hebrew *Heh* (H) to Abram's name carries a 9 vibration as well.

New Testament

In the first four books of the New Testament, Matthew, Mark, Luke and John, the writers express their Christian teachings mostly by allegory and parable. These are meant to be interpreted in various ways; some apply to the cosmic world as a whole, some to our solar system, some to the entire human race and some to individuals. Since a person is called the microcosm within the macrocosm, an individual represents, in miniature, all that is, was and will be.

As in the Old Testament, symbology is used also to point out significant hidden meanings in names and numbers. The art and science of numerology is one of the most obvious methods employed, although a deep understanding of the basic meanings of numbers is necessary for a complete unravelling of inner meanings.

The New Testament describes the path of faith. Faith is the conscious acceptance of wisdom and love. When faith is strong the mind is at peace and the body is free of tension. Faith is a mystical conviction that God is presently a power within the individual. The instinct to believe is as strong as the instinct to survive, impelling one to search for a philosophy to sustain one's hopes and desires on the journey through life. It is said that primitive people were mystics by instinct, and that modern people are mystics by intuition.

In Christian teachings Christ is the revelation of the love and forgiveness of God. The Sermon on the Mount (Matthew 5:17) is the code of mystic Christianity, and it is in the faithful heart that the Sermon is understood.

The twelve disciples of Jesus represent an extension of the twelve tribes of Israel. The seventy-two other disciples correspond to the six elders chosen from each of the original twelve tribes.

The Pythagorean dodecahedron (a twelve-sided symmetrical figure which can be compared to the twelve lines of the Divine Triangle) represents the universe as related to humanity. This indicates that the individual has within himself the potential of the twelve powers as they relate to the inherent attributes within the twelve signs of the zodiac. The search for knowledge is motivated by the desire to understand the self in relation to God.

The New Testament writers symbolically applied all the basic numbers to express their ideas, but made more references to specific numbers relating to the seven-fold human body, to the divine potential of the human mind and soul and to spiritual destiny. Many years elapsed between the writing of the Old and New Testaments which allowed time for much expansion of human consciousness. As a result, many more meanings for the numbers had accrued. The use of symbolism had grown and was liberally employed as a means of revelation.

1 IS THE ZERO made more manifest; it is the self, independence and unity. "In the beginning was the Word...and the Word was God" (John 1:1). 1 is the basis or cause of a beginning; it is a start, a creative idea for expression.

2 ENCOMPASSES ALL PAIRS of opposites—male and female, spirit and matter, heaven and hell. "No man can serve two masters...ye cannot serve God and Mammon," (Matthew 6:24). There is always a choice to be made between the pairs of opposites; thus we are warned that in duality there is danger. "A house divided against itself shall not stand," (Matthew 12:25). But, "If two agree, it shall be done," (Matthew 18:19).

3 SYMBOLIZES THE TRINITY, triad and trine—the three dimensions. In a larger sense, the 3 stands for mutliplication and growth.

Three of the disciples went with Jesus into the garden of Gethsemane. They were Peter, James and John; these three stand for light, life and love. "And Jesus went apart and prayed three times...each time He returned to find them asleep." The inner meaning is that Jesus felt that light, life and love were forsaking Him, as He said in His prayer, "Father let this cup pass from me, nevertheless, Thy will be done" (Matthew 26:37-45; Mark 14:32-41).

Jesus asked Peter three times, "Lovest thou me?" (John 21:15-17). The three inquiries refer to love on the three planes of consciousness—the conscious mind, the subconscious mind and the super-conscious mind. "If two or three are gathered together in my name, there am I in the midst of them," (Matthew 18:20). This also refers to the three parts of the mind, and avers that if all agree, the Christ power will prevail.

The story of Jesus is a story of 3's. He rose after three days and he was denied thrice by Peter. The fact that Jesus was crucified between two thieves is symbolic of the divided system of belief which has stolen many of the true teachings. Christ sat down with the twelve, a higher vibration of 3. Judas bargained for thirty pieces of silver, again a vibration of 3.

4 STANDS FOR LAW and order, measurement, the physical and material realms, reason, logic, the square and the cross. Whenever a number is made up of straight lines, it symbolizes the divine principle; therefore the 4 and the 7 are called sacred numbers. The symbols are the square and the cross. The cross is always a sacred symbol wherever found. Traditionally, the equal-armed cross represented man. With the coming of Christ, the horizontal line of the cross was raised from the umbilical center to the heart center. It is not necessarily a Christian symbol; other spiritual leaders have died on the cross such as Krishna of India, Thamus of Syria, Hesus of the Druids, Mithra of Persia and Quexalcotl of Mexico.

"And He was there in the wilderness forty days tempted by Satan; and was with the wild beasts, and the angels ministered unto him," (Mark 1:13). 40 is used in a Scripture to indicate a completed cycle of retreat from things of the world in preparation for something better to follow.

On the morning of the fourth day after he died, Lazarus (meaning lack of spiritual understanding) lay in the tomb, bound hand and foot, with grave clothes wound around him. The fourth dawning day is when spiritual understanding shall release us from the grave of materialism and bring awakening to the one light.

"At the fourth watch, just as gray dawn was breaking, they beheld one walking on the water," (Matthew 14:25). This refers metaphorically to the dawning of Aquarian Age, the age of community.

5 STANDS FOR MEDIATION, understanding and judgment. The ancients represented the world by the number 5, the explanation being that in 5 are represented the four elements earth, water, fire and air, plus the fifth essence, ether or spirit. Five became the number of humanity with the five developed senses. It is the great work of human beings to gain control over the five senses, after which the sixth sense, intuition develops.

The five wounds of Christ symbolize the suffering endured while in the flesh, which leads us to turn to God. In the parable of the five wise and the five foolish virgins (Matthew 25:3), "They that were foolish took their lamps and took no oil with them. But the wise took oil in their vessels with their lamps." The oil relates to the annointed, or those who had light. Human beings can choose the light or reject it by their actions. Interestingly, the word oil is a 9-powered word which means a completed cycle of attainment.

6 IS THE NUMBER OF BALANCE, harmony, cooperation, marriage, connubiality and beauty. "And there were set there six water pots of stone" (John 2:6) for the wedding feast. A wedding represents love (as does the number 6) at its most blissful state in earthly consciousness. The 6 expresses universal love, for out of the sorrows of personal love, the soul awakens to the higher life which leads to illumination or adeptship. Jesus's first miracle changed six pots of water to wine.

7 IS THE NUMBER OF REST, cessation but not ceasing, safety, and the full measure of the triad and the quaternary.
One of the greatest heritages from the Christian Scriptures is the seven-fold path of the Lord's prayer. The seven statements express the triad and the quaternary (Matthew 6:9-13):

1. Our *Father* which art in heaven,
2. Hallowed be Thy *Name*.
3. Thy kingdom come, Thy *will* be done, on earth as it is in heaven.
4. Give us this day our daily *bread*, and
5. Forgive us our *debts* as we forgive our debtors.
6. Lead us not into *temptation*,
7. But deliver us from *evil*.

The final statement ("For Thine is the kingdom, and the power and the glory, forever") was added much later to symbolize return to the heavenly state.

8 STANDS FOR INVOLUTION AND EVOLUTION, for cycles of ebb and flow, infinity, rhythm, advancement, strength and confidence.
The 8 is not a primary number in the New Testament. Rather, we find the 8 figures heavily in the eight-fold path of the Buddha and in occult literature.

9 REFERS TO COMPLETION, attainment, fulfillment, regeneration and revelation. Many words in the Bible are used for their symbolic meanings and teachings mystically concealed. *Bread* and *wine* are usually linked together. Bread is a 3-powered word; wine is a

6-powered word; together they form a symbol of the 9-power of regeneration. Thus the serving of bread and wine means that one is to partake of a regenerative process when taking communion.

In the Book of Revelation there are two numbers whose meanings have caused much discussion. These two numbers, the 666 and the 144,000 both vibrate to a 9. The 144,000 who were sealed as members of the Tribes of Israel refers to developed or saved humanity. The seal refers to the protective "sign in their foreheads," (Revelations 9:4). The 666, described as the "number of the beast" (Revelations 13:18), refers to humanity functioning at the materialistic unregenerated level. Thus these two numbers mystically refer to the evolution of humanity, either as "lost" (666) or "saved" (144,000).

Humanity, symbolicaly called the "hand of God," demonstrates the same principle. Hand is a 9-powered word and refers to humanity as one of God's helpers in bringing forth His Kingdom.

The nine statements of blessing in the Sermon on the Mount, which show a completed cycle, represent the essence of the New Testament teaching that the greatest of all power is love. Love is a 9-powered word. "He that loveth not knoweth not God, for God is love," (I John 4:8). "God is love, and he that dwelleth in love, dwelleth in God, and God in him," (I John 4:16). In the ninth hour—the hour of prayer—Christ on the cross said, "It is finished," (John 19:30).

The numbers 12 and 13 hold a special place in both the Old and New Testaments.

12 THERE WERE Twelve Tribes of Israel who were the sons of Jacob. When Jacob gave his blessing to his twelve sons, he was referring not only to twelve individuals, but to the development of twelve attributes to be awakened in the human soul. These paralleled the twelve characteristics of the twelve signs of the zodiac (Genesis 49:1-28). The work of these twelve sons dominated most of the Old Testament. Each tribe expressed the qualities of one sign of the zodiac and responded to a certain number. No tribe was wholly good or bad. These twelve signs and their corresponding numbers are operative in the lives of every individual, for each person indeed is a miniature universe.

Jesus chose to have twelve apostles. These also relate in character to the twelve signs of the zodiac to make a complete gathering of types of people in the inner circle of followers of Jesus. Thus the vibrational force under the number 12 belongs to the developed soul who has accumulated unusual inner strength through many and varied experiences.

13 IS A NUMBER of special significance. Note that there were twelve apostles, but Jesus, the Christ, made

a thirteenth member at the last supper. 12 is the number of solar
months in the year, but 13 is the number of lunar months. While the
solar vibrations are positive-creative in type, the lunar vibrations are
negative-receptive in type. Each, as a reflection of God, is equally important.

13 means either death through degeneration, or life and attainment
through regeneration. There are no half-way measures in 13; it requires all or nothing. If 13 is your number, face it and win!

"Choose ye this day whom ye will serve," (Joshua 24:15). In
Deuteronomy 30:16, Moses said, "See, I have set before thee this day
life and good—or death and evil—therefore choose life, and both
thou and thy seed shall live."

Incarnation in the flesh represents the soul's burial in matter, where
it loses the power it originally had in the ethereal realm where it was
created to be a companion to God. Eating of the Tree of Knowledge
of Good and Evil leads to spiritual, not physical, death. When the
soul turns from God to self it figuratively dies. We wander about on
earth in the flesh, as prodigal sons and daughters, victims of spiritual
amnesia. The prodigal, even as you and I, went from the father's
home of his own free will; the father did not send him.

Both the Old and the New Testaments contain numerous instances
of the use of numerological symbols in the form of parable and
allegory. Because every number and letter has a dual meaning, hidden
messages are discernible to readers who understand the number-letter
codes employed in biblical times.

In addition, there are three levels of meaning or knowledge which
the reader can acquire. The first level comes through the conscious
mind and applies to the material or physical world. The second level
is absorbed through the subconscious mind and is acquired by means
of parables and symbols. The third level deals with revelations on the
super-conscious plane of thought and affirms that we must rediscover
who we are from within.

The Bible is the story of humanity and its generations (growth and
attainment), of its degeneration (the prodigal who left his father's
house forgetful of his divinity) and of its regeneration through the
possible path of return to the consciousness within which proclaims,
"Thy Will be done."

II

DOUBLE-DIGIT

DELINEATIONS

Y OUR WAY OF SUCCESS and happiness is hidden in your
name and birthdate, as well as the ways to overcome the difficulties found there. These paths must be hunted out, understood
and explained when analyzing a number chart, because the way to
overcome obstacles lies alongside the indicators of success and happiness. It is always a question of action and reaction, whether the
positive or the negative choice is taken. When you understand that
you have choices, and you know what they are, you can conduct
your life in such a way as to attain any goal you set for yourself. It is
important that you choose a goal and then examine the way your
cosmic gifts have prepared you for its achievement.

The meanings of the single digits are explicit; when the single digits
are combined to form the double digits, they provide a more complete
picture of how you will express your talents. The double digits show

patterns of experience; they indicate destiny and point the way to success. These facets of your character cannot be discovered in detail except by careful consideration of the double numbers produced by your name and birthdate.

This is primarily a book on numerology, but since we use the double digits up through 78, which is the number of cards in the Tarot deck, we are including brief excerpts of the Tarot philosophy as a further dimension in understanding the numbers. The Tarot keys symbolize ways of determining the strengths and weaknesses of dynamic life forces.

Rich in symbolism, the Tarot has from ancient times been used to help people understand the laws of the universe and our relation to these laws. The twenty-two keys of the Major Arcana relate a story of our lives, of how we are constituted and what our possibilities are. If we all studied and followed these laws, our lives would improve in consciousness and inner security. The fifty-six minor keys explain the many phases of human life and symbolize ways to face our dilemmas.

The Tarot also relates to areas of the zodiac, and for those students who wish to plumb the depths of astrology, we have included in the delineations the astrological assignments for each of the seventy-eight numbers. In fact, the sciences of numerology, astrology and the Tarot coincide and confirm each other so perfectly that we have found it almost impossible to analyze a chart of any kind without somehow including concepts from each science to enhance our understanding of the chart. In their most exalted use, these three sciences will synthesize the knowledge contained in their rich symbolism, so that we may apply it in our lives toward understanding our relationship with God.

How to Read Your Number

Suppose your number is 32/5: read the delineation for the double number first, then read the delineation for the single digit that it reduces to. Keep in mind that it is the 2 working through the 3 to achieve the base number 5, which is synthesized in the 32/5 delineation. A 41/5 is an entirely different 5 vibration, with a 1 working through a 4 to achieve the base number 5.

A number always has the same meaning, no matter where it appears in your chart, but the expression of its consciousness is determined by its position as your Soul, Outer Personality, Path of Destiny or Life Lesson Number. Therefore it is important to consider where the number is operating. If the vibration is your Soul Number, then you already possess those qualities; however, if it is your Life Lesson Number, you do not possess these qualities but are here to learn them.

The numbers on the lines of the blueprint represent energies that

**Double
Digits**

will be activated at the time indicated. The same is true of the personal year number, the period number and the personal months. Realize that the numbers indicate an energy which, when activated by your life pattern, will be molded into the space in which you find it. Work with the number in that space and use it for your fullest realization.

*If the number is your Soul Number, this is what you already are.
If it is your Outer Personality Number, this is how others see you.
If it is your Path of Destiny Number, this is what you must do.
If it is your Life Lesson Number, this is what you must learn.*

If the base number of the vibration you are working under matches the base number of one of your 4 personal numbers, then read your personal number as well as the variation. For example, if one of your personal numbers is a 37/1, and you are temporarily under a 28/1, read both numbers.

1

THE MAJOR

ARCANA

1 AS A PERSONAL NUMBER VIBRATION: You are independent! You dislike restraint of any kind and need to feel free from
all encumbrances, so that your strong individuality may be expressed. You are here to build your own unique personality, which
you can do only by exercising your will. As a result, you become a
dominant force in any group to which you belong.

Recognizing that you are a natural leader, other people will look to
you for guidance and strength, so you will probably be at the head of
your organization, as a business executive, supervisor or club presi-
dent.

You need to be first and best at whatever you do. Since you have a
pioneering instinct, you are usually first, and because you have the
courage to assert yourself, you are often the best.

You will be a loner in some respects, because your assertiveness

123

tends to alienate all but emotionally secure or dependent types. You will learn to make your own decisions and stand by them, regardless of what others think. Your leadership qualities set you apart and make you acutely aware of the "weight of those splendid chains;" this is the responsibility borne by those in charge. You will meet many new and different kinds of people in your lifetime, because you are always seeking new experiences and initiating new schemes.

If you are a negative 1, you have an overpowering ego, which makes you arrogant, selfish and uncaring. You have no feeling for others and no regard for another person's point of view. Your stubborness in pursuing your own path in the face of contrary evidence sets up a series of events that will lead to failure and loneliness.

If you are a positive 1, and intellectually developed, you are quite original. Your keen, penetrating mind seeks many lines of expression, and your talents can manifest if you work as an inventor, designer or leader in any creative field. Your inventiveness allows you to solve problems creatively and constructively. This process will make you a skillful individual who expresses definite views positively. You are the pioneer setting out into the wilderness to carve a new life for yourself.

1 AS A TEMPORARY VIBRATION: **New beginnings, decisions, independence.** The period you are now entering is a time to begin again, to make a new start. You have the ability to separate yourself from your environment and choose the path you want to take. You may be required to stand alone, to think for yourself and to learn independence. The vibrations of 1 reveal the powers within, and now you must take the reins and determine your future course. If you have depended upon others in the past, you will realize that you can no longer do so.

You should set long-range goals and begin taking steps to attain them. Later, when you look back, you will realize that the events of this period were the foundation stones of your new life.

Set out to develop your talents and skills. Promote your ideas, believe in yourself and don't take "no" for an answer. Your most important experiences now will be those that you initiate; therefore, you must be decisive and firm. Great strength and self-control are required. If you fix your attention on a goal, you will attain it, because your consciousness has become an open channel of communication between your subconscious and your super-conscious. The secret is concentration. Miracles can be performed now, because you have control over all material affairs. Channel your thoughts into fertile areas where your mind's energies can set up patterns that can be transmitted to subliminal levels. The resulting subconscious reactions will bring about the desired results. Under a 1, you should be keenly aware that your results will be qualified by your real desires.

A negative use of number 1 energies can set you on a headstrong course where you insist on having your own way, regardless of the consequences. Give your individuality free rein, but guide it wisely.

Under this influence, don't be ruled by impulsiveness. Make your own plans because equal partnerships should be avoided now. Be selective in choosing friends and avoid superficial relationships. You may meet one new person who will figure importantly in your future.

Experiment with the new and untried. Remain independent and decisive, and above all, have the courage to act on your dreams.

TAROT SYMBOLISM: **Key 1 The Magician.** The Magician represents the conscious mind, which by concentration and singleminded attention to a specific idea or goal can draw upon the forces from above. In this way the idea or goal will take form and become a reality in the material world.

THE MAGICIAN.

By his posture, the central figure clearly indicates that he is merely a channel through which the life force flows. The identical ends of his wand graphically represent the axiom *as above, so below.* The horizontal figure 8 symbolizes the Holy Spirit, dominion, strength and infinity. Since a horizontal line is the ancient symbol for matter, this glyph represents the conscious mind's control over earthly things when that mind directs the life energy through fixed attention upon a specific goal.

The Magician's undergarment, symbolizing the light of perfect wisdom, is encircled by the serpent of eternity biting its own tail. The red outer garment of passion and desire, which has no binding, may be slipped on and off at will; thus the conscious mind has perfect control.

The garden is the subconscious mind cultivated by attention from the conscious mind. Red roses represent desires, while lilies represent purified thought untinged by desire. Every moment of our waking consciousness is motivated and conditioned by some kind of desire, which must be elevated to a higher plane.

The Magician has at his disposal all the elements and their human counterparts: the cup, indicating water and the imagination; the sword, indicating air and the intellect; the pentacle, earth and the body; and the wand, fire and will. These four objects represent the letters *IHVH*, which is the Hebrew word for God, and the letters *INRI (Iesus Nazarenus Rex Iudaeorum)* which appear on the Christian cross. At this point, the God energy may be translated into the world of matter to bring about perfect manifestation and harmony.

ASTROLOGICAL CORRESPONDENCE: **Mars (and Mercury).** The planet Mercury is assigned to the Magician, and Mars is assigned to the number 1. These two energies must be blended in order for the Magician to complete his task.

Mars, the red planet, supplies the fiery energy and the desire to create. Mercury is the mind, the channel through which the desire passes and the tool with which the concentration is enacted. Without the drive to accomplish, the mind is idle and useless; it needs the demanding, propelling force of Mars to spur it on to greater achievements.

When Mercury and Mars act in unison, the number 1 individual draws upon an endless source of creativity and courage. He has the vision to see what can be done, and the strength and fortitude to do it.

2 AS A PERSONAL NUMBER VIBRATION: The number 2 suggests more than one, and you, as a 2, are acutely conscious of others as opposed to yourself. Since you are socially aware of people, you tend to gather ideas and experience through others, so you would be a good diplomat, go-between, mediator or peacemaker. Your best service is through cooperation, for your mild and gentle nature is appreciated and welcomed by all sides.

You are not a forceful individual and you often prefer to stay quietly in the background. Because you are extremely aware of pairs of opposites, you find choices difficult. By remaining unobtrusive and discreet, you sometimes avoid making decisions. This quality could be a liability, but you can make it an asset by becoming an arbitrator. Your ability to see both sides of a situation, coupled with your sincerity, is a winning combination.

The number 2 also implies reflection and symmetry. Your imaginative powers are increased because you can see hidden aspects of beauty in life. Your ability to detach yourself and see separateness gives your creative and inventive potentials room to grow. When we look out into the world, we see what is in front and to the sides; we cannot see behind us without turning around. However, you seem to look into reality as in a mirror, seeing every detail, even those behind you which can be seen only with the mirror. You possess the all-seeing eye.

If you are a negative 2, you lack self-confidence, and are therefore indecisive and afraid to make decisions. You can be deceitful or two-faced. You are oversensitive and easily depressed if your surroundings are unhappy.

If you are a positive 2, you can be of great service to others because of your ability to settle situations amicably, and you may well become the power behind the throne.

2 AS A TEMPORARY VIBRATION: **Gestation, cooperation, diplomacy, self-knowledge.** You are in a gestation period in which you must not assert yourself but rather must await results. It is time to collect and assimilate the experiences of the past, giving them time

to grow slowly. This is a secretive period in which your affairs, situations and relationships are operating under an element of the unknown. You may not be aware of all the circumstances surrounding a particular situation, which may be in a fluctuating state. Therefore, you must maintain balance and equilibrium. Remain poised.

There may be meetings, conversation and comings and goings. You should be careful of what you say about your hopes and ambitions, for your words could be misconstrued by others, either unconsciously or deliberately. Use diplomacy in all your dealings and be cautious about whom you talk with and whom you put your confidence in. Carelessness and tactlessness can cause problems in relationships, which could result in angry confrontations and deceptive acts.

Be patient, considerate, tactful and receptive to other people's ideas. Practice conciliation but not at the expense of your integrity. This is a passive, receptive time in which to reflect and listen to the voice of your subconscious mind, which collects and files every piece of information it encounters. The subconscious is now potentially producing seeds that will cause either strife, dissension, disagreements and partings, or peace, cooperation, beauty and coming together.

If you exercise the positive side, you will have warm ties with other people. You can be a good mediator, go-between or agent for peace. This is a good vibration for love affairs, but be careful because you are emotionally vulnerable. Under a 2, love affairs can come and go, so maintain that balance.

The future may seem unclear during this period, because hidden energies are working that will surface later. Since choices are difficult under a 2, it is wiser to postpone important moves until your mind is more decisive. This is not a particularly good time for business ventures, again because of your indecisiveness.

Memories are a prime motivation for your actions now. Don't become trapped in unhappy memories or unconscious past conditionings. Instead use the stored wisdom from your past experiences to resolve snags in a partnership, mediation or cooperative effort. We communicate with others through the subconscious. Memories stored in that subconscious determine our response to conditions, situations and people. Examine your reactions to others now, for this period tests your ability to coexist.

Telepathic communication may be intense, as you have a subconscious knowledge of the real meaning behind events that are mysterious to your conscious mind. Therefore, you must tune in to what is formulating in your mind during this time, otherwise, you will remain in the dark. Number 2 is a two-way street, with ideas flowing between the inner self and the outer self.

A negative use of 2 makes you act petty about trivial matters. You react emotionally to confrontations, withdrawing rather than trying to settle problems peaceably. Your emotions undermine your self-confidence and upset your equilibrium.

This is a perfect time for creative people such as artists, composers, inventors and mystics to expand their consciousness through various techniques, because 2 contains latent creative powers. It is a waiting period in which the seeds of creativity are planted in the subconscious to begin the process of growth and expansion. This is also a period of wisdom in which you can see the true I AM of self by reflecting on your inner being.

You should remain passive and receptive to the present active creative forces, without vascillating or being oversensitive or withdrawn. Calm, silent contemplation of the creative potential within will help you produce exquisitely beautiful art forms, innovative ideas and unique solutions to everyday problems.

TAROT SYMBOLISM: **Key 2 The High Priestess.** The High Priestess symbolizes the subconscious mind, the receptive, reproductive and form-building power within the human organism. The curtain behind the figure connects the two pillars of light and darkness. As the balancing power between pairs of opposites, she has no preference for either and merely awaits the concentrated effort of the conscious mind. The cup-shaped crescent Moon depicts the receptiveness and retentiveness of the subconscious mind.

All memory, universal and personal, is recorded on the High Priestess's scroll, which is partially hidden because all is not yet known; God has more to reveal. The cubic stone of truth upon which she sits represents the principles of order on which the subconscious must function for perfect fulfillment. The white cross represents the proper use of the four implements on the Magician's table. The conscious mind formulates ideas which the subconscious accepts as suggestions and then sets about to make them realities in an orderly, progressive fashion.

The High Priestess is the connecting link to the subconscious through which we must pass in order to use our conscious potential, thus calling into play the powers of the Magician, the conscious mind.

ASTROLOGICAL CORRESPONDENCE: **Vulcan (and the Moon).** The High Priestess, key 2 of Tarot, (ruled by the Moon), and number 2, (ruled by Vulcan), join forces in bringing about gestation. (Vulcan is the blacksmith of the gods, the keeper of the flame and fireside. Many astrologers feel that the planet Vulcan is the rightful ruler of Virgo.) After an idea has been sown by the number 1 vibration, it must find a warm dark place where it can be properly nurtured, away from the light and clamor of the outer world. The idea seeks refuge in the depths of the Moon-ruled subconscious, where it waits to be fed by the imagination. Like Vulcan, this formation process is not seen, but it continues, fed by the fire of determination. Vulcan, the mythological tender of fire, aids the nurturing and protecting influences by making sure that the fire or desire to bring forth this seed does not flicker and die.

A number 2 individual has a quiet receptive personality, in which the seeds of cooperation, patience and prudence are nurtured. These seeds will eventually manifest in useful products and objects of beauty that will benefit the whole world.

3 AS A PERSONAL NUMBER VIBRATION: 3 is the number of the performing arts, and you are a performer. You love life, the joy of social contacts, entertainment and new experiences. Your bright active nature radiates like the Sun to warm the lives of others, and your ease with people draws them to you like a magnet. You will always have many admirers.

You are an extremely expressive person, and you should develop your skill with words and cultivate the art of conversation. You can influence others through your ability to communicate about life in a grandiose fashion. Develop and put to work your talents for entertaining and communicating. You could do well as a teacher, artist, lawyer, judge, writer, nurse, pastor or priest.

Travel will probably be an important part of your life, because you need to become involved in many experiences and investigate new opportunities. Your varied interests make your thinking broad and all-encompassing.

You like to be on stage, to entertain and live the good life. Recognition is important to you, for you need to know you are appreciated. You like to wear nice clothes, and are or should be aware of your appearance, because performing depends on how you look and project yourself.

A negative 3 does everything in a big way—eating, drinking, loving and living. You can be too self-indulgent, and extravagance could be your downfall. You tend to overact and exaggerate situations, turning mole-hill problems into mountains. Friendships will then be superficial. You may try to avoid responsibility and live just for the moment. Too much talk may make you a gossip.

As a 3, you should learn not to spread yourself too thin, which is an easy trap to fall into, with your many talents and interests. You should master at least one talent.

As a positive 3, you will be very lucky in speculative matters, investing, gambling and taking chances in general. You will have many lucky opportunities through your friends, who are most eager to assist you in every way. Your luck is derived from your positive, outgoing attitude, which induces people to want to help you.

You should avoid occupations that keep you confined in close quarters or demand long hours of isolation, because you need to

move around and express yourself in order to do your best work and
be happy.

3 AS A TEMPORARY VIBRATION: **Growth, travel, entertainment,
self-expression.** This is usually a happy time, during which previous
difficulties are overcome and resolved. You are bursting with the joy
of living; and your optimistic outlook makes you want to express
yourself socially and to indulge your desires. Many events that occur
now will add to your enthusiasm. You will definitely acquire money
during this cycle. You may receive a raise at work, a long-lost relative
might leave you an inheritance, or you might win a sweepstakes.
Luck seems to be on your side, but remember that luck is merely the
outward manifestation of your present positive attitude. You are
creating your own luck.

There is growth and expansion in all areas of your life at this time.
For some, this may mean marriage or the birth of children. For others,
birth will occur in the creative arts or in mind expansion. Recognition
of your talents in writing, painting, sculpting or acting is possible, so
now is the time to write the article, paint the picture or present the
project you've been thinking about for so long. Publication and
recognition from authorities come under a 3. Study a foreign
language, take elocution lessons or any other available means to
develop your expressive capabilities.

Spend time and money on your personal appearance, because how
others see you is extremely important now. You might attend a
weight-reducing course or yoga class to reshape and firm your body.
Pay particular attention to the way you dress, and go through your
wardrobe, replacing worn and outdated clothes. You will probably
find yourself on a buying spree.

Business mixes well with pleasure now, so involve yourself in the
social aspects of living. The people you meet will be impressed with
your manner and articulateness, and some of them will be in a position to aid your career. Give parties, join groups, attend seminars and
generally become involved in meeting and being with other people.

Don't make any commitments now that will bind and encumber
you in any way. You need freedom and time to cultivate personal
self-expression.

If you've always wanted to travel, this may be your opportunity.
Long distance travel comes under a 3, so you may have the chance to
expand through contact with other cultures or ways of life.

You will be center-stage now, so enjoy it, bask in the warmth of
others' attention and radiate the joy you feel to enhance the lives of
those you touch.

Listen to your dreams, for they can bring precognitive messages
and alert you to potential future opportunities. This is a productive
period in all areas of your life.

The negative aspects of a 3 lead to scattering your energies and overindulging in all phases of living. Talking too much can lead to gossip and deceit. Extravagance leads to dissipation. Taking unnecessary risks leads to losses. Jealousy produces loneliness. Overeating, excess drinking and indiscriminate drug consumption can have disastrous results. Be aware that exhaustion of the valuable resources of this period causes dissipation and turns potentially fertile soil to wasteland.

There is an ancient saying: "Beware of your wishes, for you will surely get them." If you desire anything strongly enough, that desire will surely come to pass. And once it is a reality, you may decide you really didn't want it after all.

During this time, your desires can become a reality, so begin now to screen your wishes. Be certain that what you desire is right and good for you and for all others concerned, and then enjoy this happy and productive period.

TAROT SYMBOLISM: **Key 3 The Empress.** The Empress is also an aspect of the subconscious mind. While the High Priestess, number 2, is memory, in number 3 we find the subconscious response to that memory which produces growth through the imagination.

In contrast to the virginal High Priestess, the Empress appears pregnant, as does the landscape around her. The Empress produces. She is the great mother surrounded by love, beauty and growth. The conscious mind, key 1, cannot produce; the subconscious mind, key 2, cannot reason; it takes a combination of 1 and 2 to produce manifestation, or key 3.

The trees, dress and wheat symbolize the ripening that takes place in the subconscious mind. The stream is the life stream, the stream of consciousness. Falling into the pool, it represents the union of the sexes or the union of the conscious and subconscious minds. Her yellow hair, symbolizing the super-concious mind, is tied by green leaves, or bound sunlight, as the leaves have captured the sun's rays. The twelve stars on her crown are the twelve zodiacal signs or the twelve months, thus representing time itself. In the same vein, it takes time to bring our desires into manifestation.

Her scepter represents her dominion over the world of creation through love, the Venus glyph. She is the epitome of creation and abundance, reminding us of the biblical passage, "And there appeared a great wonder in the heavens; a woman clothed with the Sun, and the Moon under feet, and upon her head a crown of twelve stars. And she being with child cried, travailing in birth..." (Revelations 12:1-2). Older versions of the Empress showed her with the crescent Moon beneath her feet.

ASTROLOGICAL CORRESPONDENCE: **Jupiter (and Venus).** From

the foregoing delineations of number 3 (Jupiter) and key 3 (the Empress, Venus), you can see how the attributes of Venus and Jupiter work in conjunction to bring about productivity. Venus seeks to bring harmony and beauty into whatever environment she appears. Her keen sense of justice manifests through a fine symmetry, and her loving nature seeks to make others as well as herself comfortable.

When Venus unites with Jupiter, who desires to expand services for humanity through orderly growth, an extremely productive and fertile situation results. This productivity is distinctly recognizable in number 3 individuals. They are extremely sociable and indulge not only themselves but also their family and friends. They work to bring about social harmony by using their very expressive and creative talents in such fields as acting, social work, counseling and the law. Their honesty, generosity and affability make them extremely popular with almost everyone.

4 AS A PERSONAL NUMBER VIBRATION: Symbolically, the number 4 and the four-sided square are synonymous. As a child, you spent time in a square crib and playpen. As you grew older, you drew pictures of a square house in which you and your family lived. You played with square blocks and most likely romped in a square yard. Although the perimeters of your world grew as you matured, still the boundaries defined the extent to which you could expand. Because these boundaries protected you from harm, the square became imbedded in your subconscious as a symbol of security and structure, a comfortable, productive and organized system of existence.

The earth was formed on the fourth day of Creation; therefore, symbolically, all earthly things come under a 4. As the recipient of this vibration, you are a very creative builder, an individual who puts form and structure into life. You build tangible objects because you need to see visible results from your efforts. Carpenters, masons, draftsmen and all the building trades come under a 4.

You are a good worker. An employer can rely upon your stability, steadiness, honesty and sense of responsibility. You are the salt-of-the-earth type who realizes the importance of a sound foundation upon which to build the future. By upholding the traditions of the past you reinforce your sense of security in the present and the future.

Your naturally cautious, industrious nature makes you a saver. You are a patient planner, and you insist that your finances be organized. Because of this predilection toward thrift, practicality and wise handling of finances, you would be a good banker or financier.

Law, order and regulation are keywords for a 4. You have an inborn respect for supervision and control. Many 4's work in government or law, the foundations of society. Such occupations require insight and the ability to examine situations and make judgments based upon reason, all of which you, as a 4, are extremely capable of doing.

Because a 4's insight is based on sound reasoning, this number produces the inventor who creates practical objects for the home or business. This ability also manifests itself in farming, mining, geology and gardening—those occupations which produce valuable products from the earth.

A negative 4 can be a "workaholic" whose stern and sterile outlook makes life a plodding drudgery. You can be stingy, unfriendly and alone, boxed in by secure walls of your own making, which protect you from the outside world, but also prevent you from enjoying relationships with others. This person feels limited and restrained because of a fearful need for security.

As a positive 4, you have the ability to build a useful world through sound reasoning, where your hard work and patient perseverance will benefit others in a tangible way.

4 AS A TEMPORARY VIBRATION: **Work, finances, building, practicality.** 4 brings the need to define and order things. At this time you must measure, classify, record, regulate and compose yourself as well as your affairs and your environment. You must attend to everyday, earthly matters and handle them through your own efforts and actions. You will gain materially now through honest toil, as this is a productive period in which the creative drive can be controlled and directed. For males, this time can indicate virility and fatherhood.

Controlling your daily activities will allow you to reap material rewards. Money and finances are very much a part of this cycle, so you should be economical and practical. Set up a budget and pay debts on all levels—materially, physically, mentally and spiritually. This is the ideal time to save for that special vacation or the home you've always wanted.

Surveying land, planning and building a new home, or refurbishing or reconstructing an existing one are very likely pursuits under a 4. There may be obstacles that must be solved with patience and determination, but if you have the courage to struggle through all opposition, you can make great strides.

During this period reason reigns. The number 4 is symbolic of a square window, through which we see; therefore, you must exercise vision, insight and analysis. Because you are able to see into the heart of any situation, you may be called upon to use your reason and judgment, perhaps in the judicial system as a juror or a courtroom witness. Since the judicial system is the foundation upon which a just society is built, under this vibration you may have to uphold the traditions that regulate and insure the continuity of that system.

Previously hidden aspects of the past may be revealed during this period, which allow you to correct faulty judgments from an earlier time; this is because the 4 implies the door of opportunity through which you can pass into a new life.

Since 4 rules the physical aspects of living, sensual pleasures are available to you now. You can have a physically rewarding relationship with a member of the opposite sex.

However, the crux of this vibration is responsibility, work and accomplishment. It is a time to make solid foundations—financial, physical or mental—for your life. Business and personal relationships can grow, and lasting ties of friendship may be developed now.

Financially, you will earn in direct proportion to your output. Exercise and take care of your body, your physical home. When 4 is centered on the material plane, its energies manifest as creative abilities. When these energies are spiritually centered, new psychic and spiritual realms can be contacted.

THE EMPEROR.

TAROT SYMBOLISM: **Key 4 The Emperor.** This card, ruling our conscious existence, represents reason, which is a function of the conscious mind. The Emperor therefore rules over and sets in order the reasoning, conscious elements of the material world. He supervises and controls through his ability to discern the truth in any given situation. It is his wisdom in handling affairs systematically that has placed him upon the throne.

The Emperor is the Magician grown older and now in a position where the efforts of the three previous stages bring about concrete rewards in power and dominion.

His helmet is red and gold, representing Mars and the Sun. The Sun is exalted in Aries, which rules this card, as shown by the rams' heads adorning the throne. The Emperor's thoughts have been channeled through personal effort (Mars) into productive and useful implementation, a process which has crowned him with authority (the Sun).

He holds the world in his left hand and the Tau (T) cross in his right. This cross is the T-square used in mathematics, geometry, surveying and planning. He has attained his position through proper planning. His throne, simply carved of stone, is symbolic of the body, which needs long and ardous work before it is perfected.

The Empress, 3, and the Emperor, 4, are intended to show that what you sow with your conscious mind (1) you expand through 2 and 3 and finally reap through 4. You are what you alone have made of yourself; you have the power and control. If you are dissatisfied, start with 1 and sow the proper seeds. Then follow the orderly progression through 2 and 3, and at 4, you will have what you want. This is the message of the first four cards of the Tarot.

ASTROLOGICAL CORRESPONDENCE: **Earth (and Aries).** Earth, assigned to 4, and Aries, ruler of the Emperor, key 4, are the components of this vibration. 4 is a symbol of form, manifesting in the four-sided square, or the cube, a solidified square. As such, this number logically rules all things that have form, shape and substance. The earth and all that exists as part of it fall into this category.

The abundance of the earth comes to certain individuals and not to others. By examining the astrological correspondences we can determine why this happens. Number 4 is the result of an orderly progression, just as earth-ruled Taureans are methodical types. If you make an incorrect assessment of a situation and proceed on that information, then the results will be unsatisfactory. Intelligent evaluation and proper harnessing of your personal energy are necessary for the creation of a successful conclusion. Aries, the point of beginning, is the place we must start if we expect good results. Aries has the initial thought to begin the process of manifestation and the courage to proceed. The earth vibration lends stability to the Aries desire, and the end product is a proper formation of the original thought. People with the number 4 will express these qualities, and astrologically their charts should support their 4-vibration tendencies with an emphasis on Aries and earth signs.

5 AS A PERSONAL NUMBER VIBRATION: Freedom is an absolute necessity for you. You cannot be fenced in, and your restless, adventurous nature demands that you travel physically, mentally or spiritually. Because you are an explorer, researcher and investigator at heart, your travels expose you to varied experiences which you immediately digest, dissect and file for future reference. More than others, you learn from experience. You like to probe for information and experiment, and therefore you would be a good detective.

Versatile, clever, adaptable and very creative, you can do anything you really want to do. You are extremely efficient, but you dislike monotony and cannot stand routine jobs. You perform well as long as the problem or focus of concentration holds your interest. As a constructive 5, you can go to the heights and the depths without harm. There is no limit to what you can do, if your actions are governed by reason rather than emotion.

You have inexhaustible energy which, if not controlled, can turn into outbursts of temper. When you are tired, you rebound quickly, for nothing upsets you for long. Your quick mind and instant reactions cause you to make impulsive decisions on occasion, and you tend to be impatient with people who respond more slowly. You live on nervous energy.

Hard manual labor is not your preference, so you drift into ways of making money through your mental agility. Gambling is one means of expression, and you can be very lucky if you speculate wisely but not impulsively. You could also be a mediator, peacemaker and go-between because your mind quickly performs the necessary mental gymnastics and reaches a conclusion.

Because change is a natural part of your life, you must learn to make changes in a progressive way. Otherwise you can become unstable and go in too many directions at once, becoming the proverbial jack of all trades, master of none.

You are anxious for mental growth, so you take up new studies whenever you get the urge. At these times you may become an avid student and develop intense concentration.

There are two paths open to a 5; they are indulgence on the physical plane and progress on the mental plane. As a 5, you can become immersed in the purely physical side of life, saturating your senses with drugs, alcohol, sex, food and comforts. Because you communicate well and are very witty, talkative, enthusiastic and attractive to the opposite sex, you can easily fall into the sensual life, disregarding and wasting your many talents. Negative 5's can be insincere, untruthful, selfish, irresponsible, extravagant and unpopular.

Mental development is the key to the 5, and if you choose this path, the change and variety you surround yourself with will supply answers to all your many questions. Your vast knowledge will impress people, and you will eventually accomplish the supreme task of the 5, that of cleansing the sanctuary or regenerating the body by control of the senses. Because 5 is the number of the ability to develop the powers within, you can become a sage.

5 AS A TEMPORARY VIBRATION: **Change, communication, sex, new interests, travel.** If you are operating under a 5 at this time, you feel restless and excited. Change, adventure and the lure of new vistas beckon you. Travel is very much a part of this cycle, and if you do not travel physically, then you most certainly will mentally. It is time to break out of stagnant conditions and investigate new opportunities. You are attracted to home study courses, adult education, hobbies and new mental interests of all kinds, because this is a period of mental growth and development.

You may be faced with situations that require decisions and choices, for 5 indicates two paths. This can be a turning point for you. Because this is a time of continual change in your life you must be flexible and learn to adapt, rather then make rigid plans, for they will probably be altered anyway. You must be free to meet the experience that this period has to offer because the pace is fast and events are sometimes unexpected. You will feel a nervous restless energy with this vibration, so try to avoid accidents caused by carelessness. Instead, channel your energies into constructive action through mental application.

This is a perfect time to promote yourself or a product, because you are fluent, expressive and able to communicate easily with others. You will meet new people and make friends easily. Business can be combined with social activities with rewarding results. From experiences and contacts with others, you will extract knowledge which will be filed in your subconscious and will add greater dimension to your understanding.

As this is a sensual period, you are sexually magnetic, and love affairs will be fast and intense. An old beau may show up for a last tango. There will be many opportunities for relationships with the opposite sex, one of which could develop into a marriage partnership. There can be many temptations, and you will have to use self-control and make the right decisions.

With your strong desire for change, you may very well decide, or be forced, to change jobs or partners, to move, or to alter your lifestyle considerably. At times it may seem that others are forcing a move, but it is your own need for these changes that sets up the situations. Sometimes the need for change is acted out by others, but nevertheless it is caused by your own subconscious energies.

Use self-control, channel your restless energies wisely and act decisively. This could very well be a turning point in your life.

TAROT SYMBOLISM: **Key 5 The Hierophant.** The Hierophant represents our inner teacher, our inner hearing, our intuition. Sages have always said that release from all limitation comes to those who awaken their inner awareness. True inner hearing does not involve spirits, clairvoyance and visions from the astral plane. Rather, true intuition is based upon the number 4 and key 4, the Emperor. When the conscious mind gathers all the facts and feeds them into the subconscious mind, the subconscious acts upon this information and, in a flash of intuition, sends the correct analysis back to the conscious mind. This is true intuition, based upon reason.

THE HIEROPHANT

The Hierophant's crown is triple: the row of five trefoils represents the five senses; the row of seven trefoils symbolizes the seven centers in the body and the seven original planets; the row of three trefoils stands for the three states of consciousness—the super-conscious, the conscious and the sub-conscious. His staff has the same symbolic meaning as the knob on the top: both indicate the Source, God. The ornaments attached to his crown fall just behind his ears to emphasize hearing. The crown and staff represent the four worlds—archetypal (knob), creative, formative and material.

The pale gray background represents wisdom because gray is a mixture of equal parts of black and white. Thus gray stands for perfect balance which is the practical aspect of wisdom.

At the Hierophant's feet, the crossed keys symbolize the super-conscious, which is the key to heaven, and the subconscious, which is the key to earth (or hell, if one makes it so). The robes of the two kneeling priests represent desire (roses) and purified desire (lilies), both of which must be sublimated to the conscious mind.

This card contains ten crosses representing the spiritual numbers 1 to 10, the ten aspects of the Tree of Life and the ten trees in The Empress's garden.

ASTROLOGICAL CORRESPONDENCE: **Mercury (and Taurus).** Mercury rules number 5, and Taurus has dominion over key 5, the Hierophant. These two seem unlikely partners; however, consider their attributes. Mercury, the messenger of the gods, represents movement, communication and the intellectual processes. Taurus, the first earth sign, is where we find individuals who act and react with slow deliberation, the epitome of the type who, in a leisurely manner, absorbs pleasure through the five senses.

Only through calm deliberation (Mercury in Taurus), by taking in through the senses every piece of information presented in any given situation, can the intellectual process approach its fullest potential. The jigsaw puzzle of information is then handed in pieces to the subconscious, which carefully puts them together. Once completed, the picture is presented to the conscious mind in a flash of insight or intuition. With the help of Taurus, Mercury has gathered the information, communicated it to the subconscious for analysis, and then received the answer back in the conscious mind.

Number 5 people are faced with many decisions that require intellectual discernment. They are definitely communicators and travelers, and are attracted to professions such as selling, advertising, promoting and public relations.

6 AS A PERSONAL NUMBER VIBRATION: You are an artistic individual with a fine eye for beauty and symmetry. You find art and music relaxing, rewarding and necessary for your happiness. If you choose a professional career outside the home, the creative arts would be an appropriate field.

Your innate analytical ability allows you to go right to the crux of any matter and solve problems easily and logically. Your keen perception and sense of justice would be assets for professional pursuits in law and counseling. Others sense your sagacity, honesty and fairness and seek you out to settle any differences they encounter. You are a responsible person who meets obligations and can be depended upon to follow through on anything you have promised.

6 is also the domestic vibration, indicating that you love your home and children. You may have married young in order to obtain the love you need, which a mate and children can provide. A woman with this number is likely to be a homemaker, very protective and fond of her husband and children. She prefers to be at home rather than to go out and battle the world for a living. One reason for her reluctance to go out into the world is the need for peace and harmony, which is important for all 6's. A beautiful, artistically decorated home is very important for you. You enjoy decorating and

making your surroundings attractive. You like comfort and peace and will not tolerate discord. Entertaining in your own home, if possible, is a joy for you, and you are a charming host or hostess.

You really love your friends and are concerned and sympathetic to their needs. If they require help, you generously offer whatever you have. Because of your generosity, kindness, patience and tolerance, you have many friends.

Consideration for others is basic to you personally, and you rejoice in other people's happiness and rewards as your own. You dislike jealousy intensely and cannot understand it when other people react that way. In spite of your great desire for a peaceful existence, you will fight for your beliefs against all opposition. This determination can bring you success and fame in whatever profession you choose.

A negative 6 can be very obstinate. You may become a slave to your loved ones, who use you as a doormat. You may bury yourself in your home, becoming a recluse. If you feel you have been denied the love you need so desperately, you will feel sorry for yourself, complain and whine, and indulge in self-pity. You may become discontented and jealous and play the martyr.

As a positive 6, you can be a tremendous power for good, bringing joy, love, beauty and a sense of justice into others' lives, thus establishing yourself as a snug harbor in the cold, destructive storms of life.

6 AS A TEMPORARY VIBRATION: **Marriage, change in home, redecoration and remodeling, domestic and community responsibilities.** The energies of this period center about your home and community. First look for the emphasis in the home, where changes are occurring. People may come into or leave your home, through marriage, birth, death, divorce and other occurrences, or you may change your residence.

You may marry now, or develop strong ties of friendship with someone. You feel a greater sense of responsibility toward others which people will sense; and as a result, they turn to you for assistance. They will cry on your shoulder and perhaps ask for financial aid. Some relationships could become burdensome and older people may be a responsibility now. You must accept this situation cheerfully and above all maintain harmony; put aside your own needs for a time. However, don't accept unnecessary burdens.

This vibration stimulates your artistic sense, which you could put to constructive use by redecorating or remodeling your home. Your social awareness is emphasized also, so entertaining in your home should be high on your list of things to do. Putting your house in order also includes your physical house, your body. Have a checkup, then begin a course of exercise to tighten and firm sagging muscles and generally build a healthier body.

Remember, don't take on unnecessary responsibilities, for commitments that you accept now must be seen through to their conclusion. Instead, finish up the old projects that have been on your mind. Think carefully about how to overcome the obstacles that confront you.

This can be a loving, rewarding and creative period, if you maintain balance and harmony. Make your home as attractive and warm as possible, and others will bask in its sunny radiance.

TAROT SYMBOLISM: **Key 6 The Lovers.** The Lovers is an obvious reference to partnership and marriage, the union of opposite but complementary components. The keyword is *discrimination*. When we discriminate we set apart and separate in order to see the innate differences between two categories. In this manner, we can tell the true from the false.

All creatures, including humans, have their own unique odor. This is especially important in the animal kingdom; mating, self-protection and preservation all depend upon a keen sense of smell. People discriminate through the sense of smell, which is therefore, an attribute of key 6.

The two human figures represent opposing factors of the one Source, Adam and Eva (her name in the original manuscripts), male and female, positive and negative, and the conscious and subconscious minds. These two specialized manifestations of the one life force must become equalized before attaining unity. The male, or conscious mind, looks to the female, or the subconscious mind, which in turn gazes up at the angel, or the super-conscious. Only through this step-by-step process can we reach our source and draw upon its power and inspiration.

The tree behind Adam symbolizes the signs of the zodiac. The flames on the left of the tree trunk symbolize the five senses, and those on the right symbolize the body and the original planets.

Behind Eva is the Tree of Knowledge. The serpent in the tree, the kundalini force, gives them the power to create. When the kundalini is trapped in the lower center of the body, at or near the base of the spine, only the senses are fulfilled. One must raise the kundalini, or life force, up the spine to the higher centers in the head so that the life force can be expressed on a loftier plane.

ASTROLOGICAL CORRESPONDENCE: **Venus (and Gemini).** As the ruler of 6, Venus seeks to bring together seemingly opposing factors into harmonious unit. These opposing elements are well represented by Gemini, the twins, which rules the hands, arms, lungs and shoulders; these are all pairs that must operate in unison if the body is to be well coordinated. Also, we use our hands and arms to express our love, by touching and holding. Many people cannot communicate effectively without the use of their hands.

Venus gives us the urge to create a peaceful, loving and comfortable environment, surrounded by our family and friends. Number 6 individuals are oriented in this direction. Domestic life is your highest priority, and you find comfort and fulfillment in the home, or in home-related activities. Your artistic sense is developed through the Venusian symmetry, so you may be active in the arts, fashion, or home decorating.

7 AS A PERSONAL VIBRATION: You are a dreamer and a philosopher, and your destiny is your mind. You are attracted to the mystical side of life. Your clairvoyant and psychic abilities are marked, and you will develop the intuitive, introspective side of your personality. Often your psychic hunches foretell future events. If you develop your psychic gift, you can use it for the benefit of others.

Realizing that you must leave behind the desires of the material world, you turn to the world of mind and thought. There you learn to enclose yourself behind secret walls, where your creative imagination roams freely. Poetry and music lift your spirits and transport you to other spaces. Your self-imposed periods of isolation make you something of an enigma even to yourself. You are often called a loner, and no one really knows you. Of all the numbers, you could most easily remain single, and in fact, many 7's live as hermits or recluses. When it comes to carrying out your own ideas, you can be very determined.

As a rule, orthodox religious beliefs don't offer you enough spiritual substance; therefore, you will search for your own individual belief system. However, some 7's stay with their church and rise to positions of great power. Pythagoras considered 7 to be the most sacred of all numbers, and his students took their vows or obligations by the number 7. In ancient days, a child born under the number 7 was immediately placed in the temple to become a priest or priestess. Today 7's are found in the higher echelons of the church or as leaders in mystical circles. They gain spiritual realization and become masters.

You are a perceptive person who understands human nature. When you meet someone you are not often fooled by their outer personality, but seem to scan their inner motives at once. Sometimes you make people uneasy with your ability to see right through them.

Thoughts are words of the mind, and you become close friends with words, since you understand their protective, preserving and influential power. Your cultured, studious nature is enhanced and broadened by change and travel which you love. Your mind eagerly absorbs the information you derive from contact with foreign lands and cultures. You prefer living in the country rather than in the city. In the country you can lead a leisurely life in a dignified and conservative atmosphere. You have a retiring nature and, in that environment, you can experience the periods of quiet contemplation that are necessary for your mental development.

The fastidiousness of your dress is unique; you would never wear someone else's clothes, nor would you let anyone else wear yours. You seem to be innately aware that all people have their own distinct vibrations, which are transmitted to anything they touch.

You are methodical, in keeping with the rhythm of the 7 which rules periodicity in nature. Although you have good business ideas, you should not enter into the business field, because you seldom carry out those ideas.

Unselfishness, compassion and dedication are qualities you should develop. You have an idea of what the world should be. When the world does not conform to your ideal, you may become frustrated and depressed. Generally, you dislike advice, and others find it hard to convince you of things because your mind is so individualistic.

A negative 7 is gloomy. Your disappointment in the outer world drives you to a lonely existence, where you become a hermit or recluse, and shut out the people who cannot live up to your ideals.

However, by using your will and by gaining control of your tremendous mental powers, you can be a vehicle for good in a world that desperately needs what you have to offer—a sound creative mind.

7 AS A TEMPORARY VIBRATION: **Reflection, rest, health, vacations.** It is time to rest; God rested on the seventh day, and this is your seventh day. Become quiet and receptive. Think about yourself and your station in life. Analyze your goals, projects and relationships. Spend time by yourself and listen to your inner promptings. Write down your thoughts. You can be inspired by dreams, visions, and intuitions now; therefore, any writings you produce can be creatively moving.

Use the energies of this period for mental exercise and discipline. Now you can master technical skills to aid in your profession, or benefit from philosophical and metaphysical disciplines including religion, yoga, transcendental meditation, astrology and numerology.

Do not push your financial affairs under a 7. This is not a time to be impulsive or concern yourself with business. It is a time of physical completion and attainment in the cycles because you can see the consequences of your previous efforts. Matters mysteriously complete themselves without any effort on your part. Wait and let the cycle work for you.

The number 7 rules the physical body and body functions; therefore, the forces within your body are now active. You must pace yourself wisely, rest and take care of minor problems. Abuse and overexertion can bring on physical maladies and illnesses. These discomforts force you to slow down, so that you will take the time to reflect upon yourself and your purpose in life, which is the most important reason for this cycle. Vacations are always pleasant, and now is a good time to take one.

Be careful when signing any documents or legal agreements. Check every word and look for loopholes; when you have thoroughly scrutinized all aspects, sign with confidence.

You will not feel the need to socialize at this time; rather, you prefer either to be alone or to be with people of a spiritual nature who complement and uplift your contemplative mood. Do not fight your inner urgings to rest, for that will only bring on physical problems and frustration. Instead, flow with this and look deep within yourself to discover the beautiful facets of your true inner self, the perfect jewel.

TAROT SYMBOLISM: **Key 7 The Chariot.** The Chariot represents receptivity to the will of the one Source. The keyword attributed to this card is *fence* or *enclosure*, and its sense function is speech. Every word we speak is a fence enclosing an idea or thought. An eloquent vocabulary is a powerful tool for protection and preservation, as well as advancement. When we speak we set in motion a vibration that acts upon the ethers, space and akasha. Blavatsky said, "Sound or speech is a tremendous force when directed by occult knowledge." It is only when we become still, quiet and receptive that we can be victorious. Then the primal force can work through us.

THE CHARIOT.

Symbolically, the Charioteer is the soul, directing the chariot, the body. Notice that the Charioteer has no reins. It is mentally, through the will, that he directs the sphinxes, the positive and negative senses, to draw the chariot along. The starry canopy overhead indicates that we are recipients of celestial energies. The waxing and waning moons depict time and rhythm, which are stages of mind. This can be seen by their placement on the shoulders, ruled by Gemini, which is the first air sign, symbolizing the mind.

The winged globe on the cart represents self-consciousness, elevated by aspiration. The disc with an upright rod through the center depicts the positive and negative forces joined in a working relationship. The square on the Charioteer's breast indicates an orderly attitude, and his eight-paneled skirt decorated with talismans, represents the soul's dominion over the material world.

The message here is that through control of the senses, and elevation and purification of the desires, by the use of our own free will, we can achieve complete dominion while in the physical body.

ASTROLOGICAL CORRESPONDENCE: **Moon (and Cancer).** The Moon has four seven-day cycles, and since the earth was created on the sixth day, the Moon, a satellite of the earth, could not have come into manifestation until after the sixth day. With 7 as the end of a physical cycle, we can readily see why the Moon is assigned to this number.

Cancer, the crab, rules this key, 7. The crab has a fence or shell which protects its soft body from the dangers of the outer world.

During a 7 cycle, one is sequestered away from the world in some manner, as the crab, Cancer, withdraws into its protective shell to ponder recent experiences and examine them subconsciously (Moon).

Number 7 people are quiet, introspective, analytical and very profound. They are the thinkers of the world, and are usually involved in some scientific, philosophical or metaphysical pursuit. Alone, they can mentally wander the universe, searching for the shell that will enclose their ideas with form and substance.

8 AS A PERSONAL NUMBER VIBRATION: *Strength, will* and *effort* are the keywords for your nature. You have the ability to channel your energies in order to alter any given situation, so you will ultimately be a leader. The power you exert over the material world is a product of the discipline you expend. You are the big boss type with executive abilities, and you can manage and organize efficiently. With your sound business judgment and knowledge of the value of a dollar, you prefer a big expanding business to a small enterprise.

You can be a great success in the financial world. You are shrewd, resourceful and ambitious for power, and failure just spurs you on to greater effort. You do not give up easily. You are a money maker, and will probably become wealthy. Some 8's make and lose more than one fortune in their lifetimes.

You are a down-to-earth realist. A career in finance, banking, brokerage, speculation or investment would be a good outlet for your energies. However, working for material gain alone will not provide the satisfaction you need, and you must learn to share your good fortune with others. You work zealously for the causes you adopt, and you should encourage your philanthropic leanings. Don't neglect your spiritual side, however. Develop and live by a sound policy, so that if material reverses occur, you will still have a solid basis on which to rebuild. This is where your sense of balance and judgment is most necessary.

You are endowed with originality and inspiration and you like to create so you are multi-talented in all areas of material achievement. With these qualities and your diplomacy, persistence and courage, you can accomplish anything.

Many outstanding athletes come under the number 8 vibration. They achieve distinction through discipline, effort, will and strength. Also, an athlete needs a fine sense of balance and rhythm, which are qualities of the 8.

Your marriage is likely to be based on a need for security rather than love. You want to be proud of your family, home and possessions.

If you are a negative 8, you are someone to be feared. You can be a bully, domineering, selfish and ruthless, scheming for your own advancement. You may be a revolutionary, ready to overthrow and disrupt. Upheaval is a way of life with you.

An 8 knows no halfway measures. It is either personal limitation or spiritual freedom, splendor or degradation. You must accept responsibility and handle it as well as you can. Use the positive 8 vibrations to create a stable material world in which you are willing to share your fine managerial capabilities and creative talents. Be guided by the philanthropist in you.

8 AS A TEMPORARY VIBRATION: **Responsibility, money, business, karma.** "As ye sow, so shall ye reap." This truth will be most evident under an 8. You will receive exactly what you deserve during this karmic period, because it is time to receive payments and pay debts. Since 8 rules the material plane, if you have sown wisely, you can expect recognition and rewards. You may get the raise or promotion you've been waiting for, along with more responsibility and pressure.

If you've been planning a business venture, this is the time to start by building a solid foundation for all your commercial enterprises. Face practical reality and put your finances in the black. Success on the material level is yours, so make your projects financially profitable. Be efficient, organized and concerned with tangible results. You will need energy and ambition to respond to the call you now hear. The inner drive for physical accomplishment is paramount, but you must be cautious. Don't let the strain of your present undertaking deplete your energies. Those in power will help you if you ask.

Because of the karmic implications of this cycle, you may receive an inheritance or legacy. You may have sown seeds of love and concern for someone who, in return, will give you material rewards, money, property or something of value. Whatever you receive is the result of your own past efforts.

Be helpful to those who are not operating at your high energy level. In your drive to the top, don't forget your friends and those around you. Lend them your strength and assurance, for surely this 8 cycle will show you the absolute necessity of sowing good seeds.

TAROT SYMBOLISM: **Key 8 Strength.** The keyword for this card is the *fang of the serpent*. The serpent represents the kundalini, or life force, which, in undeveloped persons lies coiled three and a half times at the base of the spine. This force must be elevated, to transform the individual into a more spiritually-oriented person. All transforma-

STRENGTH.

tions in nature are actually specialized manifestations of this kundalini force.

The only two numbers that can be written over and over without ending are 8 and 0. As such they represent divine power. The number 8 represents material power as well.

In key 8 we direct this life force through suggestion. The woman is the subconscious mind controlling body functions and directing the amounts of vital force that the body receives. She also receives and acts upon suggestions from the conscious mind. Her dominion over the lion is through gentle and spiritual power rather than by brute force.

The roses around the woman and the lion form a chain. Roses, representing desire, must be tended and properly cared for. In this context, a chain of roses is a series of cultivated desires. Any suggestion emanating from a desire sets up a chain reaction in the subconscious that eventually results in manifestation. The cosmic lemniscate (figure-8-shaped curve) over her head gives her dominion in this world.

ASTROLOGICAL CORRESPONDENCE: **Saturn (and Leo).** Saturn is assigned to the number 8 and Leo has rulership over key 8, Strength. Saturn urges the expression of concrete achievement, and represents those who have the necessary determination and discipline to rise to the top in their chosen field. Leo lifts the spirits of an overly sober saturnian attitude and bestows a sunny and magnanimous acceptance of responsibility, as well as the ability to rule in a regal fashion.

Number 8 individuals have the capacity for the top executive positions. They possess enormous reserves of strength, which can be called upon when the pressure is heavy. Many outstanding athletes also have an 8 in their personal expression.

9 AS A PERSONAL NUMBER VIBRATION: You are a humanitarian, a universalist who thinks in abstract terms. Born for service to others, you want to make the world a better place in which to live. Since 9 is the last single digit, it indicates attainment, perfection and completion, the seeds for new beginnings, the foundation for future growth in the next or higher cycle.

You have a thirst for spiritual knowledge and an urge for freedom and wisdom that transcends personal needs. You desire to live an ideal life according to your inspirations and aspirations. Through your responsive reaching out to the world, you become a beacon for others.

The number 9 is a testing number. The higher you evolve, the more difficulties you may encounter. You should be tolerant of and merciful to others on your path. In this way you will be an example for them, and they will recognize your sympathetic and compassionate nature. People will be drawn to you for your deep and broad understanding.

Your thinking is vast, and without limits. Because of your openness, your psychic abilities are well developed, and foresight, premonitions and predictions flow from you with ease. You seem to have a direct line to the mysteries of life. You have very strong emotions and feelings and could evolve a new philosophy for humanity.

You are generous and idealistic. For anyone who needs your wisdom and guidance, you are open-handed and beneficent, because you realize that knowledge belongs to those who seek it. Charitable work is close to your heart, and you are likely to be a patron of the arts and sciences.

Your associations with other people in your life are intense, but not necessarily enduring. You must learn to let friends go when their needs have been filled, because your destiny is to be a loner, a sort of recluse. You are not meant to sit alone meditating on a mountaintop, but your innate wisdom and understanding separate you from the crowd. You must share your wisdom to enlighten the world, so you cannot be bound by enduring ties that would limit your mobility. Your life cycle includes travel and associations with famous personalities who will be drawn to you by your free spirit and broad compassion. Your friendship encompasses the world. You easily acquire money and independence, so that you are free to pursue your worldly destiny.

If you are a negative 9, you are self-serving and concerned with your own needs rather than the needs of others. This self-indulgence precludes belief in a higher source and can result in faithlessness. When crossed you are quick tempered. Your keen mind makes you a formidable enemy. Since 9's have to live up to a higher standard than the other numbers, the resulting tension can cause nervous troubles. This can produce unhappy relations with others, including your mate.

Corinne Heline says in *The Sacred Science of Numbers*, "The 9 individual has run the gamut of personal experiences, including both the high and the low, the mundane and the spiritual. It is the synthesis of these experiences which produces that sympathy, compassion and rare understanding which is characteristic of the 9." Using the enhancing qualities of your number 9, you can be the visionary for whom all things are possible. Your faith in life embraces all and looks forward to evolution as the promise of the spirit.

9 AS A TEMPORARY VIBRATION: **Changes, endings, charity, inspiration.** Events take place quickly at this time, with many stops and starts, because you are experiencing a period of change and transition. As Paul Case says in *The Tarot*, "You must make the final selection between assimilable material and what is rejected as waste."

Eliminating the useless, and separating yourself from past mistakes can be an emotional experience, for we often are reluctant to let go of the obstacles in our lives. If you cannot free yourself from associations and situations that are no longer necessary for your development, then the 9 cycle will do it for you. A vacation or trip would be good therapy at this time, giving you time to think and separate yourself from the emotionalism you might encounter under this vibration.

Many of your goals will be realized during this time, and you should attempt to finish all projects that are close to completion. As this is an ending cycle, do not make new commitments. Projects begun under a 9 have little durability.

Present friendships can be cemented and made more enduring, and you may receive gifts from friends. This should be a charitable time, in which you think primarily of other people's welfare. Do something for others in thanks for the blessings you have received in this life. An old friend or lover may enter your life briefly for one last encounter, but don't expect this sudden renewal to last.

Since this is an ending cycle, you may change jobs or residence. Children may leave home for higher education or marriage, or to begin their own lives. If you are separated from the people, situations and locations with which you have lived for a long time, it is because they no longer serve your evolutionary process.

Use the creative powers of this vibration to develop your artistic abilities. You will have inspirational ideas that can be used productively in the future in a way that the next cycle's number will determine.

Don't be caught by your emotions. Hanging on to the past, wallowing in what used to be can only bring discontentment, frustration and depression. Rather, look forward with joy and high expectations to the future, for which the releasing energy of this cycle has prepared you. Use the wisdom provided by the events of this cycle to inspire your actions productively in the future.

TAROT SYMBOLISM: **Key 9 The Hermit.** The symbol for key 9 is the yod, the tongue of flame, the glyph that makes up every letter in the Hebrew alphabet. It represents the fiery energy, the life force, and the hand, opened rather than closed, of man and woman. In the body we are little serpents, containing a portion of the one Source's fiery energy. As such, we are the hands of God operating in the physical world.

The Hermit is a symbol of ageless wisdom, standing on the mountain of attainment. He has achieved. The snow represents the isolation he endures because his wisdom sets him apart from others. However, as he turns to shine his light on those who follow him, he intimates that our knowledge is empty and meaningless until we turn

and give it to others. The Hermit has evaluated, selecting the
necessary and discarding the unecessary elements along his path. He
has learned to use the Magician's wand, which he now leans on, for
he knows he can depend upon it for support. He has achieved
mastery.

ASTROLOGICAL CORRESPONDENCE: **Sun (and Virgo).** The Sun
is assigned to 9 because it is only after you carefully progress through
the previous steps, 1 through 8, that you can attain a position of
respect and leadership, as well as a full recognition of your inner
potential. The true inner self is expressed under a 9, as you become
the humanitarian, the universalist who reaches out to the multitudes
to lighten their burdens through your understanding, wisdom and
compassion.

Virgo's assignment indicates that careful, thorough analysis has
preceded this final position of authority. Any mistakes along the path
could have led the aspirant astray; therefore, keen discrimination is
necessary at all times.

10/1 AS A PERSONAL NUMBER VIBRATION: If you embrace the philosophy of reincarnation,

you will recognize that you are an old soul who has lived many lives
of both high and low degree and who has learned how transitory the
things of the earth are. You have a talent for influencing and bringing
people together, and you are a power person who has a special
spiritual mission in the world. Your word is power and your
presence, peace. Therefore, your mission could be to establish peace
and fellowship among the races and peoples of the world.

Your clear thinking and comprehension help you to grasp and to
use any situation to advantage. Leadership positions are open to you
because of your obvious control and mastery. Your productive
talents constantly revivify those around you.

With a 10, luck, success, honor and material rewards are yours, for
you easily attract and acquire those things that others struggle for so
desperately. Complete attainment and realization are possible
because you are in touch with your super-conscious although you
may describe this as a deep inner feeling. You understand other people's feelings and needs, and you have faith and confidence in
yourself. These treasures are brought over from past life experiences,
or, if you prefer, they are the capitalization of past experiences in this
lifetime. Your wise use of previous experience means that your influence will be wide and pronounced.

You take one step at a time and keep your mind on the goals you
have set. The gradual turning of the wheel assures your progress, so
your plans are likely to succeed.

If you are a negative 10, you may be fixed, stubborn and opinionated. You are inclined to overdo and exaggerate your needs and desires. You may not realize your latent abilities until you are spiritually awakened. Once you are awakened, however, your influence knows no limits. Your power for good is phenomenal.

10/1 AS A TEMPORARY VIBRATION: **Intuition, fortune, luck, a turn for the better.** What you have been waiting for may now be yours. The culmination of a series of events brings success and material accomplishment. You could call this cycle a turn for the better, the start of something new. The innovative ideas and fresh beginnings you are experiencing now are really an expression of the law of cause and effect. Events that appear accidental or mere chance result from efforts you have already expended.

This is an initiation period in which you may be required to stand alone and make decisions. Base your decisions upon precise and definite facts, then rely upon your intuition, which is based upon reason. Then you will know what to do. You can settle differences with previous enemies because of your clear comprehension of the situation and its problems.

Events now reveal your understanding of the circumstances in your life. If you have worked hard and efficiently, you can expect to receive your just reward. Progress, improvement and advancement are yours. You may be awarded a special position you have been vying for, win the lottery, or inherit a large sum of money, which will help you start a new life. Realize that any of these experiences are the product of your own efforts.

If failure and loss plague you, then understand that every circumstance in life is the result of the prior use of your energies. Decide now to begin to work and plan wisely, so that you can gain mastery over your future. The wheel of fortune keeps turning, and the next rotation can bring exactly what you want, if you begin now.

WHEEL of FORTUNE.

TAROT SYMBOLISM: **Key 10 The Wheel of Fortune.** The symbol corresponding to this card is the closed hand, indicating mental comprehension. To grasp is to own; and to grasp your place in the world is to grasp what and who you really are. Therefore you never suffer material deprivation.

The number 10 begins a new cycle, a repetition of the 1. *Rotation* and *cyclicity* are the keywords for the Wheel of Fortune. All is in the process of becoming; change is the only constant, so in due time, all things come to pass.

The bull, the lion, the eagle and the man represent the four fixed signs of the zodiac—Taurus, Leo, Scorpio (the eagle is a symbol for the higher side of Scorpio) and Aquarius. The books that they hold represent the wisdom of the ages. They indicate the laws of the universe, which are immutable, fixed, and cannot be changed. The wavy serpent symbolizes the descent of the life force into manifestation. The jackal-headed hermanubis (an Egyptian god Thoth, also a race of jackal-headed men) shows evolution of form, while the human body and animal head indicate that man has not evolved beyond the intellectual level. His ears above the horizon of the Wheel show that man's interior hearing or intution allows him to rise to a higher level. The sphinx depicts the developed human being to which we aspire. The woman's head and breast, coupled with the lion's body, show the soul in dominion over the body, in perfect harmony, hence exemplifying the union of male and female powers.

ASTROLOGICAL CORRESPONDENCE: **Jupiter (and Mars).** When we work with the astrological correspondence of the double numbers, we take the number on the right and see it work through the number on the left. Here we have the God power, 0, working through Mars, 1, to bring about new starts and a change in fortune. The Jupiter influence from key 10, the Wheel of Fortune, gives us the faith and optimism that our new beginning will ultimately bring generous rewards.

Once we have completed the basic 1 through 9 cycle, every subsequent digit merely repeats one of the original 9. Therefore, we can see why 10 is considered a new start. With the 9 we have finished a complete cycle, and in 10 we have the promise that the God power within us never ceases, but merely changes form, and that the new form still contains the life spark, Mars.

11/2 AS A PERSONAL NUMBER VIBRATION: 11 is one of the four master numbers, along with 22, 33 and 44. All master numbers are powerful because they accentuate the vibration of the base number to which they can be reduced.

As an 11, you can draw upon the cosmic forces for inspiration and for aid in attaining enlightenment and even cosmic consciousness. Your pronounced intuitive abilities can guide your original, inventive and creative mind. As you will probably be a leader in some way, you must use these higher vibrations wisely. True mastery is service, and you need to be practical as well as idealistic in the role you assume.

Foresight and acute perception make you a visionary. You are idealistic and feel compassion for all types of people, regardless of their station in life. The desire to uplift others brings out the teacher in you. You can be a memorable teacher, speaker, preacher or writer, whose deep understanding of people's needs inspires them and opens new avenues of expression within them. Your talent for educating others cannot go unrecognized for long, and probably you will become famous. You are the specialist who seeks accomplishment rather than glory, but who always seems to gain recognition at the same time.

You feel that administering the law is important, and you are not content to sit back and spout platitudes. Your devotion to the expression of wisdom must find an energetic outlet so that you can actively participate in areas of life where your philosophy can be effective. With your sense of justice, fairness and honesty, you can become a leader in public and civic affairs, where your impartiality promotes better standards of living for the people whose lives you touch.

You have the courage of your convictions and will fight legally to see them implemented. Your life will be busy and active, forever meeting tests and challenges. If you go to extremes in emotion, fortune and health, the high vibration of 11 will pull you out with renewed and surprising courage.

You are intrigued by ESP, the occult and mystical and spiritual studies. Through some metaphysical or philosophical discipline, you can more easily tap your great creative potential. As an inspirational artist you can create objects of exquisite beauty that can evoke deep feelings in the viewer. You should work with others of a like nature.

If you don't respond to the higher vibration of 11, you live life as a 2 (see the reading for that number). You become involved in the details of your work and you may be forced into a life of servitude in some capacity.

If you are a negative 11, you use your power harmfully, which will work to your own detriment by creating negative karma. You may be unfair, prejudiced and severe, and you should beware of hidden dangers. However, you can redeem yourself through charitable works.

Use your 11 to create a balanced life, in which all your actions are weighed and measured. Your great insight and inspirational devotion will be an oasis in the parched lives of many people.

11/2 AS A TEMPORARY VIBRATION: **Tests, legal dealings, inspiration, art, quick decisions.** This master number period can be experienced as a 2 vibration if you do not live up to the number 11 potential.

You will have to make decisions quickly, because sudden events will require decisive action. Experiences occurring now are exciting, stimulating and likely to make you impulsive, so you must be patient and tolerant. Get rid of past mistaken thoughts and actions that have set up negative circumstances and select the right combination of attitudes to produce more desirable results in the future.

There can be legal dealings involving money in some way. For example, you could be the recipient or the executor of a legacy. Financial settlements are possible, and agreements and partnership complications may have to be settled.

Educational considerations may arise now, for the vibrations of this period are urging you to seek a balance and weigh the meaning of life. If educational pursuits will achieve this end, then you will have opportunities during this period to enter a school, take a course or perfect a skill.

Because your mind is highly sensitized, you should develop your psychic and intuitive abilities. The power of 11 must be made into something tangible and useful. A course in some metaphysical discipline would help you organize the nervous energy that is your connecting link to the high vibration of 11. Or you could develop your creative potential by working with more than one artistic medium simultaneously, or by collecting works of art and attending the theater and concerts. Surround yourself with culture. You are likely to have dreams, visions and revelations under this influence.

If you are already prepared mentally and technically your talents may be recognized by someone who will offer you a promising position, or you may receive public acclaim for some personal effort. The spotlight is on you in some way.

This is a testing and challenging period. If you channel your intense energies into something worthwhile, you will accomplish more now than you will in any other cycle. Master numbers offer master accomplishments.

TAROT SYMBOLISM: **Key 11 Justice.** Teaching, education and guidance come under key 11, which seeks to bring about balance through justice. The scales here also symbolize the doctrine of karma—work, action and reaction, the law of cause and effect.

The outstanding lesson of key 11 is to weigh the meaning of present conditions and achieve balance by overcoming the errors of the past. Use the sword of discrimination to eliminate mistaken thoughts. Libra rules here also and shows us that we communicate only through the seventh house of cooperation and through the principle of love. Libra rules the kidneys, the organs of elimination that maintain the chemical balance of the body. Through elimination of the poisonous toxins in our lives, we ensure a balanced life.

The scales represent balance. There are seven straight lines of equal length in the scales, representing the seven centers in the body, and the seven original planets—Mercury (key 1), Moon (key 2), Venus (key 3), Jupiter (key 10), Mars (key 16), Sun (key 19) and Saturn (key 21).

ASTROLOGICAL CORRESPONDENCE: **Uranus (Libra).** The Uranus vibration is emphasized in master number 11. This is a testing vibration in which you are required to weigh and analyze the tremendous energy that is flowing through your life. If this great personal energy is used impetuously or unwisely, it can bring on accidents (a by-product of nervous energy), legal difficulties and impulsive decisions.

Libra seeks to calm the nervous Uranian energy, teaching you how to use these abilities in harmony with the environment and be a help to others. The accident potential is transformed into a specialized drive toward a specific goal; legal difficulties translate into important contracts; and impulsive actions become positively decisive. The catalyst is you, and, as always, you must decide how you will use the raw potential of the number.

12/3

AS A PERSONAL NUMBER VIBRATION: You are an unusual person who has accumulated inner strength through your unique experience. Your poise sets you apart from the common world, which looks upon you as a sort of oddity. Your thoughts are centered in spiritual analysis rather than judgment of others. You have a perfect tolerance for divergent beliefs, philosophies and life styles, and yet you walk in all things contrary to the world. You know that reality is illusion, and illusion, reality. Many people in the world are ill, in great suffering and poverty, unable to exist in harmony with others and have trouble accepting even themselves. You know that these afflictions are expressions of the law of cause and effect and that whatever happens is a result of the individual's own choice, either conscious or unconscious. Modern science and psychology have proven this. By reversing or changing your thoughts, you become free of physical encumbrances. Knowing these facts, you embrace a philosophy that the world laughs at because your thinking seems wrong. Yet, without antagonizing anyone, you have quietly reversed your way of life and at the same time come to understand other people's ways. Peace and serenity fill your being, because even though you are earthbound, you have attained a measure of freedom. Your life is free of materialism and worldly matters.

You epitomize wisdom. By crucifying the personal life, you have allowed the true self to be born. Others come to you for peace and guidance, needing your faith in life and in themselves.

Your life may be one of voluntary sacrifice in which you encounter difficulties, trials and renunciation; however, no adversity can disturb your deep serenity. You have trod the Wheel of Ezekiel, the zodiacal circle and have accumulated the courage, wisdom and presence of mind that will preserve you.

12/3 AS A TEMPORARY VIBRATION: Waiting period, change of view, reversal, submission. Stop, look and listen. This is a quiet pause in your life, when you should spend time thinking, learning to see things as they really are and not as they appear. By bringing seemingly conflicting polarities into perspective in your mind, you create an inner harmony that is reflected out to your environment. Meditate

upon the fact that the miseries of the world are self-imposed, caused by negative thought processes. If your world is in disharmony, realize that your thoughts have created the problems, and that a change of view is in order.

Meditation, trips to the seashore or countryside, classes in philosophy and mind relaxation techniques will help put you in touch with the power now working beneath the surface. By submitting your consciousness to the universal mind, you can begin to see the errors in your thinking. The important elements begin to take precedence as you center yourself in the eye of life.

Your affairs will take care of themselves now, without effort on your part. Some situations will come to a head and many will be settled, but you should suspend all decision-making. Let the cycle work for you: observe, reflect and meditate. Find the serenity offered by the vibrations of this number.

If you remain absorbed in physical matters now, you may suffer reversals in friendships and fortune. Sacrifices will be required through trial and loss. Rather than fight these forces, flow with them. You will obtain what you want by remaining passive, sympathetic and tactful, as this vibration achieves success only through acceptance.

TAROT SYMBOLISM: **Key 12 The Hanged Man.** The keyword for the Hanged Man is *reversal*. The corresponding symbol means oasis, sea, or water. According to the alchemists, water was the basis of all life, the fluid substance that solidified into physical forms. This substance which emanates from the stars and suns, is called astral fluid. The Hanged Man symbolizes the first water of the divine power.

THE HANGED MAN.

Water was the first mirror in which the reflection always appears upside down. The significance of this card is that things are not as they appear on the surface. You must look beneath the surface for true understanding.

The man is suspended by his foot, like a pendulum at rest. His crossed legs form a figure 4, indicative of key 4, Reason. His elbows and head form a triangle with the point down which is an ancient symbol for water.

The Hanged Man represents a person who is poised in consciousness and under perfect control. He is conscious of the one Power everywhere, yet centered in himself. He sees the trouble in the world—people unhappy in marriage, in trouble financially and lost because they have no goals—and he knows it is because they all see things upside down. Yet they look at him and think that he is the one who is crazy. The Hanged Man's philosophy sets him apart from the crowd and, at the same time, brings him peace of mind and perfect contentment. Perhaps the world should examine his views. The ideal is to grow out of materialism by transmuting animal passion to human compassion. The twelfth step sees a man reversed, hanging upside down by his foot. The law of reversal is the keynote here, reversal from living egocentrically to giving selfless service to others.

ASTROLOGICAL CORRESPONDENCE: **Jupiter (and Neptune).** Vulcan (2) and Mars (1) in unison produce the Jupiter (3) influence in this 12/3 number. Vulcan in mythology tended the forges in which expansion (Jupiter) occurred within the fire (Mars).

Jupiter, as ruler of Sagittarius and the ninth house, represents expansion through higher education and deeper philosophy. In a 12/3, the purpose of this mental expansion is enlightenment in the abstract secrets of life. Many people remain in a dark room (Neptune), troubled by the ambiguities they see and experience. The camouflage (Neptune) in their lives can be destroyed only by seeking the true knowledge (Jupiter) which will allow them to erase the blind spots (Neptune) in their thinking, solve the enigmas (Neptune) of existence, and publish (Jupiter) their own truths (Jupiter).

13/4 AS A PERSONAL NUMBER VIBRATION: 13 has always been feared as the death number, and indeed, it does represent death, but not in the ordinary sense. Death is merely change. When we are born into this life, we die from another level of existence. When we marry, we die as a single entity and are reborn as a duo. When the struggling artist receives recognition, he dies overnight as an unknown and is reborn as a famous individual. Change is simultaneous birth and death. The death connotation of 13 has arisen because most people respond to its lower side—immersion in fleshly desires and encapsulation in matter. Death then occurs through destruction and degeneration of the body. A few people respond to the higher side of 13, which involves complete satisfaction and attainment through regeneration or using the tremendous powers of this number to create and leave something of value with the world. There are no halfway measures with this number. There is enormous potential for ultimate attainment and equally great potential for complete destruction. It's all or nothing.

Your life as a 13 will be one of constant change. As soon as a situation seems settled and quiet, a new set of circumstances will arise to replace the old. Constant renewal keeps you on your toes and impresses on you the transitory nature of earthly things. The instability of your material world strengthens the bond between you and the invisible world. Because of this you need a secure home and secure relationships therein, for you realize that these bonds are true and lasting.

You are not a leader in the ordinary sense of the word, but you do carry on for others. You take on their problems and bravely bear burdens with little complaint. Your idealism knows no bounds, and you can transform the most desperately lost cause into a worthwhile venture through your profound philosophy and understanding of the real values in life. Your limitless creative powers discover fertile soil where others see only a wasteland. You can take a dying business and, with creative ideas, organized talents and hard work, change it into a financially profitable venture. You can salvage a relationship that seems about to break and cement it more strongly than it was. *Transformation* is your keyword, whether it be in business, relationships or social causes.

Your psychic abilities are marked, and you can see right through people and situations. It is not easy to fool you, and your perceptive analytical powers make you a formidable opponent.

If you are a negative 13, you dissipate your creativity in pursuit of transitory desires. Overindulgence in drink, drugs, unsavory relationships and destructive actions can make your life and the lives of those around you a complete disaster. Your bad temper and rash actions hurt others and can tear down those structures that you attempt to build. Stagnation and inertia set in and turn you into a revolutionary. But the change you bring about is destructive rather than regenerative. You are in a state of spiritual amnesia.

You above all others have the ability to bring about peaceful changes that will improve the living standards of the world. You can take what most people would throw away, rework it and produce a useful and necessary product. This gives tangible proof of the existence and immortality of the soul, whose presence you have never doubted.

13/4 AS A TEMPORARY VIBRATION: **Change, release, transformation.** The number 13 is associated with suspicion and misconceptions. For an understanding of this, read the first paragraph of 13/4 as a personal number. Then turn back here to see how 13/4 relates to you as a temporary vibration.

Under a 13 you can expect the changes that will bring an end to conditions that no longer serve a useful purpose in your evolutionary scheme. Any rigid thought patterns must be altered and crystalized ideas must be shattered. Only through the death of present circumstance can you be released—freed to open the door for progress. Old ideas must be swept away to make room for new and better ones.

Be prepared to meet fresh ideas, new people and stimulating conditions. A change of plans, a new location and different people open the birth channel for new opportunities. This is a reconstruction period, which can bring great happiness if you make the right decisions. The events that occur may not necessitate physical action on your part, but they will require you to make the proper assessments.

Change is the basis of earthly manifestation. Upon the wave of change you can sail to a new fertile land where a fresh lifestyle is possible. Release from the past is followed by a renewal which brings changes that promote growth. This is a time to depart, to travel and to grow. The cyclical force of nature reigns here, as the old is replaced by the new. "The king is dead; long live the king."

TAROT SYMBOLISM: **Key 13 Death.** The keywords corresponding to this card are *fish, fish's mouth,* or *mouth of the uterus.* This symbol suggests reproduction and birth, not necessarily into this world but rather rebirth of the consciousness into higher planes. In the time of Christ, the fish symbol represented those who lived in a Christlike way.

The number 13 is sacred as is every multiple of 13. It connotes an initiate or one who is reborn through the mental powers of transmutation. There are twelve disciples, Jesus was the thirteenth; there are twelve zodiacal signs with the Sun at the center. Number 13 is preserved in the measurements of the Great Pyramid.

Astrologically, this card is ruled by Scorpio, which governs the reproductive organs, birth, death and transmutation.

The skeleton is the figure of Death, which comes to all: king, man, woman and child, without respect for station. He rides astride a well-behaved white horse, a symbol of the purified desires and senses in submission to the cyclical rhythm.

However, the brilliantly shining sun between the towers in the distance promises eternal life. The life force does not die, but merely changes form.

ASTROLOGICAL CORRESPONDENCE: **Earth (and Scorpio).** The expansion (3) of the original life force (1) ultimately produces form (4, earth). And here in number 13, appropriately ruled by Scorpio, we find that Death must be understood, not feared. Of all the zodiacal signs, Scorpio has the power to transform the things of earth, and bring about new life. Other people's refuse becomes Scorpio's fuel.

Another important point that is strongly suggested here is that Death belongs only to the earth. 13 has always been feared as the death number by the uninitiated, but 13 reduces to a 4, the number of the earth. The Bible tells us we are the salt of the earth. Salt crystalizes in cubes, and *cube* vibrates to 13. Our bodies are cubes that contain the immortal spirit, the everlasting life energy. The body dies; the essence goes on.

Scorpio transforms the substance and gives it new form and new life.

14/5 AS A PERSONAL NUMBER VIBRATION: The ancient symbol for the letter corresponding to the number 14 is a scribe, an individual who copied manuscripts by hand. Books were rare and very costly; therefore the scribe was in a unique

position to glean knowledge that was otherwise denied to all but the wealthy and favored. As a result the scribe was exposed to philosophy, religion, science and the arts—all kinds of ideas that created an educated mind.

The number 14 has imbued you with a vivid imagination, teeming with ideas, energy and vitality. Narrow rigid thinking confuses you, because your exposure to the greater scheme of existence won't allow your mind to be fettered. You are willing to consider all possibilities but you won't accept theory, no matter how plausible, until you have tested it in actual practice. You have to see practical applications in order to verify the theory. You achieve understanding and truth through trial and error. You learn by experience, however, and you are always ready to listen.

The sexual principle is active under a 14. You enjoy life's sensual pleasures and can immerse yourself in fulfilling them. Temper the bodily passions and desires or your health may suffer. Overwork can bring on physical maladies and create a barrier of competition between your business and personal life. If you are cautious, you can be successful in speculation and in handling money. Business dealings can be extremely profitable if you select the proper combinations. Analyze all the contingencies and proceed with caution.

With this number your strength will be tested. If you can overcome yourself then there is no limit to your capacity for achieving greatness. You must maintain a balance among the various aspects of your life. You like continual excitement and motion but indulging in one facet of experience to the exclusion or neglect of another will bring you more problems than others would have. You must remain a positive thinker, or you can create an unstable foundation.

The number 14 can be a difficult vibration, causing you to live for sensation in such a way that the physical appetites may harm you. Envy, jealousy and divorce are common. A negative 14 has a nervous impulsive nature which propels you into problematical situations.

A positive 14 must learn to be more cautious, always on the lookout for the right mixture or perfect set of circumstances that will congeal into a proper blend of intellect and feelings. Once you have achieved this combination of energy, vitality and creativity, plus a superb comprehension gained through experience, you will be supplied with the necessary tools to bring inspired messages to the world.

14/5 AS A TEMPORARY VIBRATION: **Active sexual principle, pregnancy, social and family obligations, competition, a need to verify.** A variety of experiences will occur that urge you to slow down and think about your previous behavior. You may need to modify your lifestyle and control your desires and sexual appetites. The sexual principle is active now and can result in pregnancy. Or the creative act may be channeled to bring about a product of the mind, an invention, painting, sculpture, book or musical composition.

Competitive situations may arise. In commercial or political enter-prises, money and business dealings can be profitable if you are aware of all the alternatives. Be aware that with number 14 there are risks in-volving the loss of property or business failure. Social and family obligations could be at the root of peculiar circumstances that will need careful consideration.

Through concentration and the mental transference of your thoughts, you can easily influence others now. Your verbal sugges-tions can sway their decisions which can work to your advantage. You will gain through tact, diplomacy and persuasion. Listen to your dreams and inner promptings. ESP experiences may help you assess your situation and find the means to modify any unacceptable cir-cumstances.

TAROT SYMBOLISM: **Key 14 Temperance.** The keyword cor-responding to this card is *sustenance* or *establishment*. You should establish the foundations of your belief system through proof or verification. The keywords *verification* and *wrath* show that the desire to find the truth surfaces from within, through wrath (not temper, but strong and stern anger). This process tempers one's soul, just as steel is tempered. We become balanced by choosing the middle path between the extremes of action.

Sagittarius rules key 14. The arrow of concentration of the fiery life force brings about the manifestation of the higher ideals, which leads to elevated states of consciousness.

The androgynous angel is a perfect blending of polar opposites, of male and female. It is an angel of the Sun, the life force, as shown by the solar disk on the forehead. The red wings depict the fiery nature aspiring to higher consciousness.

The pool and the earth represent the subconscious and conscious minds, on which the angel maintains perfect balance. The mountain peaks symbolize attainment of wisdom and understanding. The crown in glory over them represents the culmination of the great work.

This key teaches you to verify your destiny as a manipulator of the life power, the kundalini. This should be verified by actual practice and testing until you feel the presence within.

ASTROLOGICAL CORRESPONDENCE: **Mercury (and Sagit-tarius).** The things of the earth (4) must be understood as manifesta-tions of pure energy (1). Unless we can consciously direct our mental energies (Mercury) toward a deeper understanding of this concept (Sagittarius), we cannot possibly hope to develop along the lines of spiritual consciousness.

We need accumulated experiences to temper ourselves into

something more fitting, and a 14/5 vibration supplies the necessary testing situations. Anyone responding to this number will surely be tested and should learn to ask of each experience, "How can I use this?" "What lesson in tempering does this experience teach me?" Strong anger is diluted—tempered—by adding another quality, such as forgiveness. The profound development that can result from the proper handling of this vibration produces great wisdom and understanding.

15/6 AS A PERSONAL NUMBER VIBRATION: You have a great deal of magnetism, plus a talent for obtaining money, gifts and favors from others. But at the same time you work for your possessions and good fortune. You are persevering and strong willed and always get what you go after. You are very conscious of other people's foibles and weaknesses, and you may tend to take advantage of them. In the process of artfully carrying out your purposes, you may step on some toes. Your attachment to worldly status and possessions is the impetus for your driving ambition.

You are a good student because you absorb knowledge easily and retain it. Knowledge thus gained allows you to proceed up the ladder of success with few slips, for you can learn from the mistakes of others. Your moves are calculated.

If you are wise you will develop a philosophical attitude toward the material world. Although you pursue material rewards, you realize that worldly attachments and cares are ridiculous and can entrap you in a prison of restraint, limitation and suffering. You see people whose mistaken estimate of their possibilities results in lasting bondage. You pity those who prefer a comfortable lie to an uncomfortable truth, who prefer to believe that this world is all there is and that the individual can do nothing but endure. You see these people as negative 15's whose obstinate adherence to materialism brings heartache and emotional disturbance, which can upset the home and marriage. They must learn emotional control. Violence and revolution, terrorism and anarchy breed as a result of their negative concepts of what they are and life is. 15 is virtue or vice; there is no middle path. You can attempt to use your knowledge and financial ability for negative purposes, or you can choose to see the paradox of materialism which at death leaves you with nothing. At death the delusion of outward appearance is erased; the grasping scrooge becomes the penniless penitent.

Laughter physiologically and psychologically relieves pressure, lightens burdens and lifts the spirits. You should learn the art of laughing in the face of difficulties. Reflect on the wisdom expressed in a hymn to the Sun god Ra "Thy priests go forth at dawn, they wash their hearts with laughter."

15/6 AS A TEMPORARY VIBRATION: **Indecision, bondage,
freedom, laughter, discernment.** The materialistic side of life is emphasized now. You may receive money and favors from others. Opportunities for progress can come through a radical change in your lifestyle that releases you from present limitations and allows you a freer expression.

Long held views may change, and newly found beliefs can set your mind at ease and eradicate old fears. You may have to make decisions and take decisive action. Under a 15, it is vital to decide whether the experiences of this period are limiting you or setting you free.

Be careful not to burn the candle at both ends in an attempt to satisfy your personal needs. Don't chain yourself to things or people who will place you in servitude. You should be cautious about signing contracts or agreements at this time.

Don't allow outward appearance to cause heartaches, trouble in partnerships or ineffective action. Look beneath the surface and see the situation as it really is. *Discernment* is the keyword here.

Learn to laugh at your own and other people's weaknesses. By lightening the seriousness of your problems, by accepting the frailties of others and by looking beyond the limitations of circumstances, you can bring about peaceful and satisfying solutions. Laughter cleanses the soul and can lead to physical healing through spiritual understanding.

THE DEVIL.

TAROT SYMBOLISM: **Key 15 The Devil.** Key 15 shows what happens when we fail to use discrimination. The Devil is a misconception of God, as God upside down or opposite. He represents the delusion of judging by outward appearances instead of by inner realities. He also represents religious dogmatism, which is ridiculous to the enlightened person. Therefore the keyword here is *mirth*. We should learn to laugh in the face of difficulties, for laughter or ridicule is sometimes the most effective defense against evil.

Capricorn, ruled by Saturn, overshadows this key. The Saturn center at the base of the spine is where the kundalini force lies coiled, and it is the life work of Capricorn to raise the kundalini, and then teach others.

The black background on this card indicates ignorance, lack of light. The inverted pentagram on the Devil's forehead is the symbol of black magic, inverted power. His torch burns wastefully and gives no light. The humans, chained loosely to the half cube could easily free themselves by refusing to be bound by darkness and imperfect knowledge—or half truth—as indicated by the half cube.

This key means we are God incarnate, but all too often we play the role in an upside down position, as undeveloped people, chained in bondage to appearance.

ASTROLOGICAL CORRESPONDENCE: **Venus (and Capricorn).** In 15/6 we find Mercury (5) working through Mars (1) to produce the basic Venus vibration (6).

The Venus awareness of opposites finds fertile ground in key 15, which casts a false image of truth. If you can examine both sides of a situation or see beyond outward appearances, you can escape the bondage of adherence to the purely physical aspects of living.

Through Capricorn, the eye of discernment raises you to the highest peak of expression in the full light of day at the apex of the natural horoscope. Capricorn's natural predilection for prestige in the material world is fulfilled by being elevated as a teacher and example for others to follow.

16/7 AS A PERSONAL NUMBER VIBRATION: You are a magnetic individual. Your forceful personality attracts others. Your talent for writing and speaking aids in the clever expression of your ideas. You are a clear-sighted intellectual with the ability to assess circumstances easily and accurately. This can lead to a tendency to speculate which will not always bring you the desired results. Overconfidence can result in material loss.

You may experience trials, defeats and the loss of material security. Sudden material and physical upsets are the outward manifestation of emotional discontent. Examine your life and your attitudes. Is your personality dominated by emotions? Have you had disappointments in love because of misplaced affections or illicit love affairs? Have your indulgences, your selfish and unsympathetic nature, brought about this emotional fall? If any of these are true you have allowed the material world to control you. Financial, professional and personal losses dominate your existence, and you experience telepathic invasion through your subconscious. Your desire for freedom and your impatience at restraints of any kind have brought on these many difficulties. Your subconscious is now urging you, through these calamities, to awaken the inner spiritual self, the real you. It is here, under extreme pressures, that a sudden bolt from the blue, an illuminating flash of insight, will lead the way to exoneration and solution.

If 16 is your Soul Number, you may be atoning for a promiscuous past when ideals were lost. Now you have to learn truth and faithfulness. If you learn freedom from dependence on the illusory material world, you will be awakened to the truth that lies deep within your soul. This is the splendor of the 16/7.

Through silence and meditation you overcome all obstacles. You have the inclination, at this point in evolution, to become a mystic. Here the 16 becomes the 7. And here, any material losses are meaningless, for you have become one with the Oneness.

16/7 AS A TEMPORARY VIBRATION: **Love affairs, health, accidents, awakenings.** The unforeseen and sudden events of this period are intended to overthrow existing conditions, especially in a material sense. Erroneous ideas and habits must be altered, and for some this has to be done in a forceful manner.

There can be losses and setbacks in business and financial affairs. This is not the time to take speculative risks. You may lose a desired position or suffer a scandal in your present position. Selfish ambitions fall under a 16, and bankruptcy may result. In extreme cases imprisonment is possible.

Deception and trouble in matters of the heart are likely. The love you give can be misplaced, and disappointments may result. Separation from close partners and trouble in relationships come from your pride and emotions. The result is personal isolation.

Do not overwork now. An overexpenditure of energy will take its toll on your health. The energy operating during this cycle is intense; therefore, do not take risks. Be careful of accidents and conflicts with others. Number 16 is not as bad as it seems at first. You can use the additional energy spurt during this period to plan wisely for the future. You are in touch with your intuition. If you listen to the generous advice of your inner self you can formulate plans to be implemented in the next cycle. Illuminating insights may reveal the insubstantial nature of the selfish materialistic approach and spark your creative talents to work toward a future goal which will inevitably bring good fortune. Bright prospects may arise suddenly. The power for loss is great under a 16, but so, too, is the potential for financial gain, fame and prosperity. All the material rewards are yours as long as you are not obsessed with ownership.

THE TOWER.

TAROT SYMBOLISM: **Key 16 The Tower.** Mars rules this card in which the keyword is *awakening.* This comes as a clear flash of understanding, a bolt from the blue bringing awareness of the true nature of the self. What inspires fear in the mind of the ignorant liberates the enlightened, just as electricity frightens the primitive but is used constructively by the knowledgeable. A flash of lightning is another symbol of the electrical serpent force, or the kundalini, the Mars force in the body.

The Tower, also called the Lightning-struck Tower, is the house of God, or the human body. It was also referred to as the Tower of Babel (Babble means confusion of understanding.) Lightning strikes the crown or head or place of understanding and knocks the man and woman out of the tower. This analogy depicts erroneous ideas being knocked out of the two parts of mind, conscious and subconscious, by the lightning of true understanding.

The twenty-two yods or tongues of flame represent the twenty-two letters in this alphabet. These tongues of flame also refer to key 9, where the one yod is the Hermit, representing the response to primal will. When we respond to the primal will, we receive a flash of illumination which bears a message that awakens us to our true source.

ASTROLOGICAL CORRESPONDENCE: **Moon (and Mars).** Basic desires (1, Mars) must be refined (6, Venus) before they become reality in the subconscious mind (7, Moon); once the subconscious receives the suggestion, the suggestion becomes a reality in the world of thought. It is only a matter of time before the suggestion manifests in the material world.

Mars is the driving force within any given mechanism, including the human body. It also rules the head, through Aries. After the kundalini or Mars force within the body is driven up the spine, there, in the head, final illumination must take place.

17/8 AS A PERSONAL NUMBER VIBRATION: You are the researcher, the scientist, the natural detective who investigates the unseen mysteries of life. You desire truth and seek solutions to enigmas. You are intuitive and fond of the occult. You delve into the secret depths of the inner consciousness in pursuit of hidden knowledge. This relationship to the secret forces of life instills in you a quiet strength and an air of mystery. Others see you as a deep individual, as indeed you are.

You are an intellectual in the beginning stages of mental unfoldment. Your intelligence and introspection necessitate periods of solitude in which to meditate. Seeds germinate in darkness before they burst into the light of day. Your ideas need the same germination period in which to unfold. After questions, research, meditation and experimentation, your ideas begin to take form.

You possess insight and a fine mind. You are very successful in pursuits which require deep concentration and enduring mental application. You deal wisely in the material world and enjoy seeing the tangible results of your mental concepts and efforts. You have hope and faith in the future and courage in the face of difficulties. You are determined to overcome any and all obstacles. Compassion for others and a desire for peace and love among all people is a product of your deep understanding of the essence of life, an understanding which surpasses worldly considerations. Your spiritual love imbues you with good health.

If you are a negative 17/8 you are stubborn. Doubts bring on faithlessness and create a pessmism so that you can see no promise or light in the world.

You have executive and leadership ability that can lead to a distinctive career. Researchers, discoverers, explorers, executives and aviators come under this number. You may travel often by sea or air.

Because of your outstanding abilities, you may achieve fame and a name that lives on after you.

17/8 AS A TEMPORARY VIBRATION: **Good fortune, rewards, travel, meditation, assistance.** This is a fortunate vibration, for you will receive all types of assistance. Money, gifts, advancements and promotions are possible, and business and public affairs turn out profitably. Intellectual achievements will be rewarded. You could receive recognition for outstanding leadership. You are the star under number 17.

If travel is in the picture, you could take a trip by sea or air. Medical problems will improve and you will enjoy good health. The law of action and reaction operating here proclaims that your positive attitude and buoyant hopes will be rewarded.

The help you receive now brings a promise of a brighter day. Hope springs within, and because you are positively expectant, positive things happen. You are determined to overcome any obstacles and you do so. Greater mental vitality and an open channel to the unconscious help you solve any problems. Your intuitive and creative powers are pronounced, and you should spend time in meditation, where ideas that have long lain fallow can now begin to emerge into the light of understanding. Secrets are revealed to you.

You must be very truthful with others. You are most persuasive now and your words can have a profound effect.

Don't allow doubts to creep into your mind, bringing on periods of depression and pessimism. Delve beneath the superficial irritants to the deeper person, the true I AM within.

THE STAR.

TAROT SYMBOLISM: **Key 17 The Star.** *Fishhook*, keyword for the Star, suggests the drawing of ideas from the universal subconscious. The hook relates to the subject selected for research or meditation. Revelation comes through meditation. You must still the conscious mind but keep a line on the subject chosen for meditation.

Aquarius rules this key, which brings the age of revelation. The Star key explains the fifth or celestial essence, which is above and beyond the four elements of fire, earth, air and water. The great star has eight points representing rotation. The seven lesser stars refer to the seven bodily centers which are really whorls of motion and vibration. The ibis is a fishing bird, again emphasizing searching and probing.

The woman represents the subconscious mind which shows that all secrets are available if you fish in the proper manner. Her left leg, holding her weight, forms a right angle or square, hinting at the number 4, order and reason. Resting on the water, her right foot shows that the mind sustains her.

She pours water, her mental powers, on land and sea, indicating the pouring of knowledge over humanity everywhere. The water on land divides into five streams representing five senses.

Ask yourself a question and seek the answer with calm expectancy. This is the right attitude for meditation and the proper method for gaining illumination.

ASTROLOGICAL CORRESPONDENCE: **Saturn (and Aquarius).** 17 has the 7 of receptivity (the Moon) and the 1 of concentration (Mars). Together they equal 8, the Saturn correspondence and the symbol of the kundalini force rising from the Saturn center at the base of the spine. These are necessary attributes for the subconscious mind to use in meditation.

The Aquarian influence brings the revelation, which 17/8 represents, and universal consciousness, both of which are the ultimate goals of meditation.

18/9 AS A PERSONAL NUMBER VIBRATION: You are an extremely active person with an unusually vivid imagination. Intense emotions and feelings well up from your subconscious and invade your conscious mind. You can probably recall your dreams in detail. Dreams are the workings of the subconscious mind; through them, you are in touch with the illuminating guidance of your being. You are receptive and intuitive and receive impressions and hunches about people and situations. As a child you may have had nightmares which caused restlessness and troubled sleep. Your subconscious may have presented fears in the form of monsters chasing you in your dreams.

It is vital that you take care of your body and health. You need rest, exercise, fresh air and sunlight; you would be wise to spend time in nature, mountain climbing, hiking, swimming, skiing, skating and so forth. Nature has healing powers to which you are attuned. Organizing your life transmits suggestions to your subconscious to organize your self. Your every action and thought affects your body physically; therefore, more than most people, your health depends upon your thoughts and lifestyle. Your intuitive powers are also dependent upon a healthy body.

You are a natural healer with a gentle touch. You are tolerant of others and would make a good counselor or advisor. You are loyal to your friends and your beliefs. You have hope and faith in life and believe in justice, integrity and truth.

The hidden forces of life are active within you. You are sensitive to their undulating motion, and sometimes your body reflects this sensitivity in the form of nervous habits.

If you are a negative 18 you allow the subconscious to surface. You become touchy and irritable. You may be deceived by others and experience losses because of hidden enemies and unforeseen dangers. You may make money from the conditions of war, but only if you are not involved in treachery or in promotion of the disputes.

You have the power to heal. Your gentle presence soothes, and your intuitive insight mends the minds and bodies of those you touch. If you develop your healing potential, you can become an influential force in the relief of suffering.

18/9 AS A TEMPORARY VIBRATION: **Caution, dreaming, healing, body care.** You must slow down the fast pace of your life. You need to pay more attention to your bodily needs; therefore, exercise outdoors, eat properly and get sufficient sleep.

Your dreams are active now, and any sleeplessness you experience is the product of an extremely vivid imagination. New plans and ideas are forming in your mind. Do not start new projects, but rather allow the ideas to germinate. They will blossom at a later date. Maintain your present status while considering changes, such as a new occupation.

Healing forces are working beneath the surface, and your health can improve if you allow periods of quiet contemplation to calm your mind. Your thoughts have a potent control over your bodily processes now.

Sign documents carefully or not at all, if possible. Be on guard against deception in business and difficulties in personal affairs. Family quarrels and accidents are caused by rashness or carelessness. Travel is not advisable. Mental unsettledness can bring a physical illness. Wars and revolutions are brought on by such vibrations.

You have a unique opportunity to organize your life now. Set your environment in order, clean your house, organize your desk, finish up odds and ends. Such actions will direct your subconscious to set itself in order as well. Then your dreams and visions will express the future direction you should follow.

TAROT SYMBOLISM: **Key 18 The Moon.** Evolutionary growth and development come under key 18. The keywords are *organization* and *sleep*. The function of the Moon is sleep, and, during sleep, waste is eliminated and new materials are woven into the body. Consciousness continues while the upper brain cells rest. It is during sleep that our aspirations and efforts are being built into the body cells. What we think and do all day goes on influencing the body while we sleep. Every cell is a center of consciousness, and every cell contains spirit. Astrologically, Pisces, the final sign of the zodiac, rules this key.

The shellfish coming out of the water represents the lower form of existence. Shaped like a scorpion, it indicates the creative force starting on the path of return, which leads to the mountain of attainment.

THE MOON.

The narrow path implies that concentration is necessary. It goes up,
then down, but always rises higher at the next step. It is meant to
show that spiritual unfoldment does not come all at once, but rather
progresses gradually.

The dog and wolf are of the same species, but one is wild and the
other is domesticated (depicting nature aided by human consciousness). The towers are human handiwork. The thirty-two rays
of the Moon indicate the thirty-two paths on the Tree of Life, and the
falling yods represent the descent of the life force from a higher plane
into the material world. Many symbols here show that we can change
the outward structure of things. They are proof that the same changes
may be accomplished within the body through organization and
cultivation.

ASTROLOGICAL CORRESPONDENCE: **The Sun (and Pisces)**. The
test of Saturn (8) is energized and supported by Mars (1), resulting in
full attainment and realization (9, the Sun).

With the combination of the Sun and Pisces, final completion is
possible under this number. The Sun, representing true individuality
finds its own true identity in key 18, which symbolizes body consciousness. By combining body consciousness and control with
realization of one's self, all things are possible.

19/1 AS A PERSONAL NUMBER VIBRATION: Your
leadership talents would be useful in public ser-
vice. You will be the head of projects as the organizer, director or
manager. You are very expressive with words and would make an effective speaker or lecturer. Art and science may also appeal to you, as
well as agriculture, nature and the simple pleasures of life.

Your tremendous vitality and intellect create a mind capable of
overcoming any obstacles. You collect, synthesize and regenerate
past errors into attitudes which assure your future success. Here, your
faith and creativity constantly renew those aspects of living which
others ignore, thereby ensuring your continuing growth. You
epitomize the quote from Ecclesiastes 8:1, "A man's wisdom maketh
his face to shine."

You attract love and money. A good marriage, contentment in the
home, material happiness, honor and esteem can be yours. There
may be many turns in your life that require new beginnings. You
must master your emotions so that emotional upheavals and uncontrolled impulses do not cause material loss and failure.

If you are a negative 19, you lead a double life. You create a
positive image of yourself as one type of personality while living a
secret life of falsity and deceit. In this respect 19 is called the spiritual
fall. Your courage is being tested. You must learn independence and

refrain from self-pity. Number 19 is karmic—the equalizer and collector.

As a positive 19/1 you have great endurance. You know that it is always darkest just before the dawn. Reason prevails. Many turn to you for guidance because you collect and distribute the power which gives light and life. You use this light to warm, to create, to urge growth and life, rather than to burn and scorch. You will find happiness, rewards and victory over adversities when a degree of adeptness has been attained.

19/1 AS A TEMPORARY VIBRATION: **Love, marriage, rewards, obstacles overcome, new beginnings.** 19 is known as the love vibration, and marriage under this number is indeed fortunate. Happiness and contentment are enhanced by good fortune in material affairs. You may experience happy reunions with friends and family. Rewards, honors, and esteem are manifestations of your past productive and creative efforts.

This period brings a brand new start for you, promising liberation and prosperity. Your energy, drive and ambition run high, urging you to step out on your own. Be independent, take a chance, for luck shines upon you. Any obstacles now can be overcome. New beginnings have life-energizing forces behind them, which promote growth and assure success.

You must restrain impulsive actions and prepare future plans carefully. If you indulge your personal desires, you could cause difficulties for others, broken engagements, invalid or troublesome contracts and loss of personal possessions. The future looks very uncertain to someone who uses number 19's energies negatively.

Watch every opportunity and keep a positive faith in your own abilities; then you can achieve whatever goals you pursue. Great happiness and satisfaction are possible here. The choice, as always, is yours.

THE SUN .

TAROT SYMBOLISM: **Key 19 The Sun.** The Sun means face or countenance. Face implies head, one who takes the lead, as the head of an organization. This card also brings to a head all the potencies of the life power. The keyword is *regeneration*. We renew our bodies when we renew our minds. "Be ye transformed by the renewing of your mind that ye may prove what is the good and perfect will of God." (Romans 12:2).

Astrologically, the Sun rules this key, bringing light and life, symbol of the divinity, the great divine power. We must control and adjust our lives through the Sun's action. As the ancients knew, the powers themselves are neither good or bad; it is how they are used. The power of the Sun is not just a physical energy but also a living power. What we see in the Sun is identical with the spiritual power behind the Sun. Everything on earth is a manifestation of the Sun.

The twenty-one rays of the Sun represent the twenty-one keys of the Major Arcana in the Tarot. The four flowers symbolize organized development: mineral, vegetable, animal and Adam-consciousness. Sunflowers always face the sun to draw their power, as we should do to develop our consciousness.

The nude child astride the horse has sublimated the animal desires and is a symbol of the naked truth and an understanding of things as they really are. "Except as ye become as little children, ye cannot enter the kingdom of heaven," (Matthew 18:3).

ASTROLOGICAL CORRESPONDENCE: **Mars (and Sun).** The personal energy, the basic life force and the driving instincts of Mars must be controlled, channeled and raised to a higher level through the developed awareness and consciousness of the true life power, the Sun. All our energy comes from the Sun, and we in turn must radiate the energy we receive.

Number 19/1 individuals must heed the advice given in the Bible, "Let your light shine," (Matthew 5:16).

20/2 AS A PERSONAL NUMBER VIBRATION: You will be faced with many decisions in your lifetime. You must learn to make judgments based on reason, not appearance. When measuring or sizing up people, see their works and not their reputations. Outward appearances can be deceiving, so you must exercise thoughtfulness before any final judgments are made.

You like to control the people in your circle of influence and prefer to shape things to the ends which you deem worthy. Such a position necessitates choices; therefore, you are constantly tested: Should I do this or that? Is it wise to take this path or that path? Shall I go with the new or stick with the old? Deep within, you have an abiding knowledge of opposites; therefore, you are continually confronted with the need to make choices. As a result, your life is one of adaptation and renewal. New plans, new purposes and new ambitions present a continuing scenario demanding decisive action. This cyclical process creates the awakened human personality because the moment of judgment is the same as the moment of awareness. You cannot make a decision until you have weighed and measured all the facts and arrived at an awareness of the situation. Through decisive action you develop yourself and overcome the difficulties in life. Let your conscience guide you.

20's have the power to make or break, save or slay. If you are a negative 20 you fear death and change from familiar habit patterns. You must learn control over your emotions. Your weakness brings on poor health, disillusionment, loss of material goods and separation from those you love.

As a positive 20, you constantly renew your life through the many decisions you must make, increasing your realization and awareness of the perpetual adaptations that life requires.

20/2 AS A TEMPORARY VIBRATION: **Turning points, decisions, awareness, adaptability, reconstruction.** Sudden events require you to make a decision that could be a turning point in your life. A change of location, a new job or fresh relationships demand new thoughts, feelings and actions from you. Be able to see the alternatives, the pros and cons. In this way you will learn much about yourself and how adaptable you are. If you accurately weigh and measure your present situation or any situation presented to you during this period, you will formulate a profitable plan that can be implemented in the near future.

Unless you act decisively to put your ideas to practical use, the influence of number 20 can make you restless and uneasy. Do not remain idle, and don't waste time. You are experiencing a period of growth; future realizations are now germinating. Ingest, assimilate and create form from the energies operating here. It is a fine planning period. Come to reasoned conclusions, and the cyclical force will see your plans manifested soon.

Do not resist the need for change. Remain adaptable, use your common sense, and come to a logical conclusion. Then you have fulfilled the requirements of this period.

TAROT SYMBOLISM: **Key 20 Judgement.** The key symbols for this card are tooth, fang, and serpent. An ancient adept was called a serpent, and when we want to invoke silence, we pronounce the sound of the letter for this key—*Sh.* This indicates the silence of the wise. "Be ye wise as serpents," (Matthew 10:16).

Teeth break food and prepare it for digestion. Wisdom, which is kept silent, destroys the forms of the outer world and reveals the hidden nature of things so that you may absorb the spiritual essence.

The cobra was the sacred symbol of Egypt and India. Its venom attacks every cell of the body instantly. The serpent's fang conveys the poison. The analogy is that wisdom can be like acid which instantly eats away everything false. Therefore, the keyword for this card is *realization.* Astrologically, it is ruled by Vulcan. When we have gained realization of spiritual things, our personal consciousness is ready to blend with the universal consciousness. We then realize our oneness with God and our unity with all humanity. This state of consciousness begins with a mental grasp of the real world, where our attitude is the reverse of most people's because we identify ourselves with the One Reality. Our subconscious minds are dominated by true will.

Our judgment day is the day we have reached our ability to judge

the true from the false. The card represents the call to judgment day.
The angel Gabriel calls those who are ready to hear the truth which
shall set them free and give them new life. Stone coffins, the human
body, arise from the deep. They are black when closed, from lack of
light, or truth. The three states of consciousness arise: man, consciousness; woman, subconsciousness; and child, superconscious-
ness. In older versions of the Tarot, their arms spell the word *lux* or
light. They have come into illumination.

ASTROLOGICAL CORRESPONDENCE: **Vulcan (and Saturn).**
Vulcan is doubly emphasized here through the double digit 20
(Vulcan is number 2) and through the base digit 2.

In mythology, Vulcan was thrown from heaven. He became the
keeper of the flame, tending the forges of heaven and earth. He was
also known as the master craftsman. Despite the lameness resulting
from his fall, he traveled frequently between heaven and earth.

The analogy in the myth represents the fall of our spirit into form,
ruled by Saturn. The spirit's freedom is hampered by the physical
body. The fiery life force must be well tended by keeping open the
line of communication between the body and the spirit.

Vulcan may eventually be assigned to Virgo, the perfect servant
and tender of health, as was Vulcan. Artisans are also assigned to
Virgo.

In 20, the God power 0, works through Vulcan, 2, to bring about
the union of what appears, in the physical form, to be separate
parts—spirit and matter.

21/3 AS A PERSONAL NUMBER VIBRATION: This
is a number of general good fortune. You have
talent, charm, and luck, all of which bring succeess. A good memory
and a positive attitude toward life are the basis of your luck. Advancements, honor and recognition are possible during your lifetime.

You are patient. The limitations that most people fear become the
cornerstone for your successes. Your administrative ability is enhanced because you know that the only way to rule nature is to first
obey its rules, its limitations. Adherence to the orderly progression of
things assures your triumph in all pursuits. The act of concentration is
a sort of limitation, and concentration is the basis of science. You see
the necessity of limits in the evolution of life and can validate these
beliefs in scientific pursuits.

The arts may call you, and many 21's have enjoyed literary success
because they are so expressive. You have achieved the union of
wisdom and love through past efforts and may now desire to reveal
these truths in an art form. Your professional pursuits may require
changes of residence. Traveling and moving satisfy your innate need
for liberation and freedom.

If you are a negative 21, you fear change of all kinds. You lack vision and become greedy and selfish. Your tenacity assures eventual loss, as others manage to take away the very things that give you security. You are stubborn and refuse to learn life's lessons.

You can be an example for others through service and material attainment. You will make a mark in life. Others see you as the ultimate realization of the personality to which they wish to evolve. 21 is the mystical number of the cosmic consciousness.

21/3 AS A TEMPORARY VIBRATION: **Travel, change, rewards, success, new worlds.** This is a very potent period in which the old order changes, making way for the new. The newly revealed world offers ultimate realization of your plans, hopes and wishes; therefore, do not overlook opportunities that arise now.

Plans already in progress may come to a successful completion, with accompanying rewards. Those plans still in the thinking stages should be carried out now, as the potential for success is high in this period. You can accomplish what you desire.

Travel may be part of this cycle, and faraway places lure you. The desires for freedom, self-expression and pleasure urge you to look to distant places for fulfillment. A change of jobs and/or residence may result from your present thinking.

Your subconscious is developing at a pace faster than usual during this period, along with a growing sense of security and protection. Many marriages take place under a 21/3. Mental or physical investments made here bear fruit.

Those who react negatively must guard against losing emotional control. They see family responsibilities as burdens. They experience delays and restrictions and neglect to grasp offered opportunities. For them, all situations must be examined carefully. Legal counsel should be employed in business dealings because material loss is possible.

For you, this period is one of reward. Realize that the opportunities opening for you now can fulfill your future dreams.

THE WORLD.

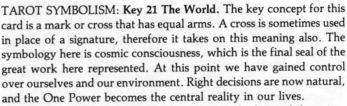

TAROT SYMBOLISM: **Key 21 The World.** The key concept for this card is a mark or cross that has equal arms. A cross is sometimes used in place of a signature, therefore it takes on this meaning also. The symbology here is cosmic consciousness, which is the final seal of the great work here represented. At this point we have gained control over ourselves and our environment. Right decisions are now natural, and the One Power becomes the central reality in our lives.

Saturn rules key 21. The Saturn center at the base of the spine, called the sacral plexus, is the storehouse of excess energy left from each day's activities. Saturn has been considered a malefic; however, it can help build for the future if one uses the energies in the sacral plexus for constructive action.

In mythology, Saturn was the father or the god who ate his children; this means that the cosmic consciousness swallows up all lesser consciousnesses. The bull, lion, eagle and man represent the four fixed signs of the zodiac and indicate that the laws of the universe are fixed and orderly. The wreath in the form of a zero or egg or seed is that from which all things issue forth. This is the divine power. The dancing figure is androgynous, a unity of opposite polarities; however, the veil hides this fact, showing that cyclicity also brings about this androgynous state. The figure stands on air, self-supported and perfectly balanced.

This picture represents the dance of life, which is never ending. 21/3 is a new heaven and a new earth or a new mind and a new body. When we have renewed ourselves through study and practice, the old order will change. New plans and a new outlook will prevail.

ASTROLOGICAL CORRESPONDENCE: **Jupiter (and Saturn).** Traditionally, the conjunction of Jupiter and Saturn prevails over the birth of avatars and holy persons, those who bring a message of inspiration to the world. Here this combination of planets seeks to unite the things of earth, under the rulership of Saturn, with the wisdom of the higher mind, under the control of Jupiter. Only then can Saturn's malefic hold on many people's lives be transformed into the highest achievement which Saturn has to offer while in the physical body to bring about elevation to the apex of the horoscope, the sacred spot closest to the Sun, the One Source.

22/4 AS A PERSONAL NUMBER VIBRATION: This is one of the four master numbers (11, 22, 33, 44), and it can be experienced as either a 22 or a 4, or as a fluctuation between the two during your lifetime.

You have the potential to accrue vast wealth and power on a world-wide scale. Your greatness can be achieved through resources, including people. You are the philanthropist whose fortune gained from material achievement is used to build a better world.

Your originality allows you to create solutions to problems that others consider unsolvable. You have a genius for thinking in broad terms while always arriving at practical solutions. You are hard working, honest in dealing with people, and above all, ethical. You are a master at directing others but be careful never to exploit them for selfish reasons. Overwork and a desire for power and control can create a negative 22 whose potential for evil can produce a ruthless and even infamous type. Overwork brings on emotional difficulties.

You have strong opinions and a great deal of wisdom, which is always directed to practical uses. You can contribute to shaping the destiny of the world through industry, politics or the professions.

Firmness in friendship and all relationships, including marriage, provides the secure base from which you meet the world. You have enormous leadership and policy-making abilities. With effort, of which you are extremely capable, you will become one of those financial tycoons whose name lives on through good works that benefit millions.

22/4 AS A TEMPORARY VIBRATION: Travel, plans, advancements, your dreams come true. 22 is a master number and the ancient numerical value for a circle. As such it implies completion, fulfillment and cyclicity. Under a 22, you are reaching your goal; the fulfillment of your secret desires can become a reality. Success on a huge scale and attainment of those impossible dreams are very possible. You should make those big plans, dare the mighty deeds you have only contemplated up to now. Traveling toward a goal can also suggest physical travel, which is a distinct possibility here.

Make sure your concepts are well organized and practical. Think in large sweeping terms, and go to the head person with your creative ideas. They have a good chance of being accepted now. Many people can benefit from the ideas you present under a 22, and as a result, you may be given a top position. You are now the known expert in your field, and others come to you for opinions and advice.

This is a very tense period when you will be dealing with groups of people. Guard against extremes; do not be too extravagant with money, and do not speculate in uncertain enterprises. Stay away from gambling. Deal only with practical matters during this period. Overindulgence may cause the dissolution of affairs which otherwise have good potential.

If in doubt about any matter, consult a professional. Do not trust just your own judgment. Once all the facts are collected, rely upon your own intuition, which is based on reason, to supply you with proper decisions. It can all be yours during this powerful material period.

THE FOOL.

TAROT SYMBOLISM: Key 0 (and 22) The Fool (before and after). The master number 22 holds a unique position in the Tarot deck. Theoretically, the Major Arcana begins at key 1 and continues through key 21. The Minor Arcana begins at 23, the King of Wands, and continues on to 78, the Ten of Pentacles. The Fool, as key 0, stands by itself, representing the God force. 22 would seem to be missing; however, since cyclicity is the essence of life, there can be no ending. Therefore, the Fool, key 0, is the life force before entering manifestation, and 22 is that same key 0, the Fool, having walked the 21 keys of the Major Arcana to complete that full cycle and step once more beyond the present incarnation. 22 is an ancient numerical symbol for a circle, and therefore represents the Alpha and Omega, by which the Lord described Himself in the Bible.

The word *fool* comes from the Latin, *follis*, meaning a bag of wind. Every genius is called a fool at some time, and that which contains air or breath could be called a bag of wind; therefore, we are the Fool in that sense. The Fool is the super-conscious, pictured here as having room to take one more step. This indicates that we never come to the limit of our potentials.

The white Sun is the universal radiant energy eternally rising, for it can never reach its zenith. The mountains indicate attainment. They are cold and uninteresting to many, but from their peaks melting snow feeds the streams and makes the valley fertile. So, too, ancient wisdom will feed your consciousness and transform your life.

The Fool's wreath symbolizes victory. His wand is a measuring tool by which we continually evaluate our accomplishments. His wallet contains memories of the past, and the eagle on the wallet symbolizes the awakening of higher vision toward loftier aspirations.

The dog under the Fool's control is the subhuman forms of life that are elevated by the evolution of the consciousness. The white rose in the Fool's left hand indicates that his desire is pure or spiritual and untainted by lower desires and passions.

The Fool here is the cosmic life force about to descend, inexperienced, into the world of manifestation.

ASTROLOGICAL CORRESPONDENCE: **Earth (and Uranus).** Since the master number 22 reduces to a 4, the earth holds dominion in this vibration, coupled with Uranus, which is assigned to key 0, the Fool.

Consciousness is a state of mind. The presence of Uranus here links the super-conscious to the earthly power indicated by the 22/4. A blending of spiritual conscious awareness with the proper use and control of the world's material offerings, including the body itself, gives the perfect state of being. Once this has been achieved, the individual is no longer bound by earthly considerations but merely uses them with reverence and respect.

2

THE

WANDS

23/5 AS A PERSONAL NUMBER VIBRATION: This number can lead you to honor, fame and material gain. Your strength is in your material ideas. You exercise intelligence in your actions and wisdom in your control. With your quick, clever brain, you learn easily and retain what you have learned. You also have the courage and daring to enforce your ideas in the material world. You enjoy exercise. Physical agility maintains good circulation and increases the brain power; therefore, your agile body and energetic mind make you a sure success. In addition, you possess healing abilities. You are gifted in speech and writing and may be known as the monarch of ideas. Thus a career in communications is possible. Researchers also come under 23/5.

Because you are loyal and passionate, you enjoy a good marriage and children. Inheritances may come to you during your lifetime.

You thrive on constant change and adventure. Learn to make each change a step in a constructive direction. You are sometimes headstrong and hasty; learn to handle this fiery energy within, and direct it accordingly.

Your friendly, honest approach to others and your ambitious nature attract people in a position to aid your progress. Through your superiors you will have opportunities to better yourself. This is a karmic reaction brought on by your willingness to help others.

If you are a negative 23/5 strict adherence to principles can create a severe, patronizing personality. You become selfish and resort to outbursts of temper when life does not go your way.

As a positive 23/5 you can look forward to a comfortable life, surrounded by a loving family, material comforts and the honor and esteem of your peers.

23/5 AS A TEMPORARY VIBRATION: **Protection, contracts, travel.** There are powerful protective forces around you now to guide you into safe ports. Follow the advice you receive from superiors or those in a position to know more about the subject in question than you do. Then your pursuits and goals will be successful.

You could inherit money and material goods through settlement of an estate or legal proceedings. You may enter into new contracts which could alter your life, and such agreements may require quick decisions on your part. Marriage is one such contract that reacts favorably to this vibration.

The changes now occurring may result in travel. It may be to fulfill the obligations of your agreements or because good fortune has increased your finances and allowed you this extra pleasure.

If others oppose your ideas, be careful not to allow the difference of opinion to degenerate into quarrels. A severe approach can alienate friends.

Be truthful and helpful during this period. Your attitudes will be well rewarded through material gain, peace of mind and contentment.

TAROT SYMBOLISM: **King of Wands.** The seated figure looking at the world indicates a mental attitude of looking toward the future, possibly deciding to change his point of view. Decorated with lions, the background screen indicates that the fixed powers of the divine law are behind him, and he is aware they are his to use. Salamanders represent spirits living in the element fire and denote that the king is able to handle fire; he can control the fire of the self and nature. He is holding the live wand of spiritual power.

KING of WANDS

ASTROLOGICAL CORRESPONDENCE: **First decan Aries.** The King of Wands presides over the first decan of Aries. (A decan is a ten-degree division of the zodiacal wheel; each of the twelve signs spans thirty degrees.) This Mars-ruled decan combines to make this a strong, driving force. You learn easily. You want to lead and be at the head of things. You have an abundance of ideas and aspire to improve existing conditions. You are ready to gain all the knowledge you can and you enthusiastically grasp opportunities to progress intellectually as well as physically. Your creative and inventive ability may express itself in the direction of science or other mechanical pursuits.

24/6 AS A PERSONAL NUMBER VIBRATION: With your magnetic personality and powers of suggestion over other people, you can attract all the material comforts and nurturing relationships anyone could possibly desire. People with authority and people of influence are always anxious to see to your needs. The help you receive promotes your success.

This is a fortunate love and family vibration. You are a good companion and helpmate, and you love your home, children and nature. Pride, ambition and a love of life make you a lively mate whose fulfillment comes through creating an abundant lifestyle where all things may be nurtured and grown. You may have many children whose religious, scholastic and physical growth you will carefully promote.

You are a stately individual, kind, generous and patient. This number allows full expression of the harmony you seek with others. A desire for truth and justice sets you in a position where others see your sincerity and respect you for it. You are a success socially and financially. You have sound business judgment and are practical with money.

Visions, dreams and ESP experiences bring you much insight and enhance your creative mind. You may also have clairvoyant experiences.

If you are a negative 24/6, you may be jealous, unfaithful and domineering to loved ones. You are stubborn, and when crossed, you can be revengeful.

24/6 AS A TEMPORARY VIBRATION: **Family matters, gain, love.** This is a highly favorable period in which all undertakings can terminate successfully. You gain financially with the help of people in authority or through members of the opposite sex. Your success can depend upon these very people. Now is the time to make plans. You may have flashes of insight on how to proceed in the future.

24/6 is a love vibration. Marriage and the birth of children are possible, and many matters concerning the family arise now. Your happiness depends on love.

You are experiencing a period of harvest, the reaping of the seeds you have sown in the past. You may receive the respect of your peers for some efforts. Financially, you stand to gain from sound practical judgment in business dealings.

Understand the feelings and emotions of other family members, and be available when they need your wise counseling. Be generous, helpful and patient with those near you, and your efforts will be rewarded.

TAROT SYMBOLISM: **Queen of Wands.** The Queen holds the wand of live power in her right hand; the sunflower which always turns to face the Sun is in her left hand. The sunflower refers to the Leo decan of Aries. The black cat in front of her throne represents clairvoyant powers. The two lions on the backdrop and the carved lions on her throne again suggest Leo and also bring in key 8, Strength. The triple peaks in the background depict attainment on three planes of consciousness.

QUEEN of WANDS.

ASTROLOGICAL CORRESPONDENCE: **Second decan Aries.** The Queen of Wands presides over the second decan of Aries which is the Leo decan, presided over by the Sun. This decan gives a high-spirited and ambitious temperament. It is a fortunate number in that your generosity and magnanimity are rewarded in kind by those with whom you deal. You attract success and assistance because of your sunny, optimistic outlook.

25/7 AS A PERSONAL NUMBER VIBRATION: You are strongly intuitive and often have prophetic dreams. You may be clairvoyant as well. These are qualities you have developed by overcoming many obstacles. Your early years may have been difficult, and these trials may have helped you overcome instability. You had to awaken to the truths within and thereby acquire wisdom. What others see in you as intuition is merely a developed talent of observation and attention to details, which allows you to piece together the whole and arrive at conclusions much faster than others. If past experiences have not taught you to develop these qualities, then you should begin now; otherwise, your impulsive nature can turn challenging situations into conflict.

You have an alert, energetic mind, which always seeks new enterprises, ideas and locations. You like nature and may prefer to live in the country rather than the city, perhaps near the water. Your adventurous disposition tends to make you more mobile than most, and you may often change your place of residence to fulfill this wanderlust.

A pioneering spirit and a quest for knowledge bring out the fiery missionary zeal within you, and you become a spiritual crusader. Remain alert to various ways to overcome the obstacles you will meet and work hard to follow through with the job; then you will achieve leadership in any business or enterprise you embrace.

If you express the negative 25/7 it will cause conflict and a loss of energy. The job never gets done. Laxity and unfulfillment can then bring on cruelty.

25/7 AS A TEMPORARY VIBRATION: **Change of residence, trials, health, success after difficulty.** You may experience trials and difficulties now which will make you draw upon your energy reserves. Success can be yours, but it won't be handed to you: it comes after hard work and perseverance.

During this period, use your mental energy positively and constructively. Visualize what you want and keep the thought ever present in your mind.

Hasty actions can cause conflicts. Sudden decisions may necessitate a change of residence, a trip or some other kind of movement. Travel should be undertaken with care; the wise person does not stay at home but travels cautiously. Annoying health conditions may arise and need attention.

Sign all documents only after consulting an expert in the appropriate field. Then proceed, assured that your enterprises will be very successful, because you have taken into account all details and mitigating circumstances.

KNIGHT of WANDS.

TAROT SYMBOLISM: **Knight of Wands.** The Knight is dressed in his suit of armor and is riding to the conquest. This indicates his burgeoning thoughts about a new enterprise and his desire to win. His crusade could be a search for the truth, because his weapon is the wand of divine power. The salamander symbol on his robe indicates his ability to handle the fiery energy.

ASTROLOGICAL CORRESPONDENCE: **Spring (Aries, Taurus, Gemini).** The Knight of Wands presides over the spring season, from the time that the Sun enters the sign Aries until it reaches the summer solstice at 0 degrees of the sign Cancer.

The Sun is exalted in Aries, and its power awakens new life as nature responds to its warming rays. Like nature, at this time of year you gain strength through mastering obstacles. There can be difficulties as you struggle to meet the Sun's promise, but you persevere through hard work.

26/8 AS A PERSONAL NUMBER VIBRATION: This is a karmic number. It designates a life in which you learn about the world around you through experience. Stressful situations eventually develop your self-confidence, at which time positive action brings prosperity and fulfillment. You have en-

thusiasm, courage and a desire for power. The power will come when you have learned wisdom and developed strength through self-control.

Your impulsiveness involves you in sudden love relationships. That same impulsiveness causes irritation in others, creating tense situations. You must learn self-control, patience and endurance. You must be subservient to the laws of nature before you can master them.

You are a gifted speaker who could become a lecturer, debater or diplomat. Communication is vital because your wide-angle vision allows a view of the whole, while others are mired in the parts. Your ideas are looking for assimilation; only through communication will your concepts find realization. Through interactions with others you will learn to form enduring relationships which will fortify your position in life. Your relationships are decidedly karmic and will be either destructive or supportive, depending on your past actions.

You could excel in sports, especially running, sprinting, high jumps, skiing, gymnastics, etc. You most likely prefer outdoor sports, pursuits which involve the legs, coordination and a sense of balance.

26/8 AS A TEMPORARY VIBRATION: **Messages, marriage, gestation, karma.** Expect some kind of message, tidings or good news. Since this is a karmic period, you may meet a marriage prospect or someone who will figure importantly in your future. Many pregnant women are under this vibration, suggesting a karmic relationship between the child and parent or parents.

This is a good time to develop your powers of expression. Take an elocution course or learn a foreign language. Study a subject that will broaden your horizons and enhance your experience.

26/8 is a splendid financial vibration; however, use good judgment. Check out all the details before making investments or going into partnership or agreements.

As a negative vibration, you may receive bad news of some kind. Partnerships or contracts may be broken and losses can occur, causing indecision.

If positive, expect the very best. Beautiful relationships can be formed now, ensuring a lifetime of happiness and fulfillment.

PAGE of WANDS.

TAROT SYMBOLISM: **Page of Wands.** The standing youth seems to be taking the measure of his power. He feels his inner strength but has yet to test and prove it on the open plain before him. Though he wears the salamander robe of protection with confidence, he nevertheless mentally inspects the working of divine power in his wand.

ASTROLOGICAL CORRESPONDENCE: **Third decan Aries.** The third decan of Aries brings in the Sagittarian co-rulership of Jupiter. You have an energetic nature and are fond of outdoor sports. Your benevolent, jovial and expansive nature tends to bring worldly prosperity, giving you the power to control others. You maintain an attitude of self-confidence even under stress because of the Jupiterian vibrations present here.

27/9 AS A PERSONAL NUMBER VIBRATION: This is a number of great spiritual strength. The beginnings of a deep spiritual understanding endow you with insight and prescience. You should follow your own intuitions rather than allow yourself to be swayed by others. You are just and wise; you wish to maintain harmony and to help others mentally, physically and spiritually.

You have a fertile, creative mind and a love of beauty and art. Energetic, inventive ideas bring unusually successful results after many attempts and changes. Others seek you out because you always have an original approach to the solution of their problems.

Your creativity extends to the physical plane: you will produce an abundant family. Civilizations are built upon the stuff of which you are made.

All business enterprises will succeed beyond expectation with you at the helm. Your mental strength and positive attitude endow you with the power to act independently. You impress other people so that they are willing to follow you and implement your ideas. Your influence over others, coupled with an ability to lead, brings you wealth and comfort.

If you are a negative 27/9, you are confused and indecisive, never knowing what path to take. You are also intolerant of the failing, or what you deem the failing, of others.

You have a tremendous opportunity in this lifetime to develop your ideas in a tangible way. There is no question that your mental capabilities are great. Now you must bring your ideas out of the realm of concepts and make them a reality. Create useful products that will benefit the world.

27/9 AS A TEMPORARY VIBRATION: **Birth, marriage, start of new business.** Things are growing, blossoming, and bearing fruit under this vibration. It is a fertile, promising period in your life. Relationships bloom and bring deeper understanding; therefore, marriage and close partnerships are a probability here.

If you have been planning to open a new business, patent an idea, have a showing or present any kind of creative enterprise, now is the time to do so. This vibration brings together all the ingredients for a successful promotion.

You will enlist the aid of others. They, in turn, will be more than happy to see that you receive what you need, because your positive attitude is infectious.

This could very well be the beginning of your fortune. The events occurring now will ultimately bring the wealth, prosperity and goals that you seek.

A negative reaction could bring delays, postponed travels, the termination of an existing business or generally unhappy feelings.

By expressing a positive, expectant attitude, you can bring about the best side of this unusually excellent number vibration. You are off on a happy new adventure in many respects. A trip is possible, but if you do not travel physically, you are at least on a journey toward your innermost dreams.

TAROT SYMBOLISM: **Ace of Wands.** The hand of God holds forth a living wand, a growing thing with green leaves. Some leaves fall to earth in the form of yods, the sparks of inspiration and creation. The wand dispenses life to all areas, for all purposes. It is pure invention, waiting to be tapped by those who would use this spiritual power.

ASTROLOGICAL CORRESPONDENCE: **The element fire (Aries, Leo, Sagittarius).** The aces of the Tarot pack preside over the elements fire, earth, air and water. The fiery element relating to the Ace of Wands indicates that you should follow your own intuition and not deviate from what you feel is right. You are inventive, creative and inspired; you bring originality to everything you touch. Art and beauty, peace and justice are very much a part of you.

28/1 AS A PERSONAL NUMBER VIBRATION: If you use care and good judgment, there are great possibilities for your life. You are ambitious and progressive, willing to lead and take responsibility. You wish to improve existing conditions. Your positive, direct approach to life instills zest in every new enterprise you initiate. You are a person of action with the ability to see things as they really are, unclouded by preconceived ideas or thoughts. You have good judgment because you have a direct link with your source of knowledge and a perfect balance between your desires and your thoughts. You are a visionary with the ability to translate your dreams into tangible products.

There is a vital, stimulating, resourceful quality in this number, always ready for action and pioneering ventures. With boldness and courage, you are the master of your fate, the sovereign of your world.

Your talent for inspiring others, your balanced mind, kindness and generosity create a karmic reaction which brings you success and satisfaction. You are attractive to the opposite sex. Money and good fortune are your payment for giving others your energy and material assistance. You may have an interest in scientific procedures.

Negatively, a 28/1 can be reckless and daring. You should practice self-control to regain a balance. You can be proud, dominating, intolerant and full of contradictions. Losses may result from poor judgment and misplaced trust in others. You probably work better if you do not work alone, and at this point you may need to begin again, profiting by experience.

Once you have determined your goal and learned to trust your intuition, you will be well on your way to a position of contentment and worldly influence.

28/1 AS A TEMPORARY VIBRATION: Contradictions, competition, surprise, unusual events. This period offers many opportunities that may result in a series of unusual or unexpected events. If you proceed with caution, your finances could improve and prosperity result. There is a competitive aspect here which suggests opposition. This could result in losses through partnerships, the law, or placing too much trust in others. Herein lies the contradictory nature of this number vibration.

Land and property dealings can bring unexpectedly good profits or surprising losses, depending on your original motives and behavior. If you have been honest, ethical and aboveboard, you can expect the former.

Be prepared for events that come up suddenly that will test your ability to judge fairly without becoming too emotional or too stern. Good judgment is essential in all transactions and agreements. If you obtain the facts and use them wisely, you can have very profitable relationships with your peers.

Some people, believing that they have all the answers, resort to sudden rash behavior. The promising beginning now offered is then lost by this lack of judgment.

The outcome of this period seems to rest solely in your hands. You have the reins; you can direct your energy down the primrose path or to the town dump.

TAROT SYMBOLISM: **Two of Wands.** A man is holding the world in his hand, indicating unlimited opportunity for achievement in any line. He is dressed in the red robe of activity and desire. He is surrounded with live power shown by the two firmly planted living wands. He looks out over the water, signifying the recognition of subconscious powers. The garden in the background shows work that has been done in previous lives. The emblem of crossed lilies and roses shows that physical desire and spiritual unfoldment are blended harmoniously.

ASTROLOGICAL CORRESPONDENCE: **First decan Aries.** There is a vitalizing, stimulating and resourceful quality in this division of the zodiac. You have courage and passion and are always ready for action and pioneering ventures. You are attractive to the opposite sex. You are emotional, generous and affectionate; at the same time, you are proud and aggressive. You understand there are many ways to accomplish any goal, and this can sometimes create difficulty in decision making. Therefore, you must learn patience, and profit by past experiences.

29/11 AS A PERSONAL NUMBER VIBRATION:

29/11 is a master number and as such requires more of you than the other number vibrations. (Read number 11 and number 2, as you may fluctuate between these two basic energies.)

This is a testing incarnation in which the strengths you have established in the past must now be put to a commercial use. You are a novice in the business world that now beckons, yet you have all the tools necessary to operate a successful enterprise. The word *wisdom* vibrates to 29/11 as does the word *light*. The positive side of the vibration endows you with the vision and foresight necessary to look beyond the ordinary world and see the uses for your many talents. You are then able to achieve wealth and success in the business world. Other business people are willing to help you achieve your goals, and you can enter a profitable financial partnership.

Just as light is physically unstable and fluctuating, this number indicates uncertainty, indecision and anxiety. This energy can draw you to unreliable friends and contracts which become testing situations. Pride, arrogance and stubborness sometimes prevent you from admitting your error. However, once fears are overcome and barriers lifted, you look back into your pool of knowledge and establish again a position of strength and stability.

You are definitely an individualist. You have vitality and a generous nature. You must learn the fine art of cooperation, since you like to have the last word.

Learn to make up your mind and stick to it. When you are able to persevere in your goals, you will, after some struggle, attain your hopes and dreams.

29/11 AS A TEMPORARY VIBRATION: **Learning period, commercial opportunities, help offered.** This is a master number period. It requires more effort from you but promises greater rewards.

Be alert. Keep your eyes open and watch for opportunities that come your way. Use good judgment and insight in evaluating the offers that are presented to you. Do not overlook or ignore any possibilities. Learn to see the advantages at hand and grasp them.

Business ventures and commercial openings offer a new approach to life. A partnership may be part of an agreement. Be open to new ideas and willing to accept the help that reputable business people extend to you.

A negative 29/11 brings uncertainties and fears. Friends prove unreliable and disappointments set in. There is trouble making decisions. Offers of help should be looked at carefully.

You can use this period to tune in to your true inner powers, bring them out into the light and test them in the world of form. See what your talents are worth by putting them to practical use. If this is done wisely, you stand to profit from such endeavors. Your peers may recognize your efforts by bestowing some honor upon you.

TAROT SYMBOLISM: **Three of Wands.** The wands stand for spiritual power. The figure is facing away from the power. He should reverse his thought and make the power available. The background is barren, showing that much cultivation is needed. His attitude is introspective to the extent that he is unaware of the advantage at hand, yet he keeps firm hold of one wand as security. The ships at sea stand for safe voyage, and water, as always, means subconscious reflection and receptivity.

ASTROLOGICAL CORRESPONDENCE: **Second decan Aries.** This is the ambitious area of the zodiac, with great drive toward your chosen goal. There is an eagerness and enthusiasm about you that affects others. You emanate a joyous vibration which spreads over people who come within your sphere of influence. This ability assures you a welcome wherever you go. You can be the life of the party in your particular circle. Your attitude could be described as regal. Take care of this cosmic gift and use it carefully. If you allow it to turn to pride and egotism, failure, rather than success, will cause eventual regret. Hold to your highest ideals and enjoy the reward of virtue.

30/3 AS A PERSONAL NUMBER VIBRATION: As in all numbers containing the 0, the God power is behind the expression of the first digit.

You seek perfection and strive for security. This is an excellent number for handling large assignments because your mind is orderly and systematic. You could be an excellent lawyer or judge because you love system and respect conventional living. You are extremely versatile and clever and could easily excel in science. You have the skill to be a physician or surgeon.

You are skillful in the arts as well. You love the theater, plays, writing, music, children and animals. All things that bring enjoyment and fulfillment appeal to you.

The rich rewards, material comforts and loving pleasures of a happy home are yours. Because you have material goods in abundance, you may be indifferent to them and turn to religious or philosophical interests. You are idealistic and have an interest in higher consciousness and prophecy.

Your sex appeal is a great asset as well as a subtle danger unless handled with a practical mind. You easily occupy the center of the stage because you are charming and agreeable. You will have the abundance that life has to offer and thus the freedom to explore and express the very best within you. You can shine as brilliantly as the brightest star in the heavens and sprinkle a little sparkle into the lives of many people.

30/3 AS A TEMPORARY VIBRATION: Work completed, celebration, romance, happy home. The projects that you have been working on reach their fullest expression in this period. If the work has been done well, the rewards will come now in abundance. It is a time for feasting and celebration, a time that has been long awaited. Your fondest hopes and dreams can now be fulfilled.

These energies are also concerned with the home and domestic relationships. If a romance is in the wind, it will blossom. Marriage will bring happiness, fulfillment and fertility.

Your mind is active. You are clever and capable of wide vision. If you have an artistic bent, the vibrations you are now experiencing will enhance anything you create. An interest in philosophical or metaphysical disciplines will also spark the fires of expression, and if you practice these mind-stimulating arts, you will improve your ability to communicate more effectively. Your mind is in a superior state.

The negative side of 30/3 may bring a delay or a diminishing of the qualities described above; however, even at its worst, this number seems to offer only good. Great joy, harmony and peace are yours, plus love, romance and the rewards of work well done.

TAROT SYMBOLISM: **Four of Wands.** The planted living wands show perfected work. Things have come to fruition. The red-roofed towers show desires realized. The two figures denote the union of two minds, and the garland of flowers and fruits is raised high on the wands, meaning prize work accomplished and hung aloft in triumph.

ASTROLOGICAL CORRESPONDENCE: **Third decan Aries.** Advantage always accrues in the third decan, for there is the essence of the combined planetary rulers of the fire trinity. You desire quality in the things you do, buy or collect. Your work or profession will be chosen with the best aim and desire to succeed. A charming personality is one of your cosmic gifts at birth, giving you the magnetism which attracts the opposite sex. This is an asset as well as a danger, according to how you handle yourself. Remember to follow the law of right and justice while creating beauty and harmony in your life. Your potential for success is best expressed by following a conventional course in life. Travel and the study of philosophy are possible outlets for your energy.

31/4 AS A PERSONAL NUMBER VIBRATION: You are a natural fighter; you fight for what you want and what you believe in. You are independent and proud and will work hard to prove your point. This intense competitive spirit often results in strife by arousing competitiveness in others. A rash scattering of energies can deplete your impact, so you must organize and direct your actions efficiently.

You have determination, energy and patience. If you learn to be practical, you will be rewarded through business and financial success. You have potential for achievement, and when you learn cooperation and direction, you will accomplish a great deal. You could establish an industry based on knowledge gained through diligent research.

You radiate love freely and powerfully; your loving nature illuminates the lives of others. You are generous and will surmount all difficulties because you have a positive attitude. You see each obstacle as an opportunity to prove your mettle.

If you are a negative 31/4, you remain disorganized and live a life of struggle, dispute, difficulties and material lack. You are nervous and high-strung and must learn to adjust harmoniously to others. Legal complications can arise through your rash behavior and pompous attitude.

You see the battle of life as a place where you can balance and express your strength by overcoming all obstacles. Your ambition urges you on to achievement, and you eventually reach the top of the mountain, where the exhilarating satisfaction you feel can be experienced only by one who has made the arduous climb. Success is yours.

31/4 AS A TEMPORARY VIBRATION: **Competition, obstacles, legal dealings, settlements.** You must learn to adjust to others now. Your energy is at a peak. A great deal can be accomplished if you direct those energies; otherwise your vitality may be misplaced and cause difficulties and dissension with others. A quarrelsome nature will cause isolation and loneliness. Positive action will open new opportunities and bring about changes for the better in business and financial speculation. Favorable factors combine to bring success, as long as you don't allow disorganization and dissipation of your precious energy.

Legal matters may need attention, and long-pending lawsuits will be settled under this vibration. Contracts and legal agreements should be approached in a calm and orderly manner. Cooperation, practicality and honesty are essential, so do not allow pride and extravagance to spoil the favorable outcome of these dealings.

Your finances can improve now if you join with others in an honest, mutual effort to bring about tangible results.

TAROT SYMBOLISM: **Five of Wands.** Five youths are shown wielding their wands in a way that expresses imbalance. This could be called the battle of life in which each one is trying to do something in his own way. If cooperation were the rule and if they joined forces, they could accomplish a great deal. This shows mental restlessness and lack of serenity. The desirability of regaining balance is the lesson depicted in this key.

ASTROLOGICAL CORRESPONDENCE: **First decan Leo.** This area of the zodiac indicates a strong will. You have determination and the ability to exert influence for what you believe is right. You are loyal and sincere, and while you desire harmony, you want to achieve it by bending others to your will and ways of action. You are dramatic and could follow a career in the theater, movies or television. You are endowed with a good memory and good vitality. You are forceful and resolute in all you do.

32/5 AS A PERSONAL NUMBER VIBRATION: 32/5 is the magical number ruling people and nations. It gives protection, and such words as *America, Christ, glory, power* and *circle* vibrate to it. You who are under the influence of this number are called the heralds of light; you have the knowledge and are commissioned to send it forth. You are a warrior for the right with a developed sense of duty and responsibility. You bring a message of good tidings for the future.

This is a number demanding action. You must be patient, determined and persistent in getting ahead. Your goals must be high. You must be mentally responsible and rely on your intuition. You have the ability to master speech and foreign languages to aid you in communication. You must use your good judgment and not allow yourself to be swayed by others.

Many friends will help you, and socially and in business you will succeed. With persistence you will be victorious, and the pleasures you have sought will be yours.

If you are a negative 32/5 you allow a haughty, proud nature to turn would-be friends into enemies who are eventually victorious over you. Your sense of superiority irritates others. This usually happens when you have attained a position of authority and feel guilty because you have not lived up to your potential. The rewards this number has to offer are delayed until you have learned the proper use of your energies.

You have a charming personality, which gives you confidence. Your dominant qualities make you a leader and take you into positions of authority. You are attracted to government work and could become a leader in government policy and law making. You have a great sense of personal power and desire to see justice done in your life work. The laurels of victory are yours if you remain untainted by ego. You will gain satisfaction only if you know how closely allied you are to the Source which sent the power through you. Self-confidence is an asset in your career, especially if this is your Outer Personality or Life Lesson Number.

32/5 AS A TEMPORARY VIBRATION: **Good news, humor, rewards, victory.** You are experiencing a very favorable period in which you may receive good news. You reach the high goals for which you have been striving, and the recognition and honor that goes with them are now yours. You can enjoy the pleasures earned from your industrial efforts.

Difficult situations are overcome and disputes are settled, and you come out on top. Settlements are made in your favor.

Friends are very helpful during this period, and you can rely upon them for whatever you need, socially or in business. Your persuasive talents are pronounced, and you can easily sway others to your way of thinking. The messages you bring now can be extremely effective in counseling others or in just plain good advice.

Do not allow pride in your accomplishments to make you overbearing, thus alienating potential and existing friends. Your pride can overturn all the good; then enemies gain the upper hand. This can cause delays in obtaining your goals.

Develop a spiritual philosophy based on the awareness that your present power has come from the Source and is only working *through* you. Enjoy the satisfaction of knowing you were able to open yourself as a channel for that source to work through, but don't mistake yourself as the source of power. This realization brings greater joy and satisfaction than the mistaken idea of the self as controller.

TAROT SYMBOLISM: **Six of Wands.** A horseman crowned with laurel and bearing a laurel wreath on his wand is riding horseback triumphantly, while footmen with wands walk by his side. This is a typical picture of victory. The inner meaning is mastery over the animal nature, and controlled spiritual energy. He is a warrior for right, duty and responsibility.

ASTROLOGICAL CORRESPONDENCE: **Second decan Leo.** This is a fortunate area of the zodiac, very progressive and expansive. It is a sort of peak period in the solar year. You have a religious or philosophical outlook, and you respect the conventions of the culture in which you live. You may be tempted to speculate in the stock market or gamble in other ways; if done without greed, these activities could turn out very well. You may experience vivid dreams, which you should make note of, for they could very well become a way to receive cosmic guidance.

33/6

AS A PERSONAL NUMBER VIBRATION: 33 is the third master number. It is considered an upper octave of Venus, a love vibration raised to the highest level—compassion. It is called the Christ vibration because the title *Saviour* reduces to 33. If lived to its ideal, this number will not be lowered to its base number 6; but if the individual cannot meet the standard it may be lived as a 6 vibration. It requires self-sacrifice and sometimes martyrdom. You are a teacher of teachers. You are required to spread your light and you must be willing to sacrifice for others or for your ideals. You are responsible for some special task; you have accepted this mission with conviction and an unfaltering steadfastness.

With your courage and tireless energy, you inspire others to follow your leadership. You show bravery in difficult situations and maintain your position regardless of consequences. You accept the burdens placed upon you with patience and forbearance, without expectation of reward or even appreciation. You may experience a crucifixion in emotions.

You are honest, self-disciplined, discriminating and law-abiding. You are also extremely versatile, creative, resourceful and imaginative. You appreciate art and beauty. Crowds disturb you; therefore, you prefer the country where you can get away from noise and turmoil. If you are not living up to the high potential of the 33, you may carry on as a 6, in which case domestic considerations take precedence.

If you are a negative 33/6, you are emotionally unstable and will sacrifice yourself for any cause, even though it be unworthy. You become a doormat for others. You are anxious, fearful and indecisive; your false bravado immediately crumbles when you are aggressively attacked. Much responsibility comes into your life for which you get no appreciation. You are incarnated for a special purpose and may be unhappy or frustrated if your particular mission is not found. You are a reformer and have a strong desire to make the world a better place in which to live.

33/6 AS A TEMPORARY VIBRATION: **Responsibility, self-sacrifice, courage.** You have entered a period in which you should maintain faith in your inner abilities. You have been given the opportunity to use your energies to help others alleviate their problems. They will seek you out and ask for assistance. You must use discrimination in selecting those tasks which require your energy. Compassion for others may be given freely; however, sacrifice for its own sake is self-defeating and wasteful if not applied to the most urgent causes.

Responsibilities will require your attention. Your home or people in the family may need your assistance, and older people might seek your shoulder to cry on. Accept your responsibilities with a loving heart and have faith and courage in the good service you are performing. The energy and strength you need will be available. Adhere to your principles in the face of all opposition, and the law of karma, as always, will repay in equal measure.

Special situations will open your eyes and allow you to see into yourself and perhaps present a purpose for your existence, a clue as to what direction your life should take.

TAROT SYMBOLISM: **Seven of Wands.** Six wands are already planted, which means that six senses (the sixth being intuition) are developed; and the seventh, the ability to leave the body at will, is being planted, or developed. The figure represents a person who is willing to work hard without thought of self, for he is dressed simply and works on a barren hilltop. He cares little for the luxuries of the world; he is interested only in higher development. Self-sacrifice and determination to give service to others are his goals. Sometimes this is a martyr's card.

ASTROLOGICAL CORRESPONDENCE: **Third decan Leo.** There is the power of the world beater in this area of the zodiac, but the problem is best expressed in the old proverb, "He who would conquer the world must first conquer himself." The fiery power of this decan (the total power of the fire trinity) may have enough impetus to propel you to extremes. You need to develop steady but progressive attitudes in making your way in the world. You have a strong pioneer spirit and innate leadership qualities. You are tireless and can inspire others to work with you for worthwhile goals.

34/7 AS A PERSONAL NUMBER VIBRATION: This number rules orderly growth and development. It is connected with the hidden mysteries of life. You can integrate the material, mental and spiritual worlds and bring about a systematic approach to your evolution.

You are practical and conventional, seldom overstepping the bounds of formal behavior. You stick to the facts as you see them. You are trustworthy, honest and patient, with a keen intelligence and discriminating mind. People can depend on you for straight-from-the-shoulder answers to their questions and sound advice for solving their problems. Your wisdom makes you a person who is much sought after.

You are philosophical and introspective, with strongly religious leanings. These inclinations to the spiritual aspects of life, coupled with an open mind, make you very intuitive. Your mind travels freely without obstruction, and you dislike any restrictive discipline.

Journeys will carry you to many places during your lifetime. You will experience all modes of travel, but flying is probably preferred.

Since you are articulate, lecturing and writing are good outlets. As expressive as you are, you have learned to be discreet and you can be trusted in all things. You have a determined approach to life, and seek your goals with a hopeful, expectant attitude. You embrace patience because you understand that progress takes time.

If you are a negative 34/7, you are impatient, impulsive and reckless. You are selfish and not above using your keen mind to outwit an opponent. At times you may resort to violence to attain your goals.

34/7 AS A TEMPORARY VIBRATION: Haste, messages, settlements. Pursuits are approaching completion, and your rewards are in direct ratio to the efforts expended. Stagnant conditions are stirred up, and final settlements are made.

This is an active, hopeful period in which you rapidly advance toward your goals. You may receive communications of all kinds, and these messages propel you onward. Your messages are dashed off in return. Romance is emphasized now, and messages of love fill the air.

A negative reaction brings about disputes, legal difficulties and delays. Business and love relationships can stagnate. Quarrels and domestic problems arise, sometimes because of jealousy or rash behavior. It requires extra effort on your part to bring about a settlement.

Travel, perhaps by air, is very likely in order to bring affairs to a successful conclusion. This period sets the wheels in motion. Your affairs are obviously progressing, and you can see that time brings all things to their designated completion.

TAROT SYMBOLISM: Eight of Wands. Eight live forces move swiftly through the air, unobstructed over open country. All follow the same direction, pointing east toward the light, and aim toward the earth and water. The lower wand is actually touching earth and water to show the blending of the three parts of mind and the four elements. It depicts the integration of the above with the below. The significance of this key is orderly growth, with much cosmic help.

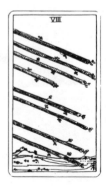

ASTROLOGICAL CORRESPONDENCE: First decan Sagittarius. You love outdoor exercise, walking, swimming, horseback riding and most games and sports. You also have a high regard for the spiritual side of life and believe that nature has a lot to offer. You have a hopeful and enthusiastic outlook on life, and you believe in right and justice. You are clever, quick-witted and humorous, while possessing a level-headed practicality that keeps you in balance with the times. Wisdom is one of your virtues. You are frank in speech, often blunt, but people know where you stand, which is admirable. You like to aim your arrow toward the stars and gain results quickly.

35/8 AS A PERSONAL NUMBER VIBRATION: This is called the inheritance 8 because its bearer usually inherits money, power or position, and sometimes all three. You have an individualistic, forceful mind, a tremendous vitality and a sense of what the public needs and how to supply it; therefore, you make a good executive, business person, teacher or researcher.

You work and play hard because you enjoy strenuous activity. You have a great deal of personal charm and are attractive to both sexes. You have many interests and could succeed in any number of professions. You are friendly, helpful and considerate. Emotional balance is important for you. You need stability to control your dynamic energy and achieve success.

Travel is one outlet for your tremendous vitality because it satisfies your need for freedom and action.

You may meet opposition during your lifetime; however, you are prepared. Inner strength and power and a healthy body give you the tools to defend your position. Through dedication and consistent force, you are eventually victorious.

The negative 35/8 produces doubt, unreasonableness and unbending judgments. You become self-indulgent and undisciplined, which brings on weakness, ill-health and many bitter emotional experiences.

However, with your vision and foresight, you have the opportunity to be a leader, who is able to supply both mind and body.

35/8 AS A TEMPORARY VIBRATION: **Preparedness, strength, inheritance, recognition, business.** This is a period when almost anything can happen; you should be prepared for whatever comes. The demand is toward more responsibility and discipline; you will need to use your stored energy source. You may be promoted and therefore have to withstand more pressure and more work. The honors bestowed now reflect past efforts.

This is a money vibration, and job advancement usually means an increase in salary. However, inheritances also come under a 35/8, so this is another source of money.

The pressures of this period will affect your health only if you work and worry too much. Allow sufficient time for rest, follow careful eating habits and relegate the demands of the material world to their proper place. Your health can improve through the exciting demands placed upon you; you will never feel more alive. So use the tremendous vitality this period has to offer. Get the job done, whatever the job happens to be.

TAROT SYMBOLISM: **Nine of Wands.** Eight firmly planted wands make a fence between the figure and the outer world. The ninth wand is held in readiness for use if necessary. This is a picture of strength and latent power, both physical and spiritual. It implies inherited strength for work well done in the past.

ASTROLOGICAL CORRESPONDENCE: **Second decan Sagittarius.** A strong independence is inherent in your nature. You are a bit impulsive and forceful. You like to be at the head of things, and you have the executive ability to back up that desire. You must not let overconfidence lead you to take on more responsibility than is comfortable. Keep your nervous energy in check and control your desire for too much expansion. You can usually find your way out of a jam, but it would be better to take the middle road and accept the simple laws of personal discipline.

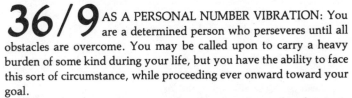

36/9 AS A PERSONAL NUMBER VIBRATION: You are a determined person who perseveres until all obstacles are overcome. You may be called upon to carry a heavy burden of some kind during your life, but you have the ability to face this sort of circumstance, while proceeding ever onward toward your goal.

Energy and common sense are part of your makeup; therefore, you preserve what resources you have. Your dependability, persistence and intensity lead you to a position of power and authority. You have a natural executive ability. You are trustworthy and can inspire and direct others. You see things from a broad viewpoint. Large and important enterprises are exciting, and you are not afraid to tackle them, for you do not fear responsibility.

Your strength is expressed in kindness. You are a believer in justice tempered by mercy. Sympathy for others increases your loving nature and blankets your life with good influences which lighten any loads you must carry.

Your quick intuition and inspired nature allow you to see into the future. This, combined with your inventive mind, creates the ability to discover. Your discoveries should be directed toward the uplifting of others. By performing service you find the Holy Grail or the Christ within your innermost being where all ideals await manifestation.

You are sometimes described as the salt of the earth, and you must be careful that your earthiness does not bring on waste and selfishness and impose additional burdens on you.

A negative 36/9 is easily upset and has continual ups and downs.

36/9 AS A TEMPORARY VIBRATION: **Obstacles, intuition, invention, leadership.** This vibration may temporarily place some burden on you; however, persevere with relentless determination. Remain in-

The Wands

tent upon your goal and have confidence that it will soon be reached; all problems will then be solved. Have joy in the prospect of this completion.

You are now endowed with great strength, intuition, vision and optimism. This can aid you in working creatively, finding solutions in research and completing projects in progress. If you wisely use these energies, you need not suffer any emotional difficulties.

The separations, endings and apparent losses in this vibration are necessary to free you for the new cycle you are about to enter. Problems may have to be settled legally during this time; by projecting optimism and honesty, a favorable outcome is assured. Any losses occurring now involve only those things that you do not need. Upon closer scrutiny, you will find that this is true.

TAROT SYMBOLISM: **Ten of Wands.** This key represents the binding of one's forces to preserve and protect them. Spiritual forces, if used as a spiritual fence between the individual and the affairs of earth, serve to blind one and lead to an attempt to escape from the discipline of matter before its lessons are learned. Thus it is not advancement but rather represents arrested development. The lesson of this key is to guard against the repression of energy and force and use it instead for invention and upliftment.

ASTROLOGICAL CORRESPONDENCE: **Third decan Sagittarius.** The ultimate decan of the fire signs sometimes brings emotions to extremes. You are impetuous and need to control your feelings when dealing with others, as they may not understand your personality. You must be careful not to be a plunger, dipping quickly into things without careful thought. You could, however, develop the ability to preserve your assets and become fortunate in speculative ventures. Your compassionate nature can be awakened so that a philosophic and prophetic nature comes to the surface, which could prove to be very beneficial for yourself and others.

3

THE

CUPS

37/1 AS A PERSONAL NUMBER VIBRATION: You are a mature, reserved individual whose calm exterior belies your desire to rule. You aspire to prominence, to be in a leadership position in which your inherent expansive and emotional nature can be expressed. Your friendly, kind and generous qualities promote goodwill among your followers.

A slight militancy emerges into a dedicated defense when you feel the insititution of the home and family is under attack either physically or intellectually. Although some 37/1's remain unmarried, they nevertheless value a home as a secure base for future happiness. The life partner you choose will be a great help toward your success, and together you will create peace and pleasant fellowship.

Business and religion are equally attractive to you. You are just as able to apply your nurturing and expansive philosophy to investments and international banking affairs as you are to the spiritual problems of others.

Travel and overseas projects intrigue you, and you could be attracted to some sort of foreign service as an ambassador or agent. Your talents and devotion bring you the position and emotional security you need. You then share your blessings with others.

If you are a negative 37/1 you have a calm exterior which conceals a dishonest, perhaps violent nature. You use all forms of trickery to gain your ends.

37/1 AS A TEMPORARY VIBRATION: Friendships, partnerships, love, family. During this calm, happy period, a friendship with an influential person can help you to achieve the results you desire. This help may come through your mate or through an existing relationship.

You will feel drawn to your family, ready to protect and defend them against any adversity. A slightly militant attitude arises when you feel they are threatened. The love vibration is strong, and if you are looking for a mate, you could very possibly find a suitable candidate. This is a fortunate vibration for making plans with the opposite sex.

You may be attracted to philosophy, science and the arts. Religious and spiritual subjects also interest you, and your creative talents find expression in these fields.

Business prospers and you benefit financially. Pursuits during this time may require travel, possibly over long distances.

KING of CUPS.

TAROT SYMBOLISM: King of Cups. The King carries both the scepter of power and the upright cup of controlled emotion. His throne, floating on water, represents the idea that his subconsious sustains him. The leaping fish on one side and the fish on the chain around his neck show his involvement in spiritual matters. The ship depicts his involvement in the world of commerce. He is the lord of wisdom and commerce because of his wise use of emotions.

ASTROLOGICAL CORRESPONDENCE: First decan Cancer. This decan is ruled by the Moon. You are mild, reserved and home-loving. The life partner you choose will be a great help toward your success. You aspire to prominence and could be attracted to some position in foreign service, such as ambassador or agent. Travel interests you. Friendships, love and partnerships are part of your lifestyle.

38/11 AS A PERSONAL NUMBER VIBRATION:
This is a powerful master number both spiritually and materially, as this vibration carries the gift of vision. You have achieved a perfect blend of the conscious and subconcious,

which grants you a rapport with spiritual things. You are poetic and imaginative and can see things that are hidden from most other people. Through dreams and visions, you see the goals you desire. You can act upon them and bring them into reality. You have an intense, powerful spirituality, with the visionary qualities of an avatar.

The security and material advantages of the world are yours. Love, success and a happy marriage blend to create the harmony you so desire, thus allotting you the leisure time in which to further pursue and develop your dreams and psychic faculties.

You are a good parent dedicated to your home and family. You receive much joy from them, and you take pride in their accomplishments and energetically back them in all their endeavors. Through your thoughtful interest, you become an influence in the lives of others. People are affected not so much by what you say as by the example you set. Your life is a pattern they wish to emulate.

Abuse of these beautiful energies through the extravagant use of your material wealth causes problems. Deception can degenerate into immorality, at which point discord disrupts the harmony of the home and business world.

You know that true happiness comes from service to others. Material donations are not enough; you have to develop the gifts of the spirit as well. You should engage in charity work or contribute to and participate in educational programs.

38/11 AS A TEMPORARY VIBRATION: **Love, marriage, dreams, visions, rewards.** This is a master number period which demands a great deal from you but promises even greater rewards. Your cup runneth over. Many advantages come your way, and your fondest desires can now be fulfilled. People in high positions not only offer you assistance but may bestow some sort of recognition upon you.

If romance has been lacking, this vibration should very nicely fill that void. The love you encounter now is deep and abiding and can develop into marriage. Existing relationships are enhanced and family members are drawn closer.

Your dreams bring messages from your subconscious. You are tuned in to secret areas of your being that are usually closed off. A powerful spiritual force is present, moving in your life to awaken a deeper part of you. This is a time to give not only of your material wealth, but also of your time, talents and compassion, the gifts that have the only true lasting value.

Metaphysical disciplines should be learned and practiced now, so that you can adequately contact your higher sources. So much of value will be found that the material benefits of this lucrative period will wane beside the glitter of the gifts of the soul.

TAROT SYMBOLISM: **Queen of Cups.** The Queen holds the ornate

QUEEN of CUPS.

cup of vision and sees in it the events in the sphere of the zodiac; therefore, the cup portrays the divine gift of reflective clairvoyance. She wears a red and blue robe that blends the conscious and subconscious minds. The cherubs on the throne represent the guardianship of the divine beings who protect and guide her.

ASTROLOGICAL CORRESPONDENCE: **Second decan Cancer.** Scorpio and Pluto are underlying influences in the second decan of Cancer. You are proud, reserved and introspective. Your perception makes you a visionary, and you tend toward spirituality. The 3, the number of Jupiter, and the 8, the number of Saturn, act in combination as if the planets were conjunct; this aspect is found in the charts of holy leaders and sages.

39/3 AS A PERSONAL NUMBER VIBRATION: You have selected a life of service to others. You offer affection, love and sympathy in order to help make the world a better place in which to live. You are a crusader who wants to feel that the world has benefited because of your sojourn in it. You are idealistic and philosophical. You desire justice and you will make a vigorous stand for your beliefs. No obstacle can deter you from finishing a project once you have begun.

A gentle poetic nature makes you a romantic. You dream beautiful unhurried dreams that inspire you to enlarge the scope of your life. Your imagination dovetails nicely with a keen intellect; together they achieve an expansiveness that inspires others.

You will live a long and healthy life, in peace and contentment, surrounded by friends and loved ones. The love you give is returned abundantly, which fills your cup even fuller, until the love must spill over into the lives of those who are in need. You exemplify the saying, "Love wasn't put in your heart to stay, Love isn't love 'til you give it away." Each time you give you are rewarded ten-fold; thus your life is ever enriched. You will communicate this love to all you contact.

If you are a negative 39/3, you live a sensual life, indulging your every need. You are lazy and sometimes insensitive to the suffering of others.

39/3 AS A TEMPORARY VIBRATION: **Love, propositions, vacations.** Thoughts of love dominate this period. You feel warm and friendly, and you desire to share these feelings with others; therefore you draw people to you. Friendships develop, one of which may deepen into a bond of love.

Messages and invitations of various kinds are possible. People seek you out, wishing to join you in a goodwill project. You may be offered a partnership or proposition.

This is a leisure time. Your unhurried attitude and general good feeling may prompt you to take a vacation or get away to a quiet spot that matches your contemplative mood. Faraway places lure you, and you should heed the call. Relaxation, love and affection are the goals of this romantic period.

A negative reaction brings contracts and propositions that should be looked into. There can be fraud and deceit. Any delays here are for the best.

Do something good for someone else now. Every effort on your part will be fully rewarded under this delightful vibration.

TAROT SYMBOLISM: **Knight of Cups.** Both Knight and horse are gentle and unhurried. The Knight approaches calmly with a cup of affection held out as an offering to humanity. His robe is decorated with the divine fish symbol. The stream, running serenely through the valley, depicts the Knight's calm emotional attitude. The entire picture is one of peace and contentment.

KNIGHT of CUPS.

ASTROLOGICAL CORRESPONDENCE: **Summer (Cancer, Leo Virgo).** Love dominates this period. Summer is a warm time of year when leisure or vacations promote affection and love. Cancer imbues you with a sympathetic and loving nature; Leo bestows powers of leadership and high goals; and Virgo demands service to the world. All these qualities combine to create an idealistic crusader.

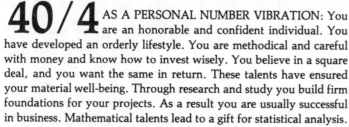 AS A PERSONAL NUMBER VIBRATION: You are an honorable and confident individual. You have developed an orderly lifestyle. You are methodical and careful with money and know how to invest wisely. You believe in a square deal, and you want the same in return. These talents have ensured your material well-being. Through research and study you build firm foundations for your projects. As a result you are usually successful in business. Mathematical talents lead to a gift for statistical analysis.

You have learned to deal wisely with people and are considerate of their needs. Your quiet, receptive nature is influenced by the feelings of those around you. Your studiousness and meditative nature find a natural channel in the study of literature.

You are a peacemaker and you handle emotions well. Love and passion have evolved into love and compassion for others. You are sure of the eternal life. Since you have the God symbol, 0, backing the 4 in 40, protection is assured. Inner guidance is always available.

If you are a negative 40/4, you see only difficulties and obstacles in your life. This creates confusion and disorder. You squander your money chasing illusive goals and build your castle upon sand.

If you maintain an orderly and secure existence, you will create a sound base from which to draw the strength to pursue realistic goals. Then you leave lasting values and substance in this world.

The Cups

40/4 AS A TEMPORARY VIBRATION: **Finances, building, birth.** This is a good planning period. New techniques can be implemented now. Building a business, a house, or both, are possible ventures. You are advised to use caution in all financial dealings; handle your money wisely. Whatever you plan can be successful if you invest wisely. Set up a budget and put your affairs in order. This period will require a systematic existence; only then will your subconscious carry out the plans you have devised.

Messages of all kinds are forthcoming. The birth of a child, the beginning of a business enterprise or a new lifestyle may be announced. These affairs all require that old habits be left behind; therefore, breaks and separations are a necessary part of this cycle.

Be discriminating about those in whom you place your confidence. Obstacles may present themselves; however, the solution to these problems will uncover past procedures that impeded your progress. With this knowledge, you realize that the obstacles are in reality a blessing.

PAGE of CUPS.

TAROT SYMBOLISM: **Page of Cups.** This quiet figure is beautifully dressed in the lotus-decorated costume of red and blue which indicates that the conscious and subconscious mind have made the wearer sure of eternal life. The lotus is a self-renewing plant, which contains both male and female elements. The Page's cup contains the fish, symbol of the divine; therefore, love and passion have turned to love and compassion for humanity.

ASTROLOGICAL CORRESPONDENCE: **Third decan Cancer.** The Piscean influence which underlies this decan of Cancer gives you literary ability. You are usually successful in business because your intuition and practical good sense make you a keen investor. You are gifted in making statistical judgments, careful in matters of finance and honest in business dealings. You are influenced by the feelings around you and prefer a peaceful, orderly environment in which to live.

41/5 AS A PERSONAL NUMBER VIBRATION: You are offered all the pleasures of the world in abundance. This number carries divine help and protection. You are extremely versatile because you are able to reflect upon the inspirations you receive. Through spiritual nourishment you translate concepts into reality; you create form where only ideas existed. You are thus able to enjoy all the material benefits the world has to offer because truly your cup runneth over.

You radiate love, faith and enthusiasm. You show courage when things go wrong. You can tackle anything, and usually do, with considerable success. Inspiration and energy combine for speedy and satisfactory results. You are a pioneer, you enjoy change, but desire practical and useful results.

Love, happiness and productivity follow you. Since you enjoy many of the pleasures of material living, you must control a tendency to indulge your senses. A pleasure-seeking personality can result and your abundant creative faculties are diffused in sensual pursuits.

Your creativity extends to the family, and you can produce many children. You will provide them with a loving, comfortable home. By applying your talents toward useful goals, you can achieve all the material wealth and comforts anyone could possibly desire. You can also create a loving atmosphere from which others can draw inspiration and nourishment.

41/5 AS A TEMPORARY VIBRATION: **Love, abundance, fertility, change.** Joy and contentment fill your life now. The abundant rewards of past efforts are available, and you radiate happiness and confidence. You enjoy the beauty and pleasure surrounding you and feel good about yourself as a person.

Creative forces are at work here, producing not only material goods but relationships as well. The love of your life may appear, or existing ties may be deepened. The birth of children brings happiness and reinforces your belief in the goodness of life.

Conditions are changing; new opportunities will alter many habits and situations. Take your time making decisions because impulsiveness can overturn all the good effects of this period. Hasty moves in business can bring losses. Love relationships may falter if the selfish appetites of one party are indulged at the expense of the other. Use the creative and potentially fulfilling vibrations of this cycle wisely, and you can expect your wildest dreams to come true.

TAROT SYMBOLISM: **Ace of Cups.** A white dove, symbolic of peace, truth and the Holy Spirit, drops the seal of Jehovah into the cup. The five streams of water emanating from the cup represent the five senses overflowing into a lotus-filled pool. When we give our sensitivities and emotions, we create an unending supply of love. The cup is held by the guardian angel or the Hand of God, from which cosmic inspiration flows. Falling drops of water take on the form of yods, the divine power.

ASTROLOGICAL CORRESPONDENCE: **The element water (Cancer, Scorpio, Pisces).** All the qualities of the water signs are built into this vibration. You have the loving, protective nature of Cancer, the deep creative understanding of Scorpio and the sensitive, reflective qualities of Pisces. You have courage when things go wrong. Your inspiration comes through receptivity and reflection.

42/6

AS A PERSONAL NUMBER VIBRATION: You have a friendly, cooperative nature. Your desire to help others and your complete dedication to peace and understanding equip you well for the ministry.

Professional work along artistic lines is your forte as well. You would be a fine singer. You have a creative imagination and a strong leaning toward the mystical. You should make an effort to train your intuition along practical lines. You need an outlet for your inner urges and a means to exercise your imagination. You could find it through writing stories. Children's stories might appeal to your sensitive nature. You see beauty everywhere and should express it in a tangible way for others to enjoy.

Your personal charm and your pleasure-loving, generous nature draw others to you. You intuitively realize their needs and work to create a happy atmosphere wherever you are. You need the sociability of friends and would not be happy living alone. Since you are hospitable and repay kindness with kindness, there is little danger that you will have a solitary life. However, those who try to fulfill their own selfish needs will, under this vibration, feel lonely and misunderstood.

Home and personal relationships are important to you; you need to be discriminating to control the emotion involved here. You believe in doing the right thing and sharing equally in all relationships and binding contracts. When you make commitments, others are assured of an honest and abiding bargain.

42/6 AS A TEMPORARY VIBRATION: **Contracts, marriage, meditation.** There is a blending of minds now, a harmony on the mental plane that seeks to bring ideas to a common meeting ground. Contracts and agreements that have been pending can be settled amicably and fairly with both sides gaining equally.

Your cooperative attitude creates an atmosphere of happiness and harmony. Worthwhile friendships will form and bring personal fulfillment. This is a vibration of love. For some it brings love affairs, for others, engagement and marriage.

This is also a meditative period in which you will be urged to give form to your inner feelings. Beauty appeals to the sense of harmony that you are experiencing. Time spent alone should be used to get in touch with those inner feelings and to bring them out where others can appreciate them. Begin to develop any creative talent you possess.

Since the keywords now are *love* and *cooperation*, you will encounter situations in which these qualities must be exercised. Do not allow misunderstandings to lead to separations; then the meditative aspects of this cycle will degenerate into loneliness. Seek peace through understanding and you will benefit from any contacts you now make.

TAROT SYMBOLISM: **Two of Cups.** The man and woman are exchanging cups to demonstrate the law of give and take. This is also the symbol of the duality of creation. The winged lion above the caduceus is a composite symbol meaning, "The adept who has power to interpret to others knowledge of the higher worlds." The woman is dressed in white with a blue outer robe to show the purity underlying the soul or subconscious. The man's costume has a yellow background which stands for consciousness and is decorated with trefoils symbolizing the trinity. The house in the background represents the creativity of humanity or the united effort of male and female.

ASTROLOGICAL CORRESPONDENCE: **First decan Cancer.** You are receptive, sensitive, affectionate and usually psychic. You meet people with graciousness and charm. You need to guard against being too sentimental or effusive, as others may misinterpret your motives. You are very creative and need interesting activity to provide balance in your life. Home decorating or other types of art appeal to you. You would be most content not being famous but rather living a happy, peaceful life, surrounded by a loving family. If there is a keyword in this decan, it is *love*.

43/7 AS A PERSONAL NUMBER VIBRATION: You are a true friend, affectionate and tolerant of others' whims and foibles. Your pledge of friendship endures many tests. Your sympathetic nature and sense of justice reach out to the young and the underprivileged; you are always willing to help someone in need.

Your gentle nature may hide a strong determination to reach your goals. You know when to be silent. Clear thinking is one of your best attributes, and it is most effectively developed in constructive activity. Your positive approach to life, temperate habits and ability to make logical decisions create an atmosphere for success. Fulfillment and abundance are the fruits you pick as the result of your clever productive actions. Your achievement of power and financial security allows you the freedom to enjoy the comforts you have earned. You enjoy being in a position of power. Your power extends to healing, in situations where the energy you possess can be transferred to the energy fields of others, thus creating a new life for them.

You are a dependable person with poise and a sense of balance. Your strong intuitive powers and discernment are based on your ability to accumulate facts. These talents will contribute to your success as a teacher, writer or speaker, if you choose any of these professions.

Whatever profession you choose, you will bring to it your constructive and creative ideas, positive attitude and fine mind. The rewards will be plentiful. However, you must control any desires to overindulge in food, drink and unhealthy relationships. Excesses will lead to physical and emotional pain. Rather, share the abundance of your life with those who are less fortunate. Such an effort increases your own store.

43/7 AS A TEMPORARY VIBRATION: Abundance, rejoicing, healing. Congratulations are in order. This is a period of rejoicing because the results of your past endeavors are now evident. You have concluded matters successfully and realized your goals. The rewards are yours.

If your pursuits have been professional, you now realize financial increases, promotion and business expansion. If health has been an issue, healing takes place. Family difficulties smooth out, and you are overwhelmed by success, peace and extra benefits that you are now enjoying.

This is a restful vibration, so loosen up and enjoy it. Follow your routine or take a vacation, but maintain the status quo. Pushing new ventures and pursuing new avenues is not part of this cycle. Sit back and relax.

Be careful that your celebration does not degenerate into overindulgence. Too much of the good life can bring on physical discomforts. If you select your partners indiscriminately, relationships can suffer. So eat, drink and be merry in moderation. You have earned it.

TAROT SYMBOLISM: Three of Cups. This key depicts the celebration of bounty and good fortune. Three maidens jubilantly toast the happy outcome of their work—the abundant harvest pictured around them.

ASTROLOGICAL CORRESPONDENCE: Second decan Cancer. The sensitivity in this area of the zodiac is subtle and inclined toward the occult. You are progressive, deeply emotional and sentimental. Your experiences become more definite; your goals, more clearly defined. You are somewhat secretive about your personal life and often silent and introspective. You know instinctively when to talk and when to listen. You may be surprised at your strength in an emergency. You prefer to lead an even-tempered life, but you can really spring into action if the occasion demands it. You fully enjoy the good things in life. You have the capacity to accomplish skilled work in valuable enterprises.

44/8 AS A PERSONAL NUMBER VIBRATION: This is a master number and, as such, demands more from you. You are a steady worker. You will persevere in your chosen goal because you exercise discipline. You conform to the demands of a situation, and make the best of it. You prefer to be in an environment where steady progress brings concrete results. Your success comes from useful enterprises.

You are extremely resourceful and cautious. You plan your actions well in advance. You could achieve distinction in political or military affairs, where self-discipline and expediency are the keys to success. You are brave in battle. You possess the will to face adversity and the energy to overcome obstacles through sustained effort.

Common sense and logic back up your judgments. You enjoy order and stability. Yours is a conventional approach to life. There is a great deal of the materialist in you. Guard against too deep a desire for fame and possessions. This can lead to overwork, poor health and material losses. You then close yourself into an ignorant, do-nothing world and become discontented and frustrated. Therefore, you should investigate new opportunities to broaden your horizons. Make room in your orderly existence for things you did not plan on.

You are well developed physically, mentally and emotionally, but you may be missing the intuitive link. The opportunity to develop this side of your character is present. Work on becoming aware of what you cannot see; tune in to your inner self. When you have achieved this awareness, you can express the master number vibration. Serve the material needs of the world through productive actions, actions first inspired on the inner plane. You can supply the comfort and common sense advice that help keep this world together.

44/8 AS A TEMPORARY VIBRATION: **Karma, reevaluation, opportunity.** In this master number period, you are being offered an opportunity to reevaluate your present circumstances. You have the time to contemplate the value of the rewards you are now receiving. If past efforts have been productive, you will see an increase in status and finances. Others will bestow kindnesses upon you; friends and family gather and increase. However, past efforts may only bring unwanted and restricting burdens. You may want to give up, sit back and do nothing. If you feel discontented and closed in, you need to establish new priorities and set worthwhile goals.

The experiences of this period may graphically depict the missing link in your makeup. Chances are the material world is well represented. Things are happening physically, and you are reacting emotionally, which sets you to work mentally. Your mind contemplates and wonders if this is all there is. At this moment you are reaching out for the Hand of God or the intuitive side of your nature. You are looking for the answer that puts your world into perspective. That answer can be found only within yourself. You can find that answer now and give it form by sharing with others the rewards or experiences this cycle has given you. Your advice and wisdom will set others upon their path of liberation.

The Cups

TAROT SYMBOLISM: **Four of Cups.** The figure is seated in quiet contemplation and concentration. He sees three full cups in front of him, and he seems unaware of a fourth cup being offered by the Hand of God coming from the cosmic cloud (hidden wisdom). If he seeks divine aid with patience, meditation, self-control and persistence, it is available to him. His calm physical appearance shows that mental activity is what brings results. He must choose a worthwhile goal or the proffered cup could be lost.

ASTROLOGICAL CORRESPONDENCE: **Third decan Cancer.** This decan will be felt more on the mystical or inner plane than on the extroverted personality plane. Thus you are more sensitive to vibrations around you or those coming into your aura from outside contacts. You are kind, hospitable and sympathetic. You may be attracted to a career in nursing, dietetics or some phase of social work dealing with the handicapped. A life of service to others befits this vibration. Your ideals are high, but you need to keep your dreams practical.

45/9 AS A PERSONAL NUMBER VIBRATION: This is a highly sensitive, mystical vibration. You will not be satisfied with worldly success alone. The positive energies of this vibration can lead to high psychic development.

You sympathize with the unfortunate and take on their heartaches. You love to teach and serve; you have the fortitude to face emergencies with courage seldom found in other number vibrations. Working with groups and organizations can be satisfying; you can effectively teach them through your own experiences.

You are secretive, reserved and proud. You are determined to successfully carry out your ambitions, as you are also receptive to new ideas, willing to work, and feel no limitations in doing so. This drive can be detrimental if it causes you to overwork.

There is conflict between your emotions and your common sense. You need to practice control and conserve your energy. Do not go to extremes in pursuit of your ideals. Emotional dissatisfacton arises only when you dwell on the past. Disappointments, sorrow and loss ensue when you stubbornly cling to old ways that have outlived their usefulness. Use the experiences of the past as stepping-stones to higher elevations. Then through your words and example you can teach others to renew their lives and build a brighter future.

You are affectionate and generous. If things go wrong, you are eager to set them right. Look at what you have as resources, rather than at what you do not have or have lost. Then you will achieve the delicate balance necessary for your happiness. With patience and hope, stressful situations can be transformed into lessons which you can teach to others.

This vibration often produces an early marriage and many children.

45/9 AS A TEMPORARY VIBRATION: **Old friends, partial gains, learning experiences.** There can be gains and inheritances during this cycle, though perhaps they are not up to your expectations. You should not brood over any partial losses that occur now. Use what you gain to initiate something new. Do not spend your energy regretting past mistakes. Learn from them and proceed onward. There will be sufficient gains here for you to realize that a better use of your personal energy will bring even more reward the next time around.

An old friend may return for a visit and remind you of your past. Use discrimination in dealing with those you encounter; don't expect too much from them. When you have successfully learned from the past and let go of it, you will form new alliances that will open doors to the future. You will become aware of some of your own resources which you have overlooked until now.

TAROT SYMBOLISM: **Five of Cups.** A cloaked figure looks sorrowfully at three spilled cups, not realizing that there are two cups left filled. This indicates that losses should not be brooded over. By turning around to face a new start, other resources are always found with which to carry on. In other words, do not waste energy regretting past mistakes; learn from them, and go ahead.

ASTROLOGICAL CORRESPONDENCE: **First decan Scorpio.** You have definite goals and a fixed determination to carry them out. You feel a sense of inner power, which may be expressed as pride or self will. You are strongly attracted to the occult. You seem to have boundless energy; you quickly bounce back from any defeat with renewed vigor and quietly go about your business. You know the power of silence. Many strongly motivated reformers or missionaries are born in this decan of Scorpio; the desire to change things for the better seems inherent. You are a tireless worker when motivated by your ideal.

46/1 AS A PERSONAL NUMBER VIBRATION: You

have a dominating personality. You work and play with equal passion. You win others through your charm and wit, cloaking your strong will under a gentle manner. You are a natural leader. You like to be the center of your world and must guard against taking advantage of those who admire your popularity, or those who could be misguided by your fine showmanship.

You have high ideals and could choose a profession in science or philosophy. With your highly developed psychic sense and strong intuition, you could also be an inventor. Any of these pursuits enable you to express your humanitarian ideals. If you choose an idealistic profession, keep your goals practical. This number often acquires money, but loses it if ideals are impractical. But this number is also willing to start again, and you can attain another fortune.

Positions of power and authority are natural for you. You are strong willed and intense. You set your goal and go after it in a steady and methodical manner. You are, however, willing to share your good fortune because you are generous, warm and tender.

Your ability, imagination and enthusiasm bring you success in work and play. A happy childhood and comforting memories give you the stability to venture forth in the world expecting, and therefore receiving, the best life has to offer.

If you are negative 46/1 you live in the past, surrounded by memories, refusing to accept the present. You can be childish and irresponsible, thereby attracting, as a natural reaction to your output, a worthless circle of acquaintances.

46/1 AS A TEMPORARY VIBRATION: **Good karma, new opportunities, success.** You are now the center of attention. You may receive gifts or inheritances of some kind from situations that existed in the past. A childhood acquaintance may appear with a gift, or a kind act in the past may bear fruit today. It seems that your attentions are riveted on the past through the happy events of the present. Joy and contentment fill your heart; you should share these feelings with those around you.

Your environment changes somehow. Either you find yourself in new places with new people, both of which promise good returns, or your old environment receives new vibrancy through fresh opportunities and relationships.

Through subtle persuasion, you can win others to your way of thinking. They will follow your strong lead because you are presently tuned in, psychically and intuitively. You can achieve any goals you set for yourself now, if you maintain a steady application of personal energy. Your enthusiastic attitude and flair for the dramatic during this cycle impresses others and aids you in gaining the support you need to be successful.

TAROT SYMBOLISM: **Six of Cups.** The six cups are brimming with flowers, showing fruition. The five-pointed-star flower indicates human emotions purified and transmuted into compassionate love. The childish male figure in the Fool's cap recalls key 0, or Uranus, which, exalted in Scorpio, here implies that the highest gift is purified love. The cross, commonly called Saint Andrew's cross, is the cross of humility. The significance is that while we "become as little children" (Matthew 18:3) or believe as little children on the earthly plane, we manifest our progress.

ASTROLOGICAL CORRESPONDENCE: **Second decan Scorpio.**
Unique experiences come into your life. Sometimes it is a sorrow
which quickens your sympathies or otherwise turns your ideas
toward the spiritual. You are willing to share with others; at all times
you perform what you believe to be your duty as a good citizen. This
area of the zodiac is at a peak of the solar year. Great creative power
is a birth endowment here. Many musical and scientific geniuses have
been born at this time of year. You get along well with others unless
they try to dominate you; then the quiet rebel within you comes to
the surface. For the most part your charm outweighs your ag-
gressiveness, and much happiness and achievement is rightfully
yours.

47/11 AS A PERSONAL NUMBER VIBRATION:
This is a master number vibration. During
your lifetime you will face many tests of character and emotional
stability. There is conflict between the emotional and practical sides
of your nature; therefore, determination, caution and tact must be
your watchwords. To perform at the most efficient level, you need to
have a goal. Once you do, your personal charm and magnetism will
sway others, and you will be offered the wealth and glamour of the
world.

Great dreams of success and wealth dance in your head; visions of
grandeur take form in your imagination. Your abilities to influence
others, inspire confidence and attract affection assures success; success that worldly people imagine they want. There is a flaw, however.
As you attain these treasures one by one, you begin to realize that
they do not bring the happiness you had expected. They do not have
any real value. You are the epitome of the adage, "To whom much is
given, much is required." You are required to use discrimination—to
weigh, test, balance and discard.

Use silence and imagination to gain wisdom and inspiration. When
your emotions are controlled, inspiration guides your life. You learn
to handle money well and would be good in financial areas, such as
banking or accounting. You also have great creative potential. You
grasp new ideas easily and work with great speed. In whatever field
you choose, you must express humanitarian qualities for a fulfilling
life.

You are adaptable, yet you have a strong will which helps you meet
unexpected challenges. Use your natural and spiritual riches to bring
stability and harmony into the lives of others. Learn the necessary
discrimination to make the right choices. Do not mistake emotion for
love or allow your illusions to affect your need for reality.

47/11 AS A TEMPORARY VIBRATION: **Discrimination, dreams
fulfilled.** This master number vibration demands additional effort

The Cups

from you but promises greater dividends. Do not sit back and build castles in the air. You could scatter your creative energies in the fanciful pursuit of success. Many of your imagined desires can become realities now if you develop realistic methods to achieve them. You need willpower and determination to implement the ideas that you select as worthy.

Many temptations can arise to distract you from the actual purpose of this cycle. These temptations will test your discriminative faculties. You will have to decide, through weighing, selecting and discarding, where your true values lie. Maintain a balance between the emotional and practical factors and make your plans accordingly.

You may have mystical or psychic experiences. Use those experiences and rely on your intuition for guidance. Make your choices wisely during this cycle; be ever aware of the true value behind the illusions you see. The proper selections can bring true love, happy marriage, material prosperity and spiritual peace.

TAROT SYMBOLISM: **Seven of Cups.** The figure stands facing seven cups filled with symbols of the gifts and tests to be handled during this life. These seven are: vanity, fame, ego, illusion, jealousy, frivolity and glamour. All are nebulous (floating on clouds). They represent what the worldly person imagines are desirable, but as they are attained one by one, it is realized that they do not bring happiness or any real value in life.

ASTROLOGICAL CORRESPONDENCE: **Third decan Scorpio.** You may experience many domestic changes which will demand that you develop patience. You have ESP, which can be developed into prophetic or healing power. Strong interest in the occult, inherent in all the Scorpio decans, is especially strong in the third because of the trinity of rulers: the Moon, Neptune and Pluto. You are a romantic. Because you are deeply affectionate and loyal, you would become deeply depressed if the object of your love proved faithless. Try to be cautious in placing your affections. Do not build up illusion over any human being; to do so opens the possibility of disappointment. You handle money well and would do well in financial pursuits. You are flexible without being wishy-washy. Weakness is no part of your character.

48/3 AS A PERSONAL NUMBER VIBRATION: Worldly success comes to you quite easily; however, as each possession is gained, you set it aside and go on searching for the satisfaction it should have brought. You yearn for something more, and when you realize that the material world alone cannot offer you the necessary fulfillment, you may turn toward the spiritual. You should not, however, turn your back completely on the mundane, for that could obstruct the practical mechanics of living. Learn to use the material, without depending on it.

You are romantic, sincere and affectionate. You have high ideals. You appreciate beauty and the arts and have your share of creative ability. Your psychic and prophetic abilities are well developed. Your impressionable nature would find the arts a good channel for success.

You are quiet, persistent and dependable. But you may be too psychic and sensitive for your own comfort. You have a good sense of values and prefer to live conservatively. You believe in giving a good day's work to your employer. If you were the boss, you would expect the same from your employees. A sense of fair play is one of your assets. You have the ability to see both sides of a problem and judge fairly.

Learning to laugh in the face of difficulties will relieve your intolerance of the purely materialistic side of life. You must remember that your keen sense of responsibility toward others, your sympathy for their suffering and your desire to do your part in the community and the world can be expressed through material means in many cases. Your love of animals and need to protect them is expressed here also. You must detach yourself from materialism, though you may be required to use materialistic means to accomplish your mission.

48/3 AS A TEMPORARY VIBRATION: **Success, success abandoned, travel.** You have reason to celebrate. Many of your goals have been reached, and the rewards are forthcoming. You feel generous and loving; you want to share the good things with those around you.

Horizons broaden, and as they do, new relationships form. Perhaps a new love is among them. Travel may be a part of the picture, lending even more excitement to an already festive time. Be aware that what seems most important now may turn out to be unimportant in the future. Know, too, that dissipation of energy can result in unstable conditions. If you find the goals you have attained bring little satisfaction, you should seek to operate from a higher level. Use your material gains to alleviate the sufferings of others. Some experience during this cycle may be the catalyst that turns your materialistic mind toward the spiritual and humanitarian realm.

TAROT SYMBOLISM: **Eight of Cups.** There are eight full cups representing the three parts of the consciousness and the five senses, all under control (because the cups are upright). Yet the lone figure is leaving all that behind and walking toward the dark mountain of the unknown. Penetrating the mysteries hidden in the mountain will bring the wisdom being sought. The robe is red to signify desire for further knowledge. Under the guidance of the Sun and Moon (eclipse symbol), he is responding to his inner urge for something higher.

ASTROLOGICAL CORRESPONDENCE: **First decan Pisces.** Sometimes you worry over things that never happen and expend unnecessary energy in doing so. Develop a philosophy of faith in yourself and in the future. You are very sympathetic toward animals; you will adopt a stray cat or dog who seems unfed and unwanted. This comes from your deep desire to help those who suffer. This same understanding includes people, of course. You are hospitable and generous. You have the gift of wisdom which makes you kind and just toward others. Poets, musicians and scientists are born in this area of the zodiac. The poet Longfellow, the pianist-composer Chopin and the scientist Copernicus were born in this decan.

49/4 AS A PERSONAL NUMBER VIBRATION: You

are a person of many gifts—executive ability, integrity, intuition and a sense of justice, to name just a few. You can apply these attributes to practical business enterprises and achieve excellent results.

You are diplomatic in your relationship with others, patient and honest in conducting your affairs. You also have a sense of when to act and when to wait, an essential ingredient of success.

You have emotional control in both business and personal matters. Material success, physical well-being and security go with this vibration. Material happiness and contentment are yours.

You love to display the good life you have attained. Your home will reflect this in the form of fine furnishings and full cupboards. This is the result of the pride and satisfaction you feel in your achievements. You enjoy good health and a hearty appetite. You are an example for others to follow by depicting what hard work and perseverence can ultimately bestow upon the achiever.

If you are a dreamy 49/4 you develop a lot of theories that are seldom carried out. This is because success seems to come too easily. Drive does not seem necessary, and inertia prevents you from attaining all that you are capable of. You are more intent on personal satisfaction than achievement, and you can become sated by your own desires. Insincerity creeps in, and your ego inflates along with your body, as a result of a gluttonous approach to life. Ill health can result.

However, the tendency under this vibration is toward a balance between the mind and emotions. This leads you onward and upward, in both mental and spiritual development.

49/4 AS A TEMPORARY VIBRATION: **Good health, satisfaction, marriage to a wealthy individual.** This is an excellent cycle for business matters, as long as you maintain an honest, persevering attitude. Through steady application, the coffers are filled, and you feel a sense of satisfaction and physical accomplishment at a job well done.

Outer comfort lends inner tranquillity, a healing balm for any ailment. Your optimistic, serene attitude will bring about improvements in health. You may put on weight; therefore, be selective of the type and amount of food you eat.

Marriage here will usually involve wealth and may be for security instead of, or along with, love. The home will be well supplied with food and material comforts.

Be careful not to overindulge in food or drink. Examine your pursuits and desires now. Will they lead to freedom from anxiety, poverty and insecurities or just replace one set of restrictions with another?

TAROT SYMBOLISM: **Nine of Cups.** The seated figure is the picture of physical and emotional well-being. His cups are full and he is protected by the blue curtain of the creative mind. A balance of mind and emotions always brings material success and inner satisfaction. This is the card of fulfilled hopes and wishes.

ASTROLOGICAL CORRESPONDENCE: **Second decan Pisces.** This is a sensitive and affectionate decan. You are unusually fond of your home and family. You are tenacious in your attachments and may have to learn to give others the same kind of freedom you want for yourself. Your psychic nature is well developed. Your intuitions are keen and helpful as you believe more and more in yourself. You work better and live more happily when practical, emotional balance is gained; otherwise you may become hypersensitive. Use your fine strength of character wisely.

50/5 AS A PERSONAL NUMBER VIBRATION: This is the vibration of lasting success and happiness.

It bestows a life surrounded by friends and affection.

You are romantic and intensely emotional. You are devoted to your family, and you seek a mate who epitomizes the perfect love. Personal magnetism makes you attractive to the opposite sex, so there should be plenty of candidates to choose from.

Your life will be one of activity and movement. You are a socializer who enjoys conversation and people. Public life may draw you. There you can use your eloquence in lecturing and public speaking for the pursuit of social betterment. You could also succeed in literature and science. You are especially good in mathematics and could work at accounting or analysis, professions that require your keen perception.

You are both creative and imaginative. Your instinctive understanding of others makes them seek your counsel. Leadership comes naturally, and your energies find constructive outlets.

With all your possibilities for achievement, you nevertheless prefer beauty and pleasure to wealth and fame. Your contentment comes

The Cups

from love of family and friends. You enjoy being able to move freely in, and communicate with, the world around you. All numbers containing 0 bestow divine protection, and your sense of security shows in your relaxed and confident personality.

A negative use of these energies brings waste, loss of or betrayal by friends, and family troubles. You will seek freedom from all responsibilities and become enslaved by this very need.

50/5 AS A TEMPORARY VIBRATION: **Love, family ties, happy changes.** This is an extremely active period of socializing with family and friends. Happiness and contentment abound. A special person may enter your life, one who represents your ideal image of a perfect mate. The love relationship that ensues will bring lasting enjoyment.

Many happy changes occur now. You may move into a new environment which promises greater fulfillment, or you may alter the present situation to your benefit.

You may receive honors and gifts. They are the rewards of past efforts, for which you could also receive public recognition. Conversations, messages, letters and meetings bring good news and promising opportunities.

However, the overall energies of this period encourage you to relax, take a trip, and enjoy the fellowship of good friends and the pleasures of close family ties. A negative use of these same energies can cause family dissension and difficulty with friends.

TAROT SYMBOLISM: **Ten of Cups.** Ten full, upright cups are elevated in the heavens. They are the rainbow of happiness fulfilled. The man and woman embrace, exalting the elevation of emotional life to a high state of consciousness. The children dance happily under the protective rainbow of promise. All good things of earth are pictured: lush green growth, water and the house, which denote permanence of achievement. Here, love has been raised to the plane of compassion.

ASTROLOGICAL CORRESPONDENCE: **Third decan Pisces.** The natives of this last Piscean cycle are endowed with a psychic and intuitive nature. The practical side needs developing. Learn to use logical thinking with your intuition to bring about wise conclusions. Learn not to be easily led by stronger and more aggressive natures. You are really more likely to be right if you follow what intuition tells you. Learn to interpret its signals.

This is the final cycle of the solar year. It contains strong vibrations for happiness if you make positive choices and form constructive habits for progressive action toward your spiritual goal.

4

THE

SWORDS

51/6 AS A PERSONAL NUMBER VIBRATION: You apply the spirit of a warrior to whatever cause you choose. Your leadership ability and your desire to uphold truth and justice qualify you for such a profession as the law, government or the military. You are intelligent and perceptive; you are able to make sound judgments, based on the facts, balanced with mercy. You adhere to the teachings of the past. You exercise firm authority that serves you well in friendships, but can often prolong enmities.

You could be successful in the sciences such as chemistry or medicine. You probably lean toward professions in the law or the military, where life and death decisions are commonplace and where you can exercise your wisdom and sense of balance.

You have an active mind, full of ideas which could bring you abundant wealth. Because of your abilities, you will advance in any under-

The Swords taking. You are cautious, yet you seem to walk through life untroubled, even in the midst of turmoil. You keep on smiling and talking cheerfully while subduing your inner fears; however, you are ever alert and observant and always prepared for all possibilities.

There is a remote possibility of assassination threats if you are in prominent public office.

An imbalance in this vibration can make you overly stern or cruel. Your harsh actions many times result in legal difficulties. You create enemies in your relentless drive for power; these rivals resent your injustices and stand ever ready to take revenge.

51/6 AS A TEMPORARY VIBRATION: **Legal dealings, justice, perception, authority.** During this cycle, disagreements and hostilities can result in lawsuits or legal dealings of some kind. You must be alert and stand guard against the harsh actions of rivals. However, injustices will be corrected. The law of balance will be rule. True and false will be separated.

Maintain a cool, impartial attitude. Weigh all cases fairly to uphold the law. Your mind is keen, perceptive and extremely active now. Rely on it now to find alternative procedures for handling your affairs. Keep a positive outlook, a cheerful frame of mind and a vigilant attitude. You are the warrior fighting for the right; you will overcome all rivals.

The challenging ideas that arise within can bring you the success and authority you desire. Listen carefully and follow your intuition.

KING of SWORDS.

TAROT SYMBOLISM: **King of Swords.** A seated figure holds the upraised sword of activity, keen perception and discrimination. The screen behind the throne displays the butterfly, symbol of recurring life and circumstances. The waxing and the waning moons symbolize ever-changing ideas and opinions. The sword divides the false ideas from the true. The king sees the crux of the matter, and with swift justice sets matters right.

ASTROLOGICAL CORRESPONDENCE: **First decan Libra.** You are intelligent and perceptive. You have the ability to judge both sides and to make keen assessments. You are likely to advance in any undertaking; you are untroubled in the midst of turmoil, for you keep smiling and talking cheerfully. You balance your intelligence with mercy; you are truly a warrior fighting for right and justice.

52/7 AS A PERSONAL NUMBER VIBRATION: You
are high minded, noble and humanitarian, uncontaminated by the sordid side of life. You stand alone because your wisdom places you above the multitudes. Supported by the experiences of the past, you face the uncertainties of the future with

confidence. Changing events and conditions do not dim your faith; you maintain your poise even under occasional emotional stress. You can always draw from your power reserve.

Most likely you are well-educated. Your liberal ideas allow your quick, perceptive mind to understand things beyond the ordinary person's ability to comprehend. This quality sets you apart, and you may decide to close the door to the material world and live a solitary existence in the spiritual realm. Because of these factors, this vibration is known as one of separation, sterility and widowhood.

You are kind, patient and courageous. You try to live a well-balanced life. You finish whatever tasks you begin. However, you are more interested in the philosophical and spiritual than the material. You love nature and prefer to live in the country.

If you express the negative side, you are narrow-minded and mean. Your jealousy drives others away, assuring that you will have a solitary life. Gossip, harsh words and a bigoted attitude further alienate even the most understanding friends. You seem determined to be alone, although the drive to be alone may be entirely unconsious.

52/7 AS A TEMPORARY VIBRATION: **Change, separation, meditation.** Changing conditions may separate you temporararily from familiar lifestyle patterns and you may experience a period of solitude in which you feel lonely and isolated. This is necessary to stimulate thoughts and ideas related to the spiritual world. You must learn to strike a balance between what appears to be real and what is real. In this manner you discover what has real value for you.

Trips into the country or to the seashore are therapeutic for you now. Take along a few books on philosophy and religion and allow your mind to travel as well.

Remember that the separations during this cycle are part of the everchanging rhythm of life, and changes bring new opportunities and challenges.

TAROT SYMBOLISM: **Queen of Swords.** The queen sits on a throne decorated with butterflies, symbols of incarnation and reincarnation. She holds the active sword raised to discriminate between true and false. Her left hand is extended toward the unknown future, but she is ready to face whatever comes. She knows she has experience as her foundation, and she can draw upon that. Although the Sun is obscured by clouds, denoting that more is to be revealed, she is confident of the future. The waxing and waning moons on her throne show changing conditions. She leans on divine protection, symbolized by cherubs on the throne. Her throne is set high where the air is pure and uncontaminated by the sordid side of life. The single bird overhead indicates the solitude she has chosen because her wisdom sets her apart.

QUEEN of SWORDS.

ASTROLOGICAL CORRESPONDENCE: **Second decan Libra.** Venus and Uranus hold sway in the second decan of Libra. They produce a high-minded humanitarian. You lean to the spiritual and prefer the quiet atmosphere of the country where your mind can meditate without the distraction of city noises. You are intelligent, quiet and introspective. Your great wisdom may set you apart from the common crowd.

53/8

AS A PERSONAL NUMBER VIBRATION: You know that you have a lot to accomplish and no effort is too great, no obstacle too difficult. You like authority and know how to assert it; however, your assertiveness may be construed as tyrannical. Because your head rules your heart, you may seem set and severe, but you rule with a pure heart and chivalrous motives.

Protection and defense against danger are your main concerns. Rather than sit back and wait, you prefer to be the aggressor. You make progress through your skill and ability to lead. Your bravery in the face of danger would make you a fine military leader.

You could also excel in law as a criminal lawyer or judge. You have the necessary intellectual and communicative skills to sway others. With your strength and fine sense of timing, you could achieve professional status in any of the aggressive contact sports.

You have the ability to separate fact from fiction; no detail escapes your notice. Your fine power of discrimination would make you an excellent detective.

If you are a negative 53/8, you always seem ready for a fight. Your cockiness alienates others, and you seem to leave destruction in your wake. Chivalry degenerates into extravagance, and you become incapable of dealing with the situations that arise in your life.

53/8 AS A TEMPORARY VIBRATION: **Sudden events, courage, discrimination.** Someone or something is about to catapult into, or out of, your life. The situation is intense. You should play the aggressor and take things into your own hands. Keep your emotions under the command of reason and act justly.

Challenging situations arise suddenly. You will need strength, courage and perseverance to handle them. Business, finance and the law may be involved. Deal wisely with whatever you encounter, and use reason to discriminate among the facts presented. Then you will overcome all problems and maintain, or achieve, a position of authority. During this period troubles come and go.

KNIGHT of SWORDS .

TAROT SYMBOLISM: **Knight of Swords.** This Knight has a lot to accomplish during the autumn season. He rides far and fast. Riding against the wind shows that no effort is too great and no obstacle too severe for him to overcome. His raised sword shows him the true path by dividing the true from the false.

ASTROLOGICAL CORRESPONDENCE: **Autumn (Libra, Scorpio,** Sagittarius). During the fall, people prepare for the long winter by storing supplies. Oversight can mean disaster. Because you have an eye for detail you would make a good detective. You are determined and may at times seem severe, but you must be able to maintain a balance and discriminate between the useful and the useless. You are courageous and have leadership potential.

54/9 AS A PERSONAL NUMBER VIBRATION: You are witty, intelligent and eloquent. Those gifts assure you the respect of your peers. You have a keen practical and perceptive mind. You pursue your education, as you have a natural tendency to seek answers. You can adjust mentally to the demands of the environment. These talents make you a prime candidate for government work or the diplomatic services.

You are always vigilant and seem prepared for any possibilities. Your subtle approach to difficulties belies your ability to arrive at swift, just conclusions. You are dedicated to the institutions and laws of the past, and you prefer to use intellectual processes rather than physical force to find solutions.

Your restless nature is something for you to overcome. You are amiable, humanitarian and conventional in your ways. These qualities help you deal successfully with your problems. You desire peace and reject the frills of life. You enjoy good health and a long, fulfilling life.

If you are a negative 54/9, you are cunning and sly. You use your fine intellect to outwit others. You scatter your energies and deplete your resources, which brings on health problems. But your scheming will be revealed, and you will be exposed for what you are.

54/9 AS A TEMPORARY VIBRATION: **Vigilance, messages, secrets.** Maintain a vigilant attitude during this cycle. Keep your imagination under control. You are unaware of some elements in certain situations, but they will be revealed to you. Adhere to your proper execution of justice, and those who work against you will be defeated. You must mentally adjust to unforeseen events which arise now. Look for the truth beneath superficial appearances, so that you will be prepared when the truth emerges.

You may receive news or messages that will demand your energy. Successful conclusions can be reached if you keep your emotions under control. Others may be observing your actions during this cycle to see how you handle yourself. If they are enemies they wait for a vulnerable moment; if friends, they wait to see how you perform. Your actions can earn you a position of authority and respect. Illness is an enemy, so take care of your body. Eat well and allow enough time for rest.

The Swords

PAGE of SWORDS.

TAROT SYMBOLISM: **Page of Swords.** This Page is without frills or decorations. He has a practical mind which is at work revealing the truth. Truth is somewhat hidden behind the clouds in the background, but the air element, symbolized by the birds as roving thoughts, will aid him in attaining his goal. However, investigation and mental application are required.

ASTROLOGICAL CORRESPONDENCE: **Third decan Libra.** This decan includes the rulers of all the air signs, Venus, Uranus and Mercury. A restless nature and an amiable disposition are found here. You are witty, intelligent, very sociable and humanitarian. You have a natural ability to communicate and you sway others with your words. You are a natural scholar, and will most likely gain the respect of your colleagues. You will live a long and healthy life.

55/1 AS A PERSONAL NUMBER VIBRATION: You are perceptive and therefore equipped mentally to explore any project, idea or concept. You have the ability to reason and the talent to write. As a dominating leader you reflect honest, high-minded and ethical ideals which inspire others to follow you.

You are a pioneer, exuberant and energetic. You react intensely and are capable of extremes in all endeavors and pursuits. You are a champion of right and seek swift justice to maintain balance. You believe in law and order and try to remain poised between mercy and severity.

This number dominates religion and morals, and you may be drawn toward the law or the ministry where you can most adequately express your keen sense of justice and mercy.

You can ferret out information that others would overlook. You are a natural researcher, and would make an excellent librarian. Words fascinate you, and writing is another area in which you can fulfill your basic need to explore and reveal the secrets of life.

Your writings would have tangible values for others. Through your love of communication you will meet many different types of individuals in your lifetime. Many children may grace your home, in keeping with your productive nature. Your children will benefit from your principles and may achieve distinction in their given fields.

Negatively, your keen ability to make fine distinctions deteriorates into a confused and chaotic lifestyle. Erratic actions create obstacles, alienate friends and produce a sterile, lonely environment. A stern attitude results.

55/1 AS A TEMPORARY VIBRATION: **Honor, birth, clarity.** You may be honored now for some achievement in which you have expressed intellectual and leadership skills. It is the culminating triumph, the reward for prolonged endeavor. Since this is a period of culminations, separations are a possibility. An affair may end and people may leave your circle, thus altering your environment in some manner. This suggests that you are through with the elements of that relationship.

Religious and legal considerations may arise here. This vibration can also bring the birth of a very special child who will in some way bring light and inspiration to the world. The triumphs of this period may set you off on a new journey that will require your energy and integrity.

TAROT SYMBOLISM: **Ace of Swords.** The Hand of God holds the upraised sword of discrimination. The golden crown studded with rubies shows the honor that comes to those who use their mental powers wisely. The holly branch hanging from the crown represents the Christmas season and therefore birth. The palm branch depicts Easter and the resurrection. The six falling yods, symbolic of the developing sixth sense, are the divine sparks that continually fall into incarnation, in a never-ending cycle of birth and resurrection.

ASTROLOGICAL CORRESPONDENCE: **The element air (Gemini, Libra, Aquarius).** As a representative of the element air, you are mentally equipped to conquer any field you choose. Your mind is your greatest weapon and tool. It will eventually place you in positions where you must maintain balance in dispensing justice. You are a pioneer in the realm of thoughts, and others will look to you for ideas.

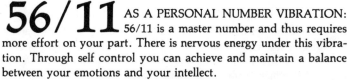

56/11 AS A PERSONAL NUMBER VIBRATION:

56/11 is a master number and thus requires more effort on your part. There is nervous energy under this vibration. Through self control you can achieve and maintain a balance between your emotions and your intellect.

You are perceptive and discriminating and do not judge by appearances alone. You make impartial decisions based on your intuition which is founded on reason. You may gain fame and fortune through the proper use of these talents.

You are a natural peacemaker, and you like to create happy conditions around you. Strife is distasteful to you, and you are able to establish harmonious conditions in the midst of changing and unexpected situations.

You are poised, modest and agreeable. You enjoy being popular so you develop one of your best qualities, which is charm. You are flexible and can yield to the opinions of others. You are affectionate and loyal to your family, sympathetic and responsive to the troubles of those around you. Military personnel and members of the government may be among your circle of friends.

The Swords

Music appeals to your finely attuned sense of rhythm. You are balanced and make an effort to stay that way. Music is a reminder of that balance. You will be successful in business. You sense what the public wants and needs, and you know how to supply it.

If you express the negative, these fine qualities are reversed and will cause indecisiveness. You will be unable to choose wisely. Associates will prove untrustworthy and trouble will result. You will live an unproductive life.

56/11 AS A TEMPORARY VIBRATION: Balance, decisions, cooperation. This is a master number cycle. It demands more from you, but it offers greater rewards in return. Balance and self-control are necessary during this period of nervous energy. You must remain impartial. Do not base decisions and judgments on appearances. A favorable financial outcome may hinge on your ability to perceive the situation as it really is.

You are attuned to the needs of others. You can play the role of peacemaker, settling disagreements at work and trouble in the family. As you project affection and understanding, you create harmony and a sense of well-being. You should be willing to help those in need, because, during this cycle, you have the insight to bring about settlements that are agreeable to all. Refusal to exercise these qualities results in indecision and stalemates. Matters go wrong because of a lack of direction which you could now supply.

Be aware of the people you deal with. Some will not be honest with you. This will require more understanding and impartiality on your part.

TAROT SYMBOLISM: Two of Swords. The figure is dressed in white to denote spiritual purity. Her hair is black (lack of light) and it is bound by the white band of wisdom. Her position is one of perfect balance. The Moon stands for the subconscious, and the rocks symbolize that which is stable, permanent or decided upon by the conscious mind. The figure is sitting on a cube of stone which shows a firm foundation for her convictions.

ASTROLOGICAL CORRESPONDENCE: First decan Libra. *Balance* and *justice* are keywords for this decan. You have clear vision and keen perception. You are artistic, graceful and congenial. You prefer mental work to physical labor. You are fastidious because cleanliness is important to you. You avoid any career that necessitates messiness or dirty hands. You like variety and may not stay long in one job. You need to learn perseverance. You are usually optimistic and pleasant. You are a peacemaker and will go all out to avoid stress and strife.

57/3

AS A PERSONAL NUMBER VIBRATION: The positive expression of this vibration results in a charitable nature, with ability to understand others and help them with their problems. If the vibration is negative, you may experience disappointment and heartache. Do not allow yourself to indulge in self-pity; rather, develop your sense of humor. This is often an outlet for the more intense emotions that can be part of your life.

You are dependable and serious and possess strength and courage in the face of adversity. Your happiness reflects your integrity in equal measure. You feel a conflict between reason and emotions; therefore, you should cultivate the art of logic to avoid being carried away by impulse.

You have the artistic ability to express your fluctuating moods. You can portray them in pantomime or on the stage. Acting and the theater provide fine outlets for your creative talents. You may prefer to work behind the scenes, as a playwright for instance, and give support to those who enjoy the limelight more than you. Some of the most interesting people under this vibration are those you may never hear of, because they have done their greatest work in the background.

You are independent and progressive, with humanitarian ideals. Become a strong force for good in the world, and you will feel that your sojourn on earth has been meaningful and well spent.

Yours is the number of the understanding heart, although it may have been gained through suffering. You mature through your experiences.

As a negative 57/3, you suffer losses and experience confusion. You become depressed and bitter and reject the extended hands of friendship because you fear being hurt. Separation and loneliness result.

57/3 AS A TEMPORARY VIBRATION: **Separation, delay, expression, growth.** Maintain a logical approach to emotional situations that arise now. Do not bemoan your fate; work on your sense of humor and try to see, from a detached point of view, the frailties of human nature. Your happiness depends on your integrity.

You may experience many ups and downs under this vibration; therefore, you would be wise to find a creative outlet to express these moods constructively. Acting, music, poetry or painting are good outlets.

There can be separations and disappointments in love relationships; those you love may be absent for a time. Expect some delays. If this is a negative vibration, your fluctuating moods could bring on confusion in deciding what to do.

Use the experiences of this cycle for growth. The wisdom you gain here should be made available to those around you who need kind words and a gentle heart.

The Swords

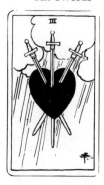

TAROT SYMBOLISM: **Three of Swords.** Three swords pierce a heart. They look like crosses, suggesting that those who bear their crosses bravely become more sympathetic and tolerant of others. The heart is also a symbol of charity. The clouds indicate that the brighter side is hidden and that all your natural attributes are not immediately apparent. There is a need to develop spiritual discernment. If negative, self-pity is your weakness.

ASTROLOGICAL CORRESPONDENCE: **Second decan Libra.** Perseverance, integrity and the drive to achieve are important attributes of this decan of Libra. You have vitality and a sense of humor. You are a humanitarian who will work to improve conditions that seem unfair. You are honest and faithful in your dealings with others and often give them the benefit of the doubt. Sometimes this results in your own heartbreak. You would rather suffer yourself, though, than cause injustice for others. You can appear aloof, but at heart you are keenly sensitive.

58/4

AS A PERSONAL NUMBER VIBRATION: You are a logical thinker and a skillful worker. A career in medicine or metaphysics is possible as this number is related to sight and insight. You are introspective and you tend to analyze a problem very thoroughly before you decide to act. You are dependable and cautious, and you use your energies carefully for constructive purposes only.

People respect you for your honesty and fairness. You have a keen sense of justice, yet you believe in mercy. You want your life to be orderly and conventional because you believe in tradition and discipline; however, you will enjoy life and its pleasures. You are charming, affectionate, careful, and yet emotionally controlled. Your creativity shows in your love of beauty, harmony and peace, which you need, and work to preserve, in your life. You could be a talented writer. You have a keen eye for details and the ability to analyze a situation and come to logical conclusions. Others seek you out for this very reason. You also have a fine sense of honor.

There is a great mental activity with this vibration, and there may be traveling. You enjoy solitude when you can relax and meditate. These periods bring things into perspective for you and help you maintain your generally good health. You may eventually decide to put away material considerations for spiritual pursuits. You are courageous and, although you prefer to live a life of peace and solitude, you are ready to take action to preserve your peace. You have earned a rest from the strains of life and will express that peace in this lifetime.

A negative 58/4 causes unrest and dissension; ill health and perpetual convalescence may be the result. Social unrest could lead to retreat and exile.

58/4 AS A TEMPORARY VIBRATION: **Rest, relief, retreat, convalescence.** This is a period of retreat in which your mind seeks rest from the cares of the world. Conflicts have ended, worries are over; now you desire peace and quiet to gather your strength. You can now analyze your situation and logically decide how to proceed. You are able to put even the smallest details of your life into perspective and clearly see what has real value.

Your solitude may be a convalescent period after an illness, a self-imposed vacation for rest and relaxation or an enforced retreat arising from social unrest. Whatever the impetus that propelled you to this space, it requires concentration and meditation on the experiences that have brought you here. If used wisely, this period can lead to a change for the better. The conclusions you arrive at subconsciously will affect your future actions.

TAROT SYMBOLISM: **Four of Swords.** The figure has assumed the proper position for rest, inferring that rest from anxiety and strain has been earned. The swords are put away; three hang on the wall, and one is placed lengthwise along the couch. This shows that, if need be, action would still be taken to preserve peace. This is a card of peace and quiet, not death. The window depicts outer activity. A man is shown kneeling before a woman, symbolizing that the conscious mind (male) is still a slave to the subconscious (female). To the resting figure all is serene; the sword of discrimination has been used and put away.

ASTROLOGICAL CORRESPONDENCE: **Third decan Libra.** The mental side of Libra is strong in this decan; therefore, intellectual pursuits will attract you. You could do well in teaching, preaching, lecturing or writing. You have an amiable disposition and a refined manner, and you are extremely adaptable. You are logical and fair and believe in mercy and kindness. This is really the most balanced of the Libra decans. You have the integrity to be a judge. Your standards are high. Your greatest desire is for order, harmony, beauty and peace in your life.

59/5 AS A PERSONAL NUMBER VIBRATION: You are passionately devoted to your convictions and will stand firm to defend your rights. You should strive to keep away from danger or injury. You are a gambler. You want to win by your wits, but you will experience defeat if you do not express yourself positively. Success as a banker or broker is possible as long as you neither take nor recommend speculative risks. Your mind is quick, and you need to guard against making impulsive decisions.

Life will be full of experiences and travels. You may find yourself doing more than one thing at a time, but doing them all well. You are creative, versatile and charming. Your lively and sparkling personality can easily influence others, especially the opposite sex.

You are critical of your own efforts and seek perfection. You are humane, refined and sympathetic. You may seek leadership positions where, as an executive, ruler or conqueror, you can use your idealism to implement social reform. Your sensitivity attracts you to the arts.

Select congenial outlets for your talents and avoid the humdrum. This will help you disperse your surplus energy and maintain the peace and serenity so necessary to your health and well-being.

A negative 59/5 deserts responsibilities. Your life becomes one of degradation and defeat. Your cruelty and unfairness in trying to outwit others brings empty victories which crumble and leave you with nothing. You, and all 59/5's, should aim for higher consciousness.

59/5 AS A TEMPORARY VIBRATION: **Travel, change, responsibility.** Do not take speculative risks under this vibration. You may tend to be more impulsive now, so make an effort to think things through before acting. This impulsiveness can also cause accidents and injury; therefore, maintain a moderate speed in your lifestyle.

There can be travel and a variety of opportunities now. Excitement, movement and romance make life more interesting. Be careful that you don't follow your impulses blindly. This can bring loss and slanderous talk, and your reputation can be affected.

Remain positive and accept your responsibilities; then you will come out on top. If you initiate changes after careful consideration, you will persevere. Situations encountered will be settled in your favor because you have the strength to stand up for what you believe.

TAROT SYMBOLISM: **Five of Swords.** The figure in the foreground represents one who has finished the job. The figure walking away has laid down his sword, but he is still not defeated; he merely shows that he knows when to fight and when to retreat. The other figure really is defeated and is weeping over this fact. This card represents three attitudes of mind. It shows that we must discriminate in all matters and stand on our convictions.

ASTROLOGICAL CORRESPONDENCE: **First decan Aquarius.** To the Aquarian could be assigned the motto, "every person a brother or sister." This is the sign of altruism. You are inspired by the concept of the Aquarian Age. You are intelligent and self-confident and determined to achieve your chosen goal. You are also willing to fight to preserve your ideals.

60/6 AS A PERSONAL NUMBER VIBRATION: You have the ability to examine reason as a human intitution and then set it aside to make room for true wisdom, un-

tainted by preconceived ideas. You may follow a literary career although you can apply your mind to various pursuits with equal success. You prefer to work independently rather than in partnership.

You are sought after for your cheerfulness, fairness, intelligence and self-confidence. You make a good lawyer because clients feel secure with you.

This vibration bestows a sense of power. You feel that you are under divine protection. People seek your advice and help because they also sense your healing qualities, both physical and mental. You are energetic and tirelessly strive toward a high goal of attainment. Nurses, advisors and managers are under this vibration. You are often deemed an idealist. You combine logic and imagination in a unique manner; this shows a fine balance between your conscious and subconscious minds. You are a leader with a sense of justice; if you find yourself becoming egotistical, balance that trend through generosity and consideration for others.

You must earn your success through sustained effort and conscientious work. Do not expect results without application. You are creative and inventive. Some notable artists have been born in this vibration, but all of them labored faithfully for their successes.

Negatively, a 60/6 is a rebel. You pursue your independent ways regardless of the needs of others. You may waste your fine mind and creative talents in selfish endeavors.

60/6 AS A TEMPORARY VIBRATION: **Passage, new home, proposals, love.** After a period of struggle during this cycle, you are on your way to a successful and happy conclusion. The job is done, and you have paid your fare.

There will be companionship, love and a meeting of minds. You may receive a proposal or invitation to join with another in a mutual endeavor which promises fulfillment. Someone may represent you in a meeting or you may deal with someone's representative. There is a coming together aspect involved here. Travel is a possibility as this vibration indicates physical movement as well as mental. A new home and environment may result.

An element of justice is present. Legal dealings may arise to bring about the peaceful settlement of unresolved issues. You may encounter lawyers, judges or the courts in some way.

TAROT SYMBOLISM: **Six of Swords.** The man, woman and child represent the trinity in consciousness. They are moving to another shore. The water of the subconscious supports them. The man has no difficulty steering the boat because the water is calm. The swords are arranged in a line to act as a shield. The points are down, indicating that the work has been done. There is harmony within the minds and they are all moving in the same direction under the guidance of the conscious mind (man).

ASTROLOGICAL CORRESPONDENCE: **Second decan Aquarius.**
You are a discriminating individual. You seek goals beyond the
material in the intellectual and spiritual realms. Your career could
take you to many parts of the world. You have the desire to see and
to investigate beyond the place of your birth. You have charm, intellect and a sense of power. Use your imagination constructively to
make logical plans and get results that will benefit many. Often this
takes place in artistic or literary fields. You have an uncanny ability
to make your projects succeed.

61/7 AS A PERSONAL NUMBER VIBRATION: The keyword for a 61/7 is *achievement*. This is a

vibration of peace and sincerity. You have control over your emotions and command over others through your calm, deliberate manner. You are patient and sensible, and will achieve many of your
goals through concentrated effort.

You are intellectual, refined and discriminating. You know intuitively that the future depends on the past, and you use past experiences to promote growth.

An interest in the occult and mystical may lead you to work in a
religious or spiritual field and live a celibate life. You are responsive
and sympathetic to the needs of others. You may be idealistic but at
the same time you are willing to work for your goals. Your creed is
tolerance and you believe that faith and spiritual development can
cure all ills.

Your well-rounded personality and high ethical standards could
lead to a position as a foreign ambassador or diplomat. Your
tolerance and idealism influence groups. You like to enjoy yourself
and you will travel because you do not like to stay long in one place.

You seek perfection and will always feel that you have not done as
much or as well as you should. People may find you elusive; just
when they think they have your number, you change unexpectedly.
Some people find your actions contradictory; others see the seeds of
greatness subtly hidden in your colorful personality.

A negative 61/7 never quite succeeds. Your plans continually fall
through, and others take what you feel is rightfully yours.

61/7 AS A TEMPORARY VIBRATION: **Health, travel, completion.**
Listen to the good advice given you during this cycle. That advice
may come from those in a position to know, or from your inner self.
Since you need a period of quiet to hear and think about this information, you will be placed in a suitable environment to do so.

Your health may require your attention. You may decide to take a
sabbatical or vacation. Past efforts and attitudes are coming to fruition now; your success depends upon how well you have handled
both. If your plans have failed or only been partially successful or if
someone else has attained what you want, then examine your pro-

cedures. Faith, integrity and concern for others must dominate all your actions. Be tolerant of the errors of others now, and partial success may ultimately become a triumph.

TAROT SYMBOLISM: **Seven of Swords.** The figure is hurrying away with an armful of swords. He turns around, wondering whether he should have taken the other two swords as well. This depicts uncertainty, hesitation and partial success. The tents also show instability for they are not permanent.

ASTROLOGICAL CORRESPONDENCE: **Third decan Aquarius.** You form strong attachments or partnerships. People seek you for advice because of your perception and sense of justice. You would make a good lawyer or judge as you can easily see both sides of a question, and would evaluate fairly. You demonstrate a cool, impersonal freedom in your own conduct. You may be considered elusive, yet you inspire confidence, perhaps beyond what you yourself may feel. To develop self-confidence, practice discipline and emotional control. Difficulties and uncertainties will then be resolved.

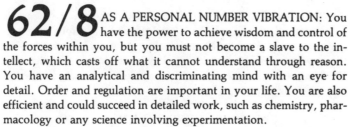

62/8 AS A PERSONAL NUMBER VIBRATION: You have the power to achieve wisdom and control of the forces within you, but you must not become a slave to the intellect, which casts off what it cannot understand through reason. You have an analytical and discriminating mind with an eye for detail. Order and regulation are important in your life. You are also efficient and could succeed in detailed work, such as chemistry, pharmacology or any science involving experimentation.

You will develop your intellect to satisfy your curiosity and desire for knowledge. You are clever, inventive and inquisitive, and are willing to research to find answers. You may want to travel, but if no opportunity appears, you will indulge in mental flights instead. You write and compile facts and statistics with equal pleasure.

You are a thinker, quick and perceptive. You dominate groups through your ability to organize and get things done; but you keep all activities running in a practical and efficient manner. You willingly accept responsibility, but you never attempt the impossible. Although aware of your limitations, you are confident that you can overcome obstacles. Through thought and care you always seem to find a solution. You are trustworthy and responsible, a good neighbor and upright citizen. You want justice to prevail and may participate in community efforts to see that it does.

You like quiet. Sometimes you like solitude so you can meditate. Study philosophy and learn to use your inner eye to see spiritual qualities. In this realm you cannot be bound by material considerations. You will find the true wisdom you are capable of attaining.

The Swords

If you are a negative 62/8, you are restricted by the appearances of your environment. You remain in bondage to trouble, sickness and burdens until you release yourself through true understanding.

62/8 AS A TEMPORARY VIBRATION: **Impasse, restriction, responsibility.** You may temporarily be involved in a situation which has reached an impasse or stalemate. You may feel restricted by your present surroundings and circumstances, or you may be censured or prevented in some way from expressing yourself.

Difficulties with relatives may come to a head. Trouble and criticism cause deeper conflicts which may result in health problems. The selfish motives of those you thought were your friends may now be exposed. However, if you are not afraid to leave old habits and circumstances behind, you will be free from fear, free to relax and enjoy your newly acquired insight. Take courses, meditate, develop a sound philosophy which goes beyond materialism—discover the joys of the mind. Look within yourself for real values in life; see beyond the superficialities. If this has been your modus operandi all along, this period will bring the honor and recognition you have earned.

TAROT SYMBOLISM: **Eight of Swords.** Although the figure is bound and blindfolded, she has found the opening through the barrier of swords (crosses). She travels the pathway of water, showing the power of the subconscious mind which is always symbolized by water in the Tarot. The castles in the background show substantial past accomplishments.

ASTROLOGICAL CORRESPONDENCE: **First decan Gemini.** The sign of the twins indicates duality. Those who are born in this area of the zodiac crave variety. You are happiest when you have several projects going at the same time. You are physically nimble, especially clever in any sort of handiwork. You easily learn to play musical instruments because of your flexible fingers. This tendency is also useful if you wish to do secretarial work. Writing, radio or TV announcing would be good outlets for your talents. When a subject captures your interest you are a very good student.

63/9 AS A PERSONAL NUMBER VIBRATION: You
are a born missionary and reformer. You worry over the sorrows of the world. You seek truth and wish to work for the good of others.

There is, in this vibration, a fine balance of heart and head. This allows you to promote your ideals but prevents you from taking on the suffering of others. You may encounter struggles in which your emotions must be sublimated if you are to be successful.

You are generous in sharing your good fortune with others. You are sensitive and sympathetic and are always ready to lend a helping hand when the occasion requires. This concern for others often leads to the development of the gift of healing. Through this you gain great happiness.

You are independent. Your greatest inner struggle may be the desire for success at the sacrifice of some personal happiness. Self-control, discipline, patience and acceptance of your finite nature is the way to balance this powerful and complicated vibration.

Artistic ability, clairvoyance and perception balance your unique personality. When you convert the threatening situations of life into tools with which to build a promising future, then you overcome all obstacles. You will have won the battle which tries to chain the spirit to the mortal world. Your inspired faith in tomorrow, against all odds, teaches and uplifts others.

If you are a negative 63/9 you become swamped in sorrows. You see nothing but pain and grief in your environment and thereby waste your promising potential as an agent for hope in the world.

63/9 AS A TEMPORARY VIBRATION: Struggles, unselfishness, healing. If doubts assail you and you find yourself worrying unduly during this cycle, it is because you must learn, through emotional turmoil, to become less emotional. As you become more attached to material things, you become increasingly sorry that you may lose them. This is a cycle of endings, when physical and mortal things must change.

The struggles and delays you endure last only as long as your persistent attachment to them. You must exercise self-control over your emotions. Become patient, quiet and receptive. You have healing powers now. Turn from your personal anxieties and share the experiences you have gained with those who need your wisdom. You can solve the problems of others and earn peace of mind and attain fulfillment.

TAROT SYMBOLISM: Nine of Swords. The woman has an attitude of despair, regret, and contemplation. The coverlet which is marked with the signs of the zodiac and the seven planets symbolizes the experiences that life has brought her. These bring sorrow only if we allow them to impel us. If we understand that difficulties are lessons for growth and development, sorrow is lessened, and courage replaces frustration. The nine swords are pointing east, toward the light; this indicates new beginnings in the dawning new day.

ASTROLOGICAL CORRESPONDENCE: Second decan Gemini. This is a more peaceful and less nervous Gemini decan, as the combined rulership of Mercury and Venus increases your sympathy and compassion for humanity. You enjoy the arts, music and poetry. A chance for harmonious partnership and love tends to produce beauty and joy in your life.

64/1

AS A PERSONAL NUMBER VIBRATION: A 64/1 is extremely individualistic and often remains single. However, your magnetic personality, tolerance, liberal views and charitable ways draw joy and affection into your life. You are especially effective with groups. Happiness and fellowship are more important to you than fame or wealth. The contacts you make will help you attain your goals, which may include wealth if you should so decide.

You want security in life and you are willing to work for it. You have fortitude, perseverance and determination; you always finish a task even though it is distasteful.

You are intuitive and a good judge of human nature. Your keen intellectual perceptions will serve you well if you decide on a literary career, or decide to become a professor or public speaker. Professional work is better for you than efforts in the commercial field.

Your conscious, subconscious and super-conscious minds work in unison, making almost anything possible for you through meditation and concentration on your life work. You are stable, honest and practical, a respected human being, who leads a proper life as a good neighbor and citizen. You know how to balance your responsibilities with recreation and rest. The lighter side of life lifts your spirits and provides a humorous respite.

Your will to win comes from your strong positive attitude and determination to let nothing get you down. Scientific and spiritual matters interest you. Once you have awakened the life force, or kundalini, within you and accepted the true nature of reality, which is change, you will have the power to overcome all negative forces.

A negative 64/1 suffers many losses and failures. You cling desperately to the material world of fear. Because you hang on, each loss brings greater suffering. You have not learned to develop a spiritual belief in what cannot be seen but nevertheless exists—faith, and the immortality of the soul.

64/1 AS A TEMPORARY VIBRATION: **Responsibility, tests, awareness.** This is a perfect time to develop your inner awareness through some form of metaphysical discipline such as meditation, yoga, TM, mind control or the like. Through spiritual pursuits you will learn that change is a constant cycle in the universe; all things must die and be reborn in new forms. Detach yourself from the experiences in your life and you will acquire the wisdom and fortitude to persevere toward your goals.

You can be your own worst enemy if you let sudden burdens and disappointments defeat you. There can be trials under this vibration.

By handling them you open a door in your life and discover the path
of your destiny. One special person may be on that path to accom-
pany you.

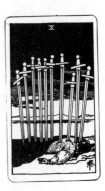

TAROT SYMBOLISM: **Ten of Swords.** The ten swords pierce the
spine at the centers. (The force centers are points of connection at
which energy flows in the etheric double of the body of a human being.) The red robe of desire drapes over the lower centers but is held
fast by the awakened discriminative sense. The background colors,
yellow and blue in equal proportions, show the balance of the two
parts of mind: conscious and subconscious. The hilts of the swords in
the form of crosses are throwing the white light of super-
consciousness, penetrating the black abyss of unknown mysteries.

ASTROLOGICAL CORRESPONDENCE: **Third decan Gemini.** A
good intellect, mental stability and balance are the gifts of this decan.
You have the power of concentration, and you very likely will pursue
a career in science. You could pioneer in electronics or in energy pro-
duction. You ability to judge human nature without prejudice or bias
is a valuable asset in your business and social life.

5

THE

PENTACLES

65/11 AS A PERSONAL NUMBER VIBRATION: This is one of the best master number 11's for obtaining material success. You will succeed through your perseverance, intelligence and maturity. By harnessing your energies and directing them constructively, you create abundance in your life. Good things seem to come to you almost without effort.

You are systematic and orderly, with a talent for organization. Others look to you for security. You are a natural leader who achieves power and authority in the business world, with control over large industries and businesses. Important people are in your sphere of influence; they can help you to advance your status and reach your goals.

You are practical and reserved and invest your riches wisely for the benefit of those around you. You are a patron of literature and the arts. You believe in education, good manners and a conventional approach to life. Your life will include a happy marriage, surrounded by comfort, productivity and powerful friends.

A negative 65/11 uses money extravagantly in speculation, gambling and frivolity. You may even use your resources for evil ends. Your power is used for self-gratification through material pleasures and possessions.

65/11 AS A TEMPORARY VIBRATION: **Promotion, risks, assistance.** This is a master number period which requires more and, in return, gives more than any other number vibration. You can expect to elevate your present status. Money, position and influence are yours. The rewards are in exact proportion to your previous output and, if this has been substantial, you will revel in the riches life gives you.

Influential people, especially of the opposite sex, will help you advance your position. You will have the power you desire in your chosen field. Maintain a practical approach to all affairs. Share your good fortune with others; you can afford to be generous now. However, extravagance and unwise speculation can lead to losses, so keep a balance. Marriage under this vibration is fruitful and successful.

TAROT SYMBOLISM: **King of Pentacles.** The King is dressed in a robe decorated with grapes; they symbolize fruitfulness and plenty. The Taurean symbols decorating the throne indicate money, possessions and material gifts. The buildings shown are not merely houses, but are castles of substantial size. Luxury is also evident in the heavy carving adorning the throne, and the golden crown topped with a wreath of roses, the symbol of elevated desires. Since the roses are on top of the crown, at the highest point of the figure, they indicate that the desires have been fulfilled. The mace in the king's right hand is a symbol of authority and power. The golden pentacle in the left hand shows an ability to handle money wisely.

KING of PENTACLES

ASTROLOGICAL CORRESPONDENCE: **First decan Capricorn.** This decan is Saturn-ruled and is the midheaven of the natural zodiac. It relates to honor, fame and ambition. If Capricorn, or any cardinal sign, is on the midheaven in your individual horoscope, some sort of prominence is indicated, depending on details in other parts of the chart. You have a talent for leadership and organization. You are persevering and thorough, thrifty and industrious, systematic and orderly. Education and the arts are important to you. You have good taste and conventional manners. You are the aristocrat of the zodiac, the most noble of the numbers, expressed in high and serious goals.

66/3

AS A PERSONAL NUMBER VIBRATION: You are intelligent, thoughtful and responsible. Your public-spirited and idealistic nature inspires you to do something to solve the social problems you see.

There is a practical side to your nature, too. You use your talents wisely and productively to achieve tangible results. Your magnetism attracts whatever you desire; as a result, you achieve great wealth and security. You are charitable and generous; you use your wealth and talents to help those who are less fortunate. You are a truly noble person.

You appreciate the finer things in life and you love to surround yourself with beauty. Your home must be comfortable and well decorated, as you enjoy splendor if it is expressed in good taste.

Flattery and deception have absolutely no place in your personality; truth and fairness rule your conduct. You are faithful and trustworthy, as you value your integrity. You are practical and determined in carrying out your plans. Others appreciate your sound business advice. Once you give your affection, you are a devoted partner and mate, supportive in every way.

As a negative 66/3, you may refuse to accept responsibility because you fear failure. You end up very dependent on others, and even worse, you allow your vast talents to lie fallow and eventually die.

66/3 AS A TEMPORARY VIBRATION: **Friends, money, travel.** This period deals with the material aspects of life and the pleasures and comforts derived from it. Money and possessions are accentuated. You will gain more affluence and prestige in some manner. An influential friend may assist you, or you could receive an inheritance or promotion. The courts and the legal profession could be involved.

Educational pursuits will bring wealth and influence. If you have dreamed of a special vacation or trip, you will now have the funds to fulfill that desire. Enough money is available for you to feel opulent and secure.

Your mind is very active now. Channel this energy to create a successful business or otherwise bring about tangible results.

TAROT SYMBOLISM: **Queen of Pentacles.** The Queen is dressed in an elegant but conservative costume, which befits her character. Her throne is decorated with symbols of fruitfulness. The goat, symbol of Capricorn, is carved into the arms of the throne. Flowers are in bloom all around her. The hare is also a symbol of fertility and productiveness. Cherubs always indicate the protection of divine beings, who radiate love, peace, happiness and contentment.

QUEEN of PENTACLES

ASTROLOGICAL CORRESPONDENCE: **Second decan Capricorn.** The second decan of Capricorn, (Taurus dominant, Earth and Venus co-ruling), produces not only a practical individual with an eye on financial gains and prestigious positions, but also a determined, loyal and sometimes stubborn individual. It would be hard to imagine anyone with these qualities who would not become successful in whatever endeavor he or she chose. Certainly, with this number, this is the case.

67/4 AS A PERSONAL NUMBER VIBRATION: You are a trustworthy, practical person and a good worker. Material progress and hard work are most important to you. You have matured to the point where you can pursue your goals without depending on others; you accept responsibility for your life and future. Persistence and hard work are your formulae for success and peace of mind.

You view the future calmly and methodically plan for it. You handle money well. It is, you feel, a tool for cultivating more resources. You have no anxiety over money because you have faith that it will increase ten-fold if invested wisely.

You have a common sense approach to life. You are artistic, creative and inventive. These talents are used to perform a service to others. You produce the products that supply our personal needs and comforts. You nurture and protect the goods of your community so that others may eventually benefit from them. You satisfy your appreciation of beauty and derive emotional satisfaction from this. You win a victory over your world and earn your rest.

A negative 67/4 is lazy and unproductive. You shirk responsibility and want others to take care of you. You never seem to have enough money or other goods to supply your needs.

67/4 AS A TEMPORARY VIBRATION: **Work, patience, firmness.** Patience is a virtue now. You must be methodical; plan each step you take. Do not depend upon others for help; rather, use your own talents and resources to get ahead.

Money is an issue, and budgeting may be necessary. Handle your finances wisely. "If you take care of money, it will take care of you." By performing services that supply vital commodities for others, you can be assured of financial success now.

Do not allow your routine to become monotonous, but do maintain a steady drive to achieve your goals. Unemployment or difficulty with your job means you should look to your work habits and your attitude toward your position. If you are in the wrong profession, make a change. If you like your work, examine different avenues of approach until you find one that will benefit you and ultimately others.

TAROT SYMBOLISM: **The Knight of Pentacles.** The Knight is pic-

The Pentacles

KNIGHT of PENTACLES

tured riding a work horse. He is contemplating work well done, while at the same time planning a course of action before he starts again. He considers the situation calmly to decide on the wisest moves. His weapon is money; he knows that a wise investment means power on the material plane. His helmet and the bridle of his horse are decorated with the leaves of the grapevine, symbolizing fruitfulness. The field ahead is an open plain, showing cultivation to be done as seasons come and go.

ASTROLOGICAL CORRESPONDENCE: **Winter (Capricorn, Aquarius, Pisces)**. This Knight presides over the winter season, when the fruits of labor have been stored for the winter's use and security. In this area of the zodiac much of the creative, inventive and artistic work is carried on, so it is with prudence that the Knight has stored the products of the harvest, allowing opportunity for other types of labor to continue.

68/5 AS A PERSONAL NUMBER VIBRATION: You have a strong attraction for money and luxuries and may become infatuated by them. You enjoy beautiful surroundings and will learn how to earn them, probably through mental rather than physical labor. Through clever planning you achieve your goals. Because clever planning requires an acute mind, you respect learning. You are willing to listen to new ideas and take advice from others.

Although somewhat of an introvert, you are a communicator whose purpose is to bring your ideas into the material world. You appear poised and confident, an image you wish to project; within, you are concerned and careful about the decisions you make. You are diligent and cautious as you build for a permanent and comfortable future. Strict attention to planning and organization account for a large share of your success.

As a negative 68/5 you can be a schemer. You become obsessed with a desire for material possessions. This creates a sense of urgency which obliterates all caution; waste and loss result.

68/5 AS A TEMPORARY VIBRATION: **Education, planning, travel, new paths.** Be careful; during this period an exaggerated materialism may prompt you to spend and react unwisely. Set about to achieve your desires through proper planning and attention to details. Your organizational ability and receptivity to new ideas can be turned to profit.

Someone you meet may be a catalyst in your decision to follow one course or another. Be flexible. Accept invitations to socialize and travel; they bring opportunities which aid you in building a sound future.

Educational opportunities may arise; accept them for they can open new doors. Communication during this cycle serves to establish priorities and strengthen financial or business dealings.

There can be ups and downs and possibly some waste or loss. These phases are intended to eliminate the unnecessary. Use discrimination, plan carefully, and the future is yours.

TAROT SYMBOLISM: **Page of Pentacles.** The Page holds the pentacle lightly, with nonchalance. On the outer surface he appears calm while within there is great care and concern that the right choices are made. The mountain of attainment is in the background. The flowers in the foreground show that the attention now is on the immediate future. The Page is nevertheless aware of the goal to be reached in the distant future.

ASTROLOGICAL CORRESPONDENCE: **Third decan Capricorn.** This is the Virgo decan which brings in the eye for detail and the fine discriminatory sense that results in good planning and organization. You have poise, confidence and good taste, but you do not believe in gaudy or showy displays.

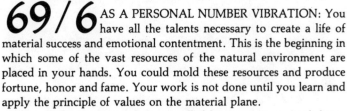

69/6

AS A PERSONAL NUMBER VIBRATION: You have all the talents necessary to create a life of material success and emotional contentment. This is the beginning in which some of the vast resources of the natural environment are placed in your hands. You could mold these resources and produce fortune, honor and fame. Your work is not done until you learn and apply the principle of values on the material plane.

The wheel of success turns, propelled by your energy and drive. You are attracted to luxury and beauty, and you have the proper attitude to attain them. To express yourself completely, you must be comfortable materially and contented mentally. You enjoy the divine protection which this vibration seems to offer.

Once you have attained success on the material plane, in the business or financial world, you share your bounty generously. Contributions are made to the arts and other pursuits that bring pleasure and culture to people. Your generosity is repaid and your riches increase, reaffirming the value you place in the earth's resources.

As a negative 69/6 you become infatuated with the pursuit of worldly possessions and, once attained, hoard them avariciously. Your greed corrupts you and assures you material comforts but little contentment.

69/6 AS A TEMPORARY VIBRATION: **Honor, fame, money, contentment.** You are showered with honor, fame, money and happiness. The fruits of your labor are in your hands for your consumption. Your past diligent efforts are rewarded.

At home, in your profession and in your community you are respected and admired. As your finances increase, you can afford to be generous; you should contribute in some measure to the environment about you.

This is such a good vibration that the negative aspect still brings material comforts and financial gains; however, the inner contentment felt with the positive side of 69/6 is lacking.

TAROT SYMBOLISM: **Ace of Pentacles.** The Hand of God is holding the pentacle as an offering to those who will learn to grasp its meaning. It seems to suggest that all may partake of material goods and reach the mountain of attainment after recognition that the universal consciousness is offered to all who seek it. The lilies in the foreground represent purified desires. The roses represent the energetic drive behind the desires of the flesh. The twin mountains of attainment, seen through the arch of roses, indicate that the goal is in sight, although still in the distant future.

ASTROLOGICAL CORRESPONDENCE: **The element earth (Taurus, Virgo, Capricorn).** Since the aces rule the elements, the Ace of earth bestows the material wealth and security which is so greatly needed and desired during the life sojourn. Fortune, honor and fame are the goals of earthly consciousness. Material and mental contentment and divine protection seem to completely express what we most strive to attain.

70/7 AS A PERSONAL NUMBER VIBRATION: This is considered a fortunate vibration because it offers business opportunities. You are thoughtful, prudent, ambitious and diplomatic. You are well liked in your business and social life. You believe in being fair in all your dealings and are probably the only 7 that should attempt a partnership. The 0 gives divine protection.

Your creativity has commercial value. You devise ingenious methods to solve problems and promote products. You also know how to get the most out of your money.

Changing situations will continually confront you; at all times, be ready to handle these circumstances and bring about harmonious solutions. You are aware of opposing forces and have intuitive understanding of other people's emotions. While skillfully controlling your own feelings you bring about peaceful and satisfactory settlements. You are thrifty and practical. Your poise, self-confidence, and managerial ability should earn you an executive position.

You may do a great deal of traveling for business, or, at the very least, be actively involved in communication. Messages and exchanges are the crux of your work.

Your perseverance and endurance prevail, and you become successful. Be sure to balance your personality by allowing equal time for work and play.

As a negative 70/7, you live a life of pretense. You cannot handle more than one situation at a time, especially if they are conflicting. You are moody; your life reflects your instability by its many ups and downs.

70/7 AS A TEMPORARY VIBRATION: **Partnership, travel, business.** This is a period of business activity. You may be offered a partnership that will be financially profitable in the long run. If both parties deal with fairness and integrity, the union will have cosmic protection. Creative ideas emerge to offer unique ways to solve difficulties or promote products. This will enhance your business.

Remain alert to changing conditions around you. Fluctuating trends need to be considered. Messages and communications regarding business abound. Travel for business purposes may be necessary.

You can settle disputes or difficulties amicably because you have insight into the opposing forces at work. Keep your imagination under control, and don't envision problems where there are none. If you allow imaginary troubles to block the positive flow here, you will lose out financially and professionally. Your health may then suffer.

TAROT SYMBOLISM: **Two of Pentacles.** The person pictured is a clever juggler. His material is money. The horizontal 8, the cosmic lemniscate, means infinity. Here it signifies a desire for balanced and continuous activity rather than struggle and strain in attaining ambitions. This is an ongoing process. The ships in the background on the crests of the waves seem to be skillfully piloted, denoting prosperous ventures or success in commerce. The figure's outer garment is made of leather which shows a desire for lasting qualities, dominance and good use of the animal and lower kingdoms.

ASTROLOGICAL CORRESPONDENCE: **First decan Capricorn.** This decan bestows ambition and diplomacy, with plenty of perseverance and endurance. You handle management positions with ease and will eventually work your way into executive positions. Because you are confident, thrifty and practical you do well in leadership roles.

71/8 AS A PERSONAL NUMBER VIBRATION: This is a number of constructive material accomplishments. You are dynamic, determined and forceful. With your persistence you finish whatever you decide to do. You work within the accepted norm, learn your trade, and become skilled in your craft. You do not allow dogma or frivolity to distract you.

Although disciplined, sensible and aggressive, you sometimes attempt the impossible; however, you realize your limitations and overcome them through sheer hard work.

You are dependable, a rock of Gibraltar, inspiring others with your stability. You must remember to take time off for vacations, rest and recreation, to prevent tension from building up, which would be the case if you insist on constantly applying your energy to work alone. Think what the word recreation means—to re-create. You need leisure time to recharge and tap your creative sources. Exercising out-of-doors and communing with nature have healing effects on you.

You are affectionate and sympathetic and instinctively understand the situations which are presented for your solution. Your skills, your desire to acquire wealth and your willingness to progress slowly and steadily to that end assure you financial success.

As a negative 71/8, you are indifferent to the development of your skills, and therefore you accomplish little. You pay the price however, because it will all catch up with you.

71/8 AS A TEMPORARY VIBRATION: **Opportunity, advancement, gain.** Apply yourself diligently and develop your skills, and you will obtain employment which will ensure your financial security. This can only be obtained through hard work, so use this period for professional development.

Be dependable, steady and reliable. Those in authority will be impressed by your cleverness, skill and persistence. Business contracts and job promotions can result.

Think big, expand your horizons, allow your creative potential a chance to show what it can do. You are on your way to the top. As you climb, be sure to take time to help those along the way who may not be operating under the powerful influence you are. The honor and recognition bestowed upon you now will increase your bank account as well.

If you are a negative 71/8, you allow the opportunity for professional development to pass. As a result of your laziness, opportunities will be lost forever.

TAROT SYMBOLISM: **Three of Pentacles.** A laborer is shown working on a cathedral, symbolizing that one should work to improve the temple or the person as a whole. The laborer earns success and rewards for good and faithful work. He pays little attention to the two figures seeking to distract him either through dogma or frivolity.

ASTROLOGICAL CORRESPONDENCE: **Second decan Capricorn.** This area of the zodiac gives a desire to acquire worldly goods. You are willing to progress slowly and steadily towards that goal. You go about your work quietly, but steadily, to attain the heights you have set for yourself. Real estate, agriculture, or mining would be suitable professions for you.

72/9 AS A PERSONAL NUMBER VIBRATION: You seek satisfaction through directing mundane affairs and accumulating earthly power. You are keenly analytical and see things in terms of material advantage. This is one of the most practical vibrations for handling material matters skillfully and constructively. You want to amass a fortune, and you have the practical ability, ambition and conviction to do so.

The urge here is to build on a large scale and make every penny count. You cannot stand loss through carelessness or wastefulness. You are generous and merciful but have the tenacity to hold onto money and to accumulate the material goods you desire. You are cautious lest the goal you have set for yourself be interfered with; at the same time, your diligent efforts provide services for others.

You have a strong character. Your standards are high, and you possess an innate stability—a gift of balanced and logical thinking, through which you achieve harmony and happiness. Through generosity you overcome your fear of poverty. You want your life to be one of usefulness and constructive accomplishments. Then others look to you as a model of practical earthly success.

As a negative 72/9, you can be selfish, clinging to your possessions out of fear that someone may take them from you. Your miserliness shuts you into a lonely and desolate existence where your wealth offers little pleasure because you spend every moment guarding it.

72/9 AS A TEMPORARY VIBRATION: **Increase, wealth, satisfaction.** Your attention is turned toward material matters. By keenly analyzing your financial condition, you can amass a fortune. You need to build major enterprises with an eye toward every detail and a hand on the purse strings. Be persevering; let nothing deter you from your goal, a goal that is practical and useful to others.

If you suffer setbacks or losses, examine your motives. Material achievement to satisfy your own need for security and allay your fear of poverty can bring failure. If you strive for success through the sustained effort and skillful execution of your talents and organizational abilities, you will achieve the material success which you seek. You can then rest upon your earned laurels.

TAROT SYMBOLISM: **Four of Pentacles.** The figure is shown very much closed up within himself. Every extremity is bound by material value; his attitude is that of one who is grasping and holding on. Skillful handling of money is shown by the perfectly balanced pentacle on top of the unadorned crown on his head. He has little regard for personal adornment, as shown by the carelessly laced shoes and

the ragged cloak or shawl thrown about his shoulders and waist. The buildings behind him show much past material accomplishment, yet he is still clinging to his material values, wanting to accumulate and build more. The lesson here is that earthly riches do nothing for the inner soul, for the figure looks poor in spite of his many possessions.

ASTROLOGICAL CORRESPONDENCE: **Third decan Capricorn.** This area of the zodiac produces a practical, ambitious person who is adaptable and discriminating. You want your life to be one of usefulness and constructive accomplishments. You see things in terms of how they will fit into your financial scheme of advancement. By learning to share the abundance you receive from life, you will overcome any fear of poverty.

73/1 AS A PERSONAL NUMBER VIBRATION: The keyword here is *wisdom*—the wisdom to acquire harmony within, to grasp the inner light, to know that to work for material reward alone brings impoverishment, while work for the deed itself brings spiritual fulfillment. You are well aware that you would have to endure the misery and burdens of the world if you took an avaricious approach to life and denied the spiritual light within. You have a fine flow of energy, enduring stamina and the ability to self-start and recharge yourself. Because fear is not part of your language, your self-confidence is superb and serves as an inspiration to others.

You are strong-willed, affectionate and patient. Your good business sense and financial ability will bring you blessings. A powerful combination of factors operate to give you a personality that can sometimes produce miracles. You should always use your abilities with honesty, idealism and integrity. You can become a power for good in the world and make it a better place in which to live.

If you are a negative 73/1, you are obstinate, self-willed, and slow to develop. Your wisdom is attained only through physical, material and financial hardships in which you must choose between material pursuits and spiritual riches. When you look to the light within, a change in consciousness takes place, and the material aspects of life flow easily.

73/1 AS A TEMPORARY VIBRATION: **Work, meditation, values.** Be aware that a preoccupation with the purely material side of life can bring only disappointment. Work and personal endeavors are emphasized here, however, you should pursue them with a delight in the accomplishment itself and not out of a need for the material rewards.

Indulging yourself out of a subconscious need for self-importance can bring temporary gains that will ultimately end in misfortune. The losses that can occur during this cycle serve only to place your purposes and aims in proper perspective. The transient nature of the material world should encourage you to look for deeper values. You should obtain some books on philosophy, spend time in meditation or sign up for a course in some metaphysical discipline which will expose you to other ways to deal with the circumstances in your life. The positive result of this cycle is wisdom.

TAROT SYMBOLISM: **Five of Pentacles.** The two figures in the picture represent physical and mental poverty. They serve as a warning to seek the light within, which is indicated by the lighted window. The card is meant to show that inner riches far outshine any material fortunes. The message here is: turn to your inner powers for guidance and avoid the poverty of consciousness to be found if attention is on the outer world alone.

ASTROLOGICAL CORRESPONDENCE: **First decan Taurus.** This area of the zodiac is noted for its strong will and great endurance. You have good business and financial abilities. You are fond of ease, good food and the luxuries of life. Artistic talent may be present in the form of singing or other creative abilities.

74/11 AS A PERSONAL NUMBER VIBRATION:

This is a master number vibration. It requires more than most number vibrations, but, as a result, it returns more. The most important element in this vibration is the balancing of debts, both present and karmic. You feel a need and desire to set things right in your life, in your community and in the world, as far as your influence and responsibility can take you. You are idealistic, with a firm faith that you can make your dreams come true. You balance charity with justice, willingly sharing your material prosperity with others out of concern and a desire to balance the scales. In adjusting your values, you expiate karmic debts through positive action.

It is your job to control and maintain the economic factors that keep our society alive and functioning. Your scientific and social inclinations could lead you into chemistry, medicine or professions connected with food and hygiene. Whatever you choose, you need to maintain a fine emotional balance so that your moods will not fluctuate from ecstasy to gloom.

You are popular with the opposite sex because of your grace, charm, self-confidence and independence. You have a keen sense of your own worth. You can direct group activities and inspire confidence because you always give a fair deal.

When you keep your many talents balanced, material success is assured. Then you must become the philanthropist, sharing your prosperity and influence with the needy of the world. Only in this manner will your worldly attainment possess any real value.

If you are a negative 74/11, you can be unscrupulous in the pursuit of financial success and security. You need money in proportion to your insecurities, and you can become a miser, drawing jealousy and resentment upon yourself by your actions.

74/11 AS A TEMPORARY VIBRATION: **Gifts, inheritances, balance, sharing.** This is a master number vibration. You are given more opportunity for achievement, and you will reap greater rewards if you fulfill the extra demand. This is a karmic period that requires balancing and sharing. This implies that there has been an imbalance prior to this that must be atoned for and settled. The resulting rewards, be they material or spiritual, must be shared with others.

You will attract others who will be inspired by your charm and self-confidence. You can perform effectively in group activities. You have the ambition to pursue your goals; great rewards come from the expression of your talents.

Material prosperity is now bestowed on you. You may receive gifts from an admirer, honor from your peers, or perhaps an inheritance. Remember, the lesson now is sharing.

A negative use of 74/11 brings undesirable friendships and jealousy. You accrue debts and suffer losses. Your unscrupulous methods bring only sorrow.

TAROT SYMBOLISM: **Six of Pentacles.** The central figure holding the scales is the benefactor, as indicated by the master number and the area of the zodiac's relationship. The key pictures the condition when values are learned and the material substances of life are shared. The other figures depict the opposite condition, when the positive side is neglected and the negative condition (objects of charity) results from carelessness. You can choose to create the positive or the negative in your own future.

ASTROLOGICAL CORRESPONDENCE: **Second decan Taurus.** This decan includes the scientific influence of the Virgo vibration. You have a discriminating and critical mind. You could be a career analyst or follow a line in the social services, or choose chemistry as related to health matters, such as hygiene, food or diets. You could also be a sympathetic nurse or doctor. You could develop methods of preserving and handling foods for market.

You are popular with the opposite sex because of your grace, ability and idealism.

75/3 AS A PERSONAL NUMBER VIBRATION: This vibration brings growth if you remain firm and independent. Much depends upon your persistence and effort. You have potential, but attainment calls for hard and steady work, which

inwardly you know is necessary. You know that it takes time for your efforts to bear fruit, that you must be calm and patient while waiting, and you must unceasingly apply yourself to the task at hand. Under this number you will really reap what you have sown.

Everything from prizefighters to editors, from dramatic actors to musicians, is covered under this number. All, however, had to maintain persistent effort to achieve their fame and position. You have what it takes to become successful: fortitude and discipline.

Your practical nature is coupled with ambition. You get along well with your contemporaries. You could become interested in metaphysics or philosophy but you would keep everything on a practical basis. You want to see concrete proof before you accept controversial concepts. You are serious about life, sober and sensible. With both feet firmly on the ground, you accomplish your goals.

Opportunities for more responsible positions come to you, and you accept the challenges with courage. You reach a higher status in life than was present at your birth through your determination and stamina. With all the material success you attain, you still realize the need for the investigation and development of your spiritual side.

A negative 75/3 worries over money or lack of it. You are impatient when rewards are not immediately forthcoming; your anxieties can affect your health and cause you to give up easily.

75/3 AS A TEMPORARY VIBRATION: **Money, travel, patience, hard work.** During this cycle you must exercise patience and perseverance. You have to learn that rewards come only after hard work. A steady application of energy toward a positive goal is necessary. Once these lessons have been learned, the success you strive for is yours. Karma has control here because your success is in direct proportion to the effort you extend.

You should unite practicality with ambition. See the situation as it really is and decide if it has any real value. If it does, proceed with determination to see the job accomplished. Always opt for concrete results. Your contemporaries are willing to assist you, so reach out to those on whom you can depend.

Positions of authority can open for you; meet them with confidence and a sense of responsibility. Always keep in mind the ethics and morality of your actions. New opportunities may require travel, so be flexible.

A negative reaction brings frustration over financial matters. There are delays, and you may feel impatient and restricted. The only solution is a calm acceptance of time as the eternal healer and a resolution to get down to business and work with a positive attitude.

TAROT SYMBOLISM: **Seven of Pentacles.** The young man pictured has attained a considerable show of success through his diligence. He

now contemplates his work and notices the lack of fruit on the beautiful full-leaved vine. He realizes it has borne only leaves. He has arrived with his cutting blade to reap the harvest; now he contemplates what could have been lacking in his efforts. He is made to realize that material things are not enough to feed the soul. The nourishment of life comes only through spiritual cultivation.

ASTROLOGICAL CORRESPONDENCE: **Third decan Taurus.** This area of the zodiac has produced many different types of individuals, all of whom have applied determination and persistence to achieve their goals. You have an independent and disciplined attitude; the Taurean plodding is here sparked with ambition. You accept challenges and responsible positions and go on to even higher achievement.

76/4 AS A PERSONAL NUMBER VIBRATION: You are endowed with the ability to be a genius in your given field. You are accomplished in a craft or trade, and are a self-made person who works not for others but for yourself. You do not look for support but painstakingly apply yourself to the task at hand. You take life seriously and are both honest and modest about your accomplishments.

Gain comes through clear thinking rather than emotional desire. You use logic in making decisions because you are accurate and analytical, a good planner and organizer, always adhering to orderly and steady growth as the proven way of advancement. You are not a world-beater as far as worldly attainment is measured, but you show progress by the example of your lifestyle and thus quietly teach others a sure way to successful achievement. What you do accomplish will be of great benefit in the long run, both to yourself and others.

You should guard against all work and no play. Overwork can give way to anxiety and worry. Relax at proper intervals and take regular vacations to preserve your health. Allow time for spiritual awakening; this is also important for total happiness and gracious living. You exemplify wisdom evolving from quiet work.

If you are a negative 76/4 you either never develop your skills and remain unproductive, or else you develop them for evil gains through fraud or forgery. This can only mean failure.

76/4 AS A TEMPORARY VIBRATION: **Training, employment, skills.** You now have the ability to develop your skills through some kind of training, apprenticeship or job opportunity. You should apply yourself to the task with concentration and dedication, resolving to improve your talents carefully and painstakingly.

Do not allow emotions to gain the upper hand. Proceed with a clear head, use logic and organization to achieve your goals. Work quietly and unassumingly, for bravado is not the method of approach here. Your accomplishments during this cycle will prove valuable in long-range goal planning.

Be sure to set aside periods for rest and relaxation. The tendency here is to push too hard, work too long and become overtired. This can bring on health problems. Balance your work with play; you are in a training period which is preparing you for future employment.

TAROT SYMBOLISM: **Eight of Pentacles.** A workman dressed in plain garments, covered with a leather apron, is diligently carving a golden pentacle, symbol of money. The large stack of work piled high shows that he has kept at the job faithfully. His back is turned to everything else in the world; his attention is on his work alone. This picture shows honesty, attention to fine details and expert skills. It may also suggest that all work and no play makes a dull life, although pleasure and satisfaction may come from the acquisition of wealth.

ASTROLOGICAL CORRESPONDENCE: **First decan Virgo.** The modesty of Virgo shows through your quiet desire to be an example for others. You accomplish your goals by proceeding carefully and showing concern that the job is done properly and orderly. You must watch a tendency to overwork and become so embroiled in your profession that you do not allow time for leisurely pleasures.

77/5 AS A PERSONAL NUMBER VIBRATION: *Fruitfulness, productivity* and *physical perfection*
are the keywords for this vibration. You have all the comforts of life. Your good fortune may have come from thrift and industry, or through unexpected and mysterious means, such as legacies or gifts of appreciation. At any rate, you are very comfortable and protected which allows you periods for reflection and pleasurable pursuit.

You have the insight to understand others, and you draw people to you. You are popular and self-confident. Emotionally you adjust to circumstances. You can be free and humorous or extremely cautious and serious as the occasion demands. Although you are shrewd and prudent, there is an imaginative and creative side to you in this highly sensitive vibration.

Practicality and thoroughness are your foremost traits. Your ambition may arouse a desire to rise in station through responsibilities in social service or public life. Your urge for higher achievement prods you onward; your tact will aid you in this climb. You handle all affairs with skill.

There is something of the aristocrat here, for you have all the material needs and physical enjoyments one could desire, but you nevertheless feel a duty to offer your services to bring about higher accomplishments for the world.

If you express the negative 77/5, you may lose through extravagance the possessions you love so dearly. You thereby forfeit the privilege of indulging your personal pleasures. Your family and friends may be among your losses.

77/5 AS A TEMPORARY VIBRATION: **Good fortune, popularity, achievement.** From an unexpected source, you may receive gifts, money or an inheritance. This good fortune can evolve in mysterious ways, or it may be the result of your prudence and industriousness. However it comes, you will now have the resources for travel, entertainment and other pleasurable ventures.

You will attract many friends, improve your social life and find yourself the center of attention. You are bright and charming; however, if circumstances demand, you can immediately become serious. Your creative side is awakened now.

Enjoy this affluent period, but also be practical in all you do. Extravagance can cause dissipation and loss of money. Look at the goals you can achieve now that you have been released from financial cares.

TAROT SYMBOLISM: **Nine of Pentacles.** A woman is shown elegantly dressed, with symbols of love, wealth and abundance in unmistakable evidence. The key depicts luxury and ease. The falcon on her hand is a symbol of aristocracy, as only those who have wealth and leisure can indulge in the art of falconry. The vines in the background are lush with fruit, thus completing this picture of ample wealth and security.

ASTROLOGICAL CORRESPONDENCE: **Third decan Virgo.** This area of the zodiac bestows a great awakening of ambition, a desire to be more persevering and an urge for high achievement. This reflects a period in the life when further opportunity for advancement will be offered. Tact and diplomacy are attributes of your personality that make you skillful in handling your affairs. For those who are aggressive there will be opportunity to serve and to gain honor and recognition. This period often brings wealth and all around better conditions.

78/6 AS A PERSONAL NUMBER VIBRATION: Here is ultimate attainment of desires on both the material and spiritual planes. 12 is considered the number of the perfect cycle as in the twelve months of the year and the twelve signs of the zodiac. The extension of 12, arrived at by adding together the numbers 1 through 12, is 78. In this number there is a high potency indeed.

You know that you have reached attainment by extraordinary effort. You used great strength and persistence to reach a high material goal. Diligence and a well-ordered life round out the effort. Emotions are kept in a proper place in the midst of your luxury. Your high idealism and finely balanced nature create a desire to serve. Surrounded by family, tradition, wealth and comfort, you are now released from the vicissitudes of labor and are able to pursue philanthropic endeavors which will aid humanity.

You are an extrovert: confident, secure in your possessions, ready to utilize your mental sagacity to establish fine living conditions and a semblance of justice in the world around you. Your love of art and beauty prompts you to support cultural endeavors financially. You will not work for the sake of work but only to establish and add an element of beauty to the better side of life. You have the financial influence to bring about such results. Harmony in the material world is a measure of what the balance between spirit and matter can produce—a fulfilling and comfortable life.

If you express the negative 78/6, you can lose more than others because you have the potential to gain so much more. Since misfortunes and burdens can plague you, use caution in all your endeavors.

78/6 AS A TEMPORARY VIBRATION: Great fortune, happy family, the arts. You can acquire a great fortune during this cycle, both materially and spiritually. The seeds of ultimate fulfillment lie here, a fulfillment achieved through personal effort and tremendous perseverance. Leisure time, pleasure and the satisfaction of sensual desires create a feeling of well-being and self-confidence. You should maintain a level head in the midst of this opulence and set your sights on cultural achievements which can bring an uplift to the soul. Pursue creative work now, and support the world of beauty and art.

A happy family life can be established here. Family lineage and prestige gain significance, and children abound.

The idealistic structures you build under this vibration will have lasting and profound effects upon those who come in contact with them. They are monuments to the perfect balance between the material and spiritual.

Do not allow yourself to degenerate into a state of idleness and dissipation because of the luxury bestowed on you now. The material life is only temporary; eventually one has to confront the soul.

TAROT SYMBOLISM: Ten of Pentacles. This scene depicts both plain and intricate structural designs. There are also shown three phases of humanity which stand for three states of consciousness. The man, woman and child are symbolic of conscious mind, subconscious mind, and super-conscious mind. Off to the side is the Ancient, observing and knowing the future of those he sees through the arch. The two gray dogs denote the development of the animal kingdom. (Gray is the result of mixing black and white; this shows balance.) Notice the balance scales built solidly on the arch, above the Ancient's head. This implies that balance is won and the scales can no longer be tipped. The pentacles are arranged in the pattern of the Tree-of-Life design, showing that the greatest attainment comes from achieving balance while on the earth plane. This is a picture of success and fulfillment in every way.

ASTROLOGICAL CORRESPONDENCE: **Third decan Virgo.** Financial prospects are good in this area of the zodiac if combined with the ability to use this influence properly. You have a sense of purpose without being too obstinate and serious. This comes from a combination of Saturn, Venus and Mercury. These qualities bring pleasure, art and practicality together; this results in service and sympathy in whatever affairs you meet during your lifetime.

APPENDIX

SYNTHESIS
OF NUMEROLOGY,
ASTROLOGY
AND THE TAROT

N UMEROLOGY, ASTROLOGY AND THE TAROT are different ways of exploring the cycles of life experience. In this Appendix the material presented in Part II of this book is summarized in table and chart form so that you can more easily see how each of these three ancient systems relates to the others.

As you know, the seventy-eight keys of the Tarot are divided into two groups, the Major Arcana and the Minor Arcana. The Major Arcana correspond to the numbers 0 to 22. These numbers are: the God-powered 0, the base digits 1 to 9 and the first cycle of double-digit numbers up to the second master number, 22. These numbers and their corresponding Tarot keys represent archetypal life patterns and are linked astrologically with the signs of the zodiac and the planets. This information is contained in Table 1.

In Tables 2 to 5, we present the information contained in Chapters

2 to 5 of Part II, which deal with the numbers 23 to 78, the Minor Arcana and the yearly astrological cycle. To clarify the relationship of these numbers to the Minor Arcana and the astrological cycle we have included Figure 7, which presents the information of Tables 2 to 5 in wheel form.

In astrology we speak of Aries (fire), Cancer (water), Libra (air) and Capricorn (earth) as the *cardinal* signs. The cardinal signs govern the seasons and mark the equinoxes and solstices. For example, the astrological year begins with the Vernal Equinox; this occurs when the Sun enters the sign Aries, and marks the beginning of spring.

In Figure 7 you will see that the king, queen and page of each suit correspond to the cardinal sign which governs the same element. The King of Wands (cardinal, fire) corresponds to Aries (cardinal, fire).

You will also note in the tables and in Figure 7 that in the cardinal signs the kings, queens and pages of each suit are assigned the same astrological correspondence as the twos, threes and fours of the same suit. For example, in Table 3 and in Figure 7, the King of Cups (37/1) and the Two of Cups (42/6) both correspond to the first decan of Cancer (0° to 10° Cancer). Here the King acts in a role of royal protectorship, overshadowing the Two, which is at an earlier point in the cycle. Each card represents different manifestations of the same astrological energy.

There are two other important cards in each suit: the knights and the aces. Each knight is pictured on horseback, representing movement and energy, and because of this symbolism the knights have come to represent entire seasons. Thus the Knight of Wands governs the spring, carrying the initial burst of Aries energy through the spring months of Aries, Taurus and Gemini, until the Sun reaches 0° Cancer and the Knight of Cups begins his journey through the summer season.

Just as each knight rules an entire season, each ace rules an entire element. The power inherent in the ace corresponds to all the manifestations of an element. Thus, the Ace of Swords corresponds to the entire element of air and rules the air signs Libra, Aquarius and Gemini.

Table 1

The Numbers 0-22, the Major Arcana, the Signs and Planets

Number	Tarot Key	Astrological Correspondence
0	The Fool	Uranus
1	The Magician	Mercury
2	The High Priestess	Moon
3	The Empress	Venus
4	The Emperor	Aries
5	The Hierophant	Taurus
6	The Lovers	Gemini
7	The Chariot	Cancer
8	Strength	Leo
9	The Hermit	Virgo
10/1	The Wheel of Fortune	Jupiter
11/2	Justice	Libra
12/3	The Hanged Man	Neptune
13/4	Death	Scorpio
14/5	Temperance	Sagittarius
15/6	The Devil	Capricorn
16/7	The Tower	Mars
17/8	The Star	Aquarius
18/9	The Moon	Pisces
19/1	The Sun	Sun
20/2	Judgement	Vulcan
21/3	The World	Saturn
22/4	The Fool	Pluto

Table 2

The Numbers 23-36, the Wands, the Fire Signs

Number	Tarot Key	Astrological Correspondence
23/5	King of Wands	0°-10° Aries
24/6	Queen of Wands	11°-20° Aries
25/7	Knight of Wands	Spring (Aries, Taurus, Gemini)
26/8	Page of Wands	21°-30° Aries
27/9	Ace of Wands	Fire (Aries, Leo, Sagittarius)
28/1	Two of Wands	0°-10° Aries
29/11	Three of Wands	11°-20° Aries
30/3	Four of Wands	21°-30° Aries
31/4	Five of Wands	0°-10° Leo
32/5	Six of Wands	11°-20° Leo
33/6	Seven of Wands	21°-30° Leo
34/7	Eight of Wands	0°-10° Sagittarius
35/8	Nine of Wands	11°-20° Sagittarius
36/9	Ten of Wands	21°-30° Sagittarius

Table 3

The Numbers 37-50, the Cups, the Water Signs

Number	Tarot Key	Astrological Correspondence
37/1	King of Cups	0°-10° Cancer
38/11	Queen of Cups	11°-20° Cancer
39/3	Knight of Cups	Summer (Cancer, Leo, Virgo)
40/4	Page of Cups	21°-30° Cancer
41/5	Ace of Cups	Water (Cancer, Scorpio, Pisces)
42/6	Two of Cups	0°-10° Cancer
43/7	Three of Cups	11°-20° Cancer
44/8	Four of Cups	21°-30° Cancer
45/9	Five of Cups	0°-10° Scorpio
46/1	Six of Cups	11°-20° Scorpio
47/11	Seven of Cups	21°-30° Scorpio
48/3	Eight of Cups	0°-10° Pisces
49/4	Nine of Cups	11°-20° Pisces
50/5	Ten of Cups	21°-30° Pisces

Table 4

The Numbers 51-64, the Swords, the Air Signs

Number	Tarot Key	Astrological Correspondence
51/6	King of Swords	0°-10° Libra
52/7	Queen of Swords	11°-20° Libra
53/8	Knight of Swords	Autumn (Libra, Scorpio, Sagittarius)
54/9	Page of Swords	21°-30° Libra
55/1	Ace of Swords	Air (Libra, Aquarius, Gemini)
56/11	Two of Swords	0°-10° Libra
57/3	Three of Swords	11°-20° Libra
58/4	Four of Swords	21°-30° Libra
59/5	Five of Swords	0°-10° Aquarius
60/6	Six of Swords	11°-20° Aquarius
61/7	Seven of Swords	21°-30° Aquarius
62/8	Eight of Swords	0°-10° Gemini
63/9	Nine of Swords	11°-20° Gemini
64/1	Ten of Swords	21°-30° Gemini

Table 5

The Numbers 65-78, the Pentacles, the Earth Signs

Number	Tarot Key	Astrological Correspondence
65/11	King of Pentacles	0°-10° Capricorn
66/3	Queen of Pentacles	11°-20° Capricorn
67/4	Knight of Pentacles	Winter (Capricorn, Aquarius, Pisces)
68/5	Page of Pentacles	21°-30° Capricorn
69/6	Ace of Pentacles	Earth (Capricorn, Taurus, Virgo)
70/7	Two of Pentacles	0°-10° Capricorn
71/8	Three of Pentacles	11°-20° Capricorn
72/9	Four of Pentacles	21°-30° Capricorn
73/1	Five of Pentacles	0°-10° Taurus
74/11	Six of Pentacles	11°-20° Taurus
75/3	Seven of Pentacles	21°-30° Taurus
76/4	Eight of Pentacles	0°-10° Virgo
77/5	Nine of Pentacles	11°-20° Virgo
78/6	Ten of Pentacles	21°-30° Virgo

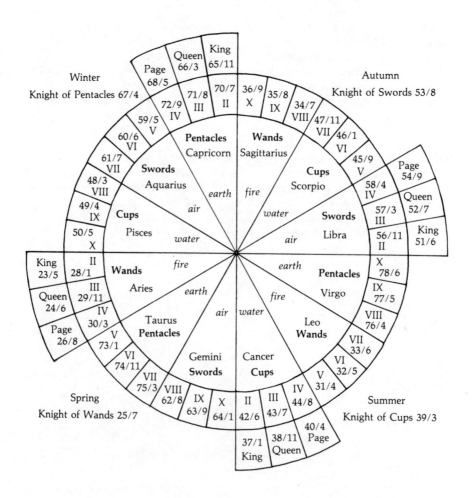

Figure 7: Synthesis of Numerology, Astrology and the Tarot. Each ace corresponds to an element: Ace of Wands (27/9), fire; Ace of Cups (41/5), water; Ace of Swords (55/1), air; Ace of Pentacles (69/6), earth.

Bibliography

Association of Research Enlightenment. *Search for God.* Vols. 1, 2, 3. Virginia Beach: A.R.E. Press, 1942.

Bailey, Alice. *Esoteric Astrology.* New York: Lucis, 1951.

Bills, Rex E. *The Rulership Book.* Virginia: Macoy Publishing, 1971.

Blavatsky, Helena Petrova. *Secret Doctrine.* California: Theosophical University Press, 1946.

Book of Enoch. London: S.P.C.K., 1952.

Bucke, R.M. *Cosmic Consciousness.* New York: Dutton, 1974.

Case, Paul Foster. *The Tarot.* Virginia: Macoy Publishing, 1947.

Cayce, Hugh Lynn. *Venture Inward.* New York: Harper & Row, 1964.

Cheney, Sheldon. *Men Who Have Walked with God.* New York: A.A. Knopf, 1945.

D'Olivet, Fabre. *Golden Verses of Rhythm.* New York: Samuel Weiser, 1813.

Encyclopedia of Jewish Religion. New York: Holt, Rinehart & Winston, 1965.

Fillmore, Charles. *Mysteries of Genesis.* Kansas City, Missouri: Unity School of Christianity, 1952.

Graves, F.D. *The Windows of the Tarot.* New York: Morgan & Morgan, 1973.

Gray, Eden. *A Complete Guide to the Tarot.* New York: Bantam Books, 1970.

Gray, William G. *The Ladder of Lights.* Great Britain: A Helios Book, 1971.

Hall, Manly P. *Man, Grand Symbol of the Mysteries.* Los Angeles: Philosophical Research Society, 1937.

———*The Mystical Christ.* Los Angeles: Philosophical Research Society, 1956.

———*Old Testament Wisdom.* Los Angeles: Philosophical Research Society, 1957.

Heard, Gerald. *The Code of Christ.* New York: Harper & Brothers, 1942.

Heline, Corinne. *The Bible and the Tarot.* Los Angeles: New Age Press, 1969.

———*The Cosmic Harp.* Santa Barbara, California: Rowney Press, 1969.

———*New Age Bible Interpretation.* 6 vols. Los Angeles: New Age Press, 1936.

———*Sacred Science of Numbers.* Los Angeles: New Age Press, 1971.

Hodson, Geoffrey. *Hidden Wisdom in the Holy Bible.* Vols. 1, 2, 3. Illinois: Theosophical Publishing House, 1967.

Hoeller, Stephan A. *The Royal Road.* Wheaton, Illinois: A Quest Book, 1975.

Appendix

Javane, Faith and Bunker, Dusty. *13 Birth or Death?* Hampton, New Hampshire: Association for Inner Development, 1976.

Jordan, Juno. *Romance in Your Name.* Santa Barbara, California: Rowney Press, 1965.

Lind, Frank. *How to Understand the Tarot.* London: The Aquarian Press, 1969.

Metaphysical Bible Dictionary. Kansas City, Missouri: Unity School of Christianity, 1962.

Michell, John. *View Over Atlantis.* New York: Ballantine Books, 1969.

Millard, Joseph. *Edgar Cayce: Man of Miracles.* Greenwich, Connecticut: Fawcett, 1956.

Newhouse, Flower. *Disciplines of the Holy Quest.* Vista, California: Christward Ministry, 1959.

———*Insights into Reality.* Vista, California: Christward Ministry, 1975.

Oliver, George. *The Pythagorean Triangle.* Minneapolis, Minnesota: Wizards Bookshelf, 1975.

Pelletier, Robert. *Planets in Aspect.* Rockport, Massachusetts: Para Research, 1974.

Pike, Albert. *Morals and Dogma.* Supreme Council of Southern Jurisdiction of U.S.A., 1871.

Ram Dass. *The Only Dance There Is.* New York: Doubleday, 1974.

Regardie, Israel. *The Tree of Life.* New York: Samuel Weiser, 1969.

Richmond, Olney H. *The Mystic Test Book.* Chicago, Illinois: A.L. Richmond, 1946.

Seton, Julia. *Western Symbology.* 1944.

Stearn, Jess. *Edgar Cayce, The Sleeping Prophet.* New York: Doubleday, 1967.

Stebbing, Lionel. *The Secrets of Numbers.* London: New Knowledge Books, 1963.

Sugrue, Thomas. *There is a River.* New York: Henry Holt, 1942.

Taylor, Thomas. *The Theoretic Arithmetic of the Pythagoreans.* New York: Samuel Weiser, 1816.

Werner, Keller. *The Bible as History.* New York: William Morrow, 1956.

NUMEROLOGY AND YOUR FUTURE

Dusty Bunker

In her second book, Dusty Bunker stresses the predictive side of numerology. Personal cycles including yearly, monthly and even daily numbers are explored as the author presents new techniques for revealing future developments. Knowledge of these cycles will help you make decisions and take actions in your life.

In addition to the extended discussion of personal cycles, the numerological significance of decades is analyzed with emphasis on the particular importance of the 1980s. Looking toward the future, the author presents a series of examples from the past, particularly the historical order of American presidents in relation to keys from the Tarot, to illustrate the power of numbers. Special attention is paid to the twenty-year death cycle of the presidents, as well as several predictions for the presidential elections.

ISBN: 0-914918-18-4
256 pages, 6½" x 9¼", paper

$12.95

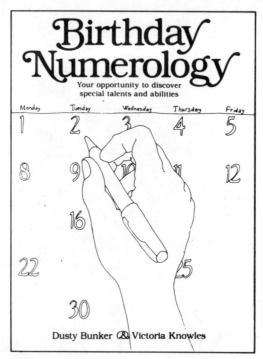

Birthday
Numerology
Your opportunity to discover
special talents and abilities

Monday	Tuesday	Wednesday	Thursday	Friday
1	2	3	4	5
8	9	10	11	12
	16			
22				25
	30			

Dusty Bunker & Victoria Knowles

BIRTHDAY NUMEROLOGY

by Dusty Bunker and Victoria Knowles

One of the unique things about you is the day on which you were born. In *Birthday Numerology*, well-known numerologist Dusty Bunker and psychic counselor Victoria Knowles combine their knowledge of numerology, symbolism and psychic development to present a clear and coherent presentation of how the day you were born affects your personality.

Unlike other methods of divination, the beauty of this book lies in its simple and direct presentation of the meaning behind personal numbers. Rather than having to perform complicated calculations, all you need to do is know your birthday. The book is uncannily accurate, written in a warm and engaging style and, above all, is easy to use.

The introductory chapters discuss the foundation and validity of numerology and will help you discover why the date of your birth is crucial in determining your personality. From there, *Birthday Numerology* examines the traits and characteristics inherent in people born on each day of the month.

Dusty Bunker and Vikki Knowles have written a book that is much more than just a delineation of various personalities, it is truly a guidebook to your journey through the 31 days.

ISBN 0-914918-39-7
225 pages, 6½" x 9¼", paper

$13.95

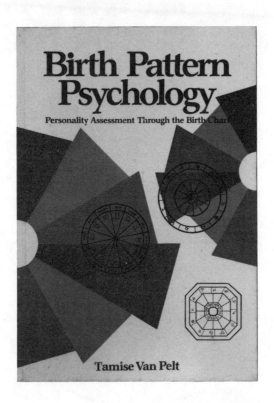

BIRTH PATTERN PSYCHOLOGY
Personality Assessment Through the Birth Chart

Tamise Van Pelt

Birth Pattern Psychology presents a holistic method for looking at the birth chart that combines some of the basic tenets of astrological measurement with the type of personality research basic to psychology. The book takes the reader through a step-by-step method for understanding the effect of birth on the developed personality.

The basis of Tamise Van Pelt's application of astrological principles to personality assessment is the division of the twelve astrological houses into four major triangles. When a planet appears in one of the houses that makes up one of these trines, it influences one of the four basic psychological needs: Growth, Security, Stimulus and Love.

Van Pelt postulates that a preponderance of planets in a specific "Need Triplicity" will cause the search to fulfill that need to be a primary motivating factor in the person's life. Lack of planets in any of the triplicities does not indicate a lack of desire in that specific area; it merely means the need will not be stressed in the individual's personality or actions.

In researching *Birth Pattern Psychology*, Van Pelt analyzed hundreds of charts to formulate and test her theory. Numerous charts of noted people are included in the book to help the reader understand the traits and needs the author discusses.

Tamise Van Pelt has taken a major step outside the typical boundaries of astrology and psychology. In so doing, she has produced a book which provides critical insights for each discipline.

ISBN 0-914918-33-8
256 pages, paper

$14.95

HOROSCOPE SYMBOLS

Robert Hand

Horoscope Symbols, Para Research's latest book by leading astrologer Robert Hand, explores astrological symbolism. Hand, with twenty years experience in the field, analyzes traditional meanings, considers alternatives and uses his own experience to develop and clarify these symbols. He thoroughly explains astrological symbolism—its history as well as its application for modern astrologers. In this new work, Robert Hand continues to build his reputation as the major new voice in humanistic astrology.

The author covers such basics as signs, planets, houses and aspects, illuminating their core meanings. In addition, Hand discusses midpoints, harmonics, the effect of retrograde planets and other often confusing areas for the astrologer.

Previously announced as *Planets in Synthesis*, *Horoscope Symbols* is the culmination of four years work. If you are new to astrology, this is the book to grow with. If you have already studied the basics, Robert Hand's approach will give you new perspective, insight and wisdom.

To quote the noted astrologer Alan Oken reviewing Robert Hand's *Horoscope Symbols*: "As usual, his writing is very clear, . . . what is most noteworthy is his ability to synthesize his comprehensive understanding of astrology from his basic scientific viewpoint . . . in humanistic prose.

ISBN 0-914918-16-8
400 pages, paper, 6½" x 9¼"

$19.95

COMPENDIUM
OF ASTROLOGY
by Rose Lineman and Jan Popelka

The more you understand astrology, the more you can do with your life. You can gain insight into human behavior, attain self-understanding and achieve full self-development. The *Compendium of Astrology* is all about astrology—the most comprehensive astrology book ever published. The *Compendium* contains the basic information needed to build a horoscope, provides a step-by-step guide that will lead beginning astrologers to in-depth knowledge of principles, calculations, and encourages them to pursue further study and research.

Part I presents a thorough grounding in the principles and theory of horoscope analysis. It explores familiar topics and detailed subjects like Vertex, East Point and asteroids. It covers the finer points of theory as well as the meanings of signs, planets and houses.

Part II introduces astrologers of all levels to several house systems and presents alternative mathematical methods with easy-to-follow examples.

Part III shows how to assemble and synthesize the astrological factors contained in a horoscope. Numerous examples clarify delineation techniques. Interpretations are given for all major aspects formed by planets. Special techniques help astrologers understand relationships and reveal future trends.

A large two-column format enhances the presentation and allows more material per page than any similar book.

This book belongs on every astrological student's bookshelf and on every astrologer's desk for easy reference. The *Compendium of Astrology* is the most complete astrological book on the market today.

ISBN 0-914918-43-5

304 pages, 8 × 9¼", paper, $14.95

WORLD EPHEMERIS
FOR THE 20ᵀᴴ CENTURY

by Para Research

Preface by Robert Hand

The *World Ephemeris for the 20th Century* is the first computer-calculated and computer-typeset ephemeris with letter quality printing. Now ease and clarity in reading is combined with accuracy and precision of data to provide the most complete and convenient ephemeris available for astrological calculation and analysis.

Available in either Midnight or Noon calculations, the *World Ephemeris* presents the Sun's position accurate to the second of arc; the Moon's mean Node and the nine planetary positions are given to the minute of arc.

Positions are reported for every day of the 20th Century. One hundred and one years in all.

Midnight Edition: ISBN 0-914918-60-5
624 pages, 8 x 9¼", paper $13.95

Noon Edition: ISBN 0-914918-61-3
624 pages, 8 x 9¼", paper $13.95

Name_____

Birthdate _____

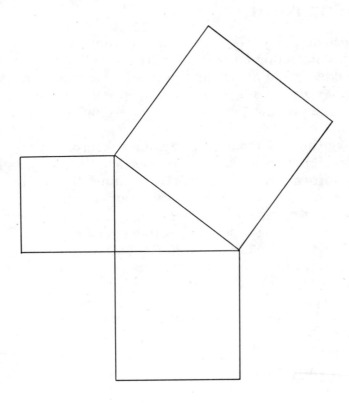

NUMEROLOGY
Key to the Tarot

Sandor Konraad

In *Numerology: Key to the Tarot*, Sandor Konraad investigates the cosmic connection between the art of reading the Tarot and the hidden meanings behind numbers. He reveals the secret of that relationship in a way that will appeal to beginning students as well as experienced numerologists and Tarot readers.

Using the card readings and numerological analysis for Sherlock Holmes, the author presents both these arts in a lively, informative and instructive manner. By teaching the Tarot spreads and numerological interpretations for a familiar character, Konraad shows you how to use the same techniques to deal with money, career, creative endeavors—most matters of life.

Through the connection between Tarot and Numerology, you'll discover why Dr. Watson had to be a character of secondary importance, why Holmes was given to drug abuse and why Holmes' brother had even greater powers of deductive reasoning. From the analysis of Holmes, you'll learn to construct the astro-numeric chart based on the numeric vibration affecting your life. Also of interest is the conflict between Holmes' personal numbers, a conflict that made for a split personality.

This book provides numerological guidance for anyone thinking about changing his or her name. For example, Konraad explains that William Shakespeare could not have had a better name for a writer, and he examines what might have happened if Sir Arthur Conan Doyle had used the name he originally intended for Holmes.

Numerology: Key to the Tarot offers an eclectic approach to these two popular disciplines and makes learning the Tarot much less formidable than other books. Sandor Konraad calls the Tarot the great "unbound bible" of Numerology and his book will help you use both disciplines.

ISBN: 0-914918-45-1
240 pages, 6½" x 9¼",

$13.95

CLASSIC TAROT SPREADS

Sandor Konraad

Classic Tarot Spreads presents one of the most comprehensive collections of card spreads available in one book. It includes 22 classic spreads that provide a key to the history, mythology and metaphysical meanings of the cards.

The book not only covers the practice and ritual of card reading, it treats the Tarot deck as a magical tool and counseling medium that can be used to resolve basic life issues. Sandor Konraad includes spreads for opening a reading—answering questions about health, love, marriage and money—as well as spreads for ending a reading.

Illustrated with the beautiful Oswald Wirth deck, *Classic Tarot Spreads* provides clear and essential meanings for all 78 cards of the Major and Minor Arcana. Also included are seven esoteric spreads rarely found in print.

A 30-day program uses repetition and slow, methodical addition of each new card to provide an easy method for learning the entire deck. And the author has included sections that introduce beginning students to the basic concepts, and sections with spreads designed to challenge the technique of Tarot experts.

ISBN: 0-914918-64-8
176 pages, 6½" x 9¼",

$12.95

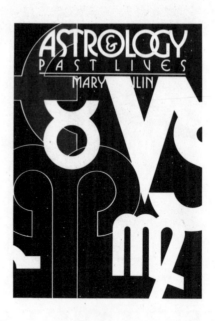

ASTROLOGY & PAST LIVES

Mary Devlin

This unique and original book is the first to examine birth charts for previous incarnations. Devlin shows you how to interpret past-life charts and compare them to your present one. By studying astrological patterns that repeat in chart after chart, lifetime after lifetime, you'll discover that many of your current experiences, relationships and attitudes are rooted in past existences.

Astrology & Past Lives is the result of ten years of research and hundreds of case studies. More than sixty charts and corresponding case histories—of both famous and ordinary people, past and present—are included as examples.

0-914918-71-0
304 pages, 6½" x 9¼", paper $18.95

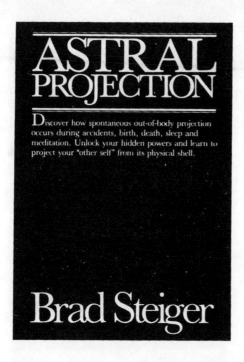

ASTRAL PROJECTION

Brad Steiger

Parapsychological researchers have established that one of every one hundred persons has experienced out-of-body projection (OBE). These experiences are not limited to any single type of person, but rather they cross all typical boundaries.

In *Astral Projection*, Brad Steiger, investigates the phenomenon of OBE and correlates those events into broad categories for analysis and explanation. In his clear and non-sensational style, Steiger relates how these spontaneous experiences occur and when they are likely to re-occur. In addition to the standard and well-documented categories of spontaneous astral projection at times of stress, sleep, death and near-death, Steiger devotes considerable time to the growing evidence for conscious out-of-body experiences, where the subject deliberately seeks to cast his or her spirit out of the physical shell.

Along with his study of astral projection, Steiger sets guidelines for astral travellers, tells them the dangers they may face and how this type of psychic experience might be used for medical diagnosis, therapy and self-knowledge.

Author Brad Steiger is your guide to controlling astral projection and using it for your own benefit.

ISBN 0-914918-36-2
234 pages, 6½″ x 9¼″, paper $12.95

KAHUNA
MAGIC

How Max Freedom Long rediscovered an ancient
Hawaiian religion that delivers new insights into your
hidden powers. Learn of your low self's innate control,
how your middle self can receive telepathic messages
and how your high self can change the future.

Brad Steiger

KAHUNA MAGIC

Brad Steiger

Based on the life work of Max Freedom Long, *Kahuna Magic* lays open
the secrets of the Kahuna, the ancient Hawaiian priests. Long used the
secrets of the Hawaiian language to unlock the secrets of this powerful and
mystical discipline.

Long was a much-respected psychic researcher. His student Brad
Steiger chronicles Long's adventures on the way to understanding the
magic of the Kahuna. By following Long's trek, the reader will learn how
the Kahunas used their magic for both the benefit of their friends and the
destruction of their enemies.

Central to the Huna beliefs was the thesis that each person has three
selves. The Low Self is the emotive spirit, dealing in basic wants and
needs. The Middle Self is the self operating at the everyday level. The
High Self is the spiritual being that is in contact with every other High
Self.

The subject matter of *Kahuna Magic* is contemporary and compelling.
The book incorporates many of the concepts and concerns of the modern
Western psychological tradition of Jung and Freud while bringing in
subjects as diverse as Eastern philosophies and yoga in a manner that will
help the readers understand themselves and those around them.

ISBN 0-914918-34-6
127 pages, 6½" × 9¼", paper

$10.95